Natural Aristocracy

Natural Aristocracy

History, Ideology, and the Production of William Faulkner

KEVIN RAILEY

THE UNIVERSITY OF ALABAMA PRESS : TUSCALOOSA AND LONDON

See the Acknowledgments section for a continuation of the copyright page.

∞

The paper on which this book is printed meets the minimum requirements of American National Standard for Information Science-Permanence of Paper for Printed Library Materials, ANSI Z39.48-1984

Jacket design by Ken Botnick

Library of Congress Cataloging-in-Publication Data

Railey, Kevin, 1954–
        Natural aristocracy : history, ideology, and the production of William Faulkner / Kevin Railey.
    p. cm.
    Includes bibliographical references (p.) and index.
    ISBN 0-8173-0956-X (alk. paper)
    1. Faulkner, William, 1897–1962—Knowledge—History. 2. Literature and history—Mississippi—History—20th century. 3. Literature and society—Mississippi—History—20th century. 4. Faulkner, William, 1897–1962—Political and social views. 5. Aristocracy (Political science) in literature. 6. Southern States—In literature. I. Title.
PS3511.A86 Z94685   1999
813'.52—dc21   98-58100

British Library Cataloging-in-Publication Data available

To my parents,
George Railey and Joan Bauer,
who have always been there,
Janet Railey,
who aided and abetted;
and to my brother, Keith,
enough said

Contents

Preface

This book proceeds on the assumption that William Faulkner was deeply affected by the sociohistorical forces that surrounded his life, and it portrays his
artistic development as occurring within the larger historical development of
the United States. Various critics over the years, notably Myra Jehlen, Carolyn
Porter, and John T. Matthews, have also been fascinated by Faulkner's immersion in history, and my work has been directly influenced by theirs. Yet, no systematic study identifying and historicizing Faulkner's specific authorial ideology
has been undertaken. This book, then, attempts to fill that void.

William Faulkner was obsessed with history and with his place in history.
Not surprisingly, then, my own interest in Faulkner originated in a curiosity
about the relationships between literature and history. My initial sense that
many Faulkner characters have strong class allegiances and are defined by historical conflict caused me to explore the interrelationships between American
history and Faulkner's fiction. A sensitivity to working-class concerns caused
me to sense that the historical narrative in Faulkner was being told from a particular vantage point. This impression pushed me to discover the roots of that
vantage point, leading to an investigation into biography and the relationship
between Southern history and Faulkner's subjectivity. My fascination with
Faulkner led, then, to three different investigations: (1) to discover as much as
possible about the history whirling around Faulkner; (2) to figure how he was
situated within that history (and to see if this position was static or mobile); and
(3) to determine the relationships between his position and the fiction. Through
these processes I discovered Faulkner's struggle with the most prominent ideologies affecting Mississippi and his own family as well as an underlying matrix of values—Faulkner's authorial ideology—through which he resolves this
struggle. This authorial ideology closely resembles the notion of natural aristocracy articulated in America by Thomas Jefferson, and it contains the same promises and problems as Jefferson's ideal.

My enterprise has been inspired by materialist criticism, which envisions literature as a discourse necessarily interactive with other forces in the world. It claims that literary texts have an ideological character and function, that accounts of history should always be grounded in the analysis of class structures, and that literature exposes the ideological complexity of the historical situations it presents in unique ways. Working from these assumptions, I interpret the history of the South in terms of its class and ideological structures, and I utilize the theory of ideology to explain the relation between this history and Faulkner's subjectivity. I come to see Faulkner's novels as situated, on one hand, within a larger historical unfolding and, on the other, within the conflict Faulkner experiences between the ideologies of his historical moment and his sense of himself. In my account, the man and the artist are one and the same in complex but definitive ways. I pose a basic Marxist question about Faulkner himself: How does Faulkner exist *in* ideology and history? How did material reality shape, produce William Faulkner?

Because an authorial ideology is a specific representation of more general ideological formations, an understanding of Faulkner's authorial ideology requires a complete picture of the history of Mississippi. Only by unpacking the general history—my task in chapter 1—can we understand which forces influenced him and which did not.

Though there has been a long-running debate among historians about the exact form of social formation characterizing the antebellum South—plantocracy or market capitalism—I am more concerned with the history of ideologies. This history clearly includes clashing ideological formations purporting different world views. Even if the Old South was a market economy fully entrenched in a global capitalist system, its ruling, plantocrat class was always composed of various class fractions that did not share the same self-conception, the same set of values, the same ideology. Though by necessity I will explore economic, social, and political developments in Mississippi after the Civil War, I will focus on the ways in which different class fractions sought to define themselves, seeing ideology as a relatively distinct mode of production.

The most important ideologies operating in the South and Mississippi during Faulkner's lifetime were paternalism, liberalism, and populism, and the first two have definitive effects on Faulkner and the production of his canon. These terms have come to be used in various, general ways in historical, literary, and journalistic discourse. I will be using them throughout the book, however, to describe very specific conceptions of distinct and coherent world views. A clear understanding of them, then, is essential. I detail these terms in chapter 1 and refer back to them throughout the first section.

In chapter 2 I read Faulkner's life and artistic career as occurring within the larger historical conflict between paternalism and liberalism, understanding the development of his authorial ideology as a working through of his identifications with these forces. He was, as Louis Althusser (1971) would say, interpellated by the conflict between these two ideologies as it manifested itself in early-twentieth-century Mississippi, and by the historical fact that paternalism was a fading, residual ideology and liberalism an increasingly emergent, then-dominant one. The story I begin to tell about Faulkner is one that shows him struggling, intellectually and artistically, with these historical developments. They threatened his own very deep sense of himself until he found a way to cope and to change, somewhat, in order to endure and prevail, as he might say. Despite the necessity of changing, Faulkner always held fast to paternalistic notions, and I will argue that his authorial ideology and his social vision remain deeply influenced by them. In fact, Faulkner's questions about the emerging society were based on a distrust of liberal, democratic notions. He feared that society would crumble or revert to primitive states if people were left unchecked by moral arbiters of law and civilization. Under this light, Faulkner's fiction can be seen to be exploring social concerns about the demise of paternalism, questions of leadership within liberalism, doubts about both an aristocracy of heritage and one of wealth. Faulkner's developing authorial ideology and his social vision, then, have much to do with the debates and conflicts at the heart of America: How does the dynamism of social mobility become reconciled with the preservation of order, deference, and society itself? How do we allow for justified mobility based on achievement and merit while prohibiting other means of social ascent?

Investigating these questions and the relationship between the larger historical process and Faulkner's Yoknapatawpha County reveals that Faulkner was more concerned with intra-class conflicts than with social conflicts in general. That is, Faulkner was concerned with conflicts *within* the ruling class of the South. Much Marxist criticism analyzes conflicts between the ruling class and the working class, between dominant and repressed ideologies, but this conflict is not important in Faulkner's fiction; therefore, I direct the tools of ideological analysis to the more predominant political agon. Philip Weinstein (1992) has argued that "the construction of the white male subject [exists] at the core of Faulkner's fiction" (82), but close inspection reveals that Faulkner is more concerned with the internal fabric and fiber of the upper classes than he is with white male subjectivity in general. His concerns focus more on those who hold or should hold positions of social power and responsibility and those who undeservedly move into these positions than on portraying both sides of the more general conflict between the ruling and the working class. This identification with the ruling class explains, in a preliminary way, why Populist, working-class, and integrationist voices are so absent from Faulkner's canon.

As I move in part 2 to the specific discussions of the novels, I begin, as many do, with *The Sound and the Fury*. For me, *The Sound and the Fury* is the novel in which Faulkner first explores sociohistorical voices with some distance and perspective; thus, it can be seen as Faulkner's first historically mature book. Here, he begins to separate himself from a close association with the residual ideology of paternalism—one that offered him no possibility of feeling anything but alienated in the world—and begins to explore liberalism for the first time. I discuss Faulkner's movement away from paternalism into a more questioning attitude about his Southern ideological heritage. The conflict within the upper class is clearly revealed in the contrast between Quentin, a sympathetic character, and others in his milieu such as Gerald Bland and Herbert Head. In this novel, immortalized for its artistic ingenuity, I read important historical resonances.

In *The Sound and the Fury, As I Lay Dying, Sanctuary,* and *Light in August* Faulkner explores various manifestations of paternalism and liberalism as well as the intense conflict between them, and the whole of part 2 explores these areas. Faulkner's depictions of Quentin Compson and Horace Benbow reveal Southern paternalism as no longer viable as a set of values and prescriptions for behavior in early-twentieth-century America. Meanwhile, depictions of Jason Compson and Anse Bundren reveal a continuing, deep distrust of liberalism and what it means for Southern, American society. Explorations of identity formation in a world of intense social mobility—the major concerns of *As I Lay Dying* and *Light in August*—do not bring Faulkner very close to liberal, capitalist values. All these books serve as symbolic histories of developments in the South and as testaments to Faulkner's early authorial position regarding these ideological formations. His struggle with America takes active form.

Chapters 6 and 7 focus on *Absalom, Absalom!* and the formation of Faulkner's authorial ideology. Chapter 6 discusses Thomas Sutpen's relationships to the other so-called white characters in the novel. In this aspect of the story, I argue that Faulkner attempts to confront the question of what happens to society if people's actions are left unchecked by the recognition and adoption of paternalist values. Only one character in *Absalom, Absalom!*, General Compson, is identified by paternalism, and the results of the other characters' actions all lead to death or depravity. Faulkner, thus, seems worried about the future of democracy when all arbiters of morality and civilization have lost social power. Faulkner's depiction of Thomas Sutpen shows a marked difference in perspective toward liberalism, especially when one compares Sutpen to the earlier character with whom he has so much in common, Jason Compson, and certain aspects of liberalism are here even supported and sanctioned by the narrative. Yet, at the same time, Faulkner fears the world in which social mobility is based on strength and money alone. Refusing to fill that void within society left by the loss of all paternalist values seems to lead to apocalypse. General Compson becomes, then, the first manifestation of the natural aristocrat in Faulkner's fiction.

Chapter 7 focuses on the intense issues of race raised by *Absalom* and on the way Southern responses to this question affected the South's destiny. Sutpen is allowed to enter the upper class, I contend, not just because of his wealth but also because of a Southern ideology of race that said people were either white or black. This intensely strict and rigid ideology led to compromises within the upper class, and these permitted those like Sutpen to succeed and progress while destroying those like Charles Bon. Bon exists for Faulkner as another example of the natural aristocrat figure, but one who cannot survive the South's ideological matrix. In this text, where imagination and history intersect, imagination reaches the more noble conclusion.

Seemingly accepting the version of history embodied in *Absalom*, at the midpoint in his career Faulkner primarily leaves the question of race and remains focused on how the upper class made those compromises that led to its sacrifice of values. Chapter 8 explores the Snopes trilogy, explaining how these books reveal Faulkner's sense of a world in which no aristocratic paternalist exists. Faulkner reveals that the conflict within the upper class of the South had been won by the Redeemers—the non-paternalist members of the upper class, here represented by Will Varner—and how this group was complicitous with the lower class, usually seen as rednecks, due to their addiction to the power of money. In the trilogy Faulkner theorizes the results and ramifications of the Redeemers' victory. Implied in the demise of Flem Snopes, at the hands of Mink Snopes and Linda Snopes-Kohl, are the parameters and limitations of Faulkner's social vision. Faulkner borders on a cooperative, communal vision of society in the enactment of justice on Flem; however, the lesson Faulkner wishes to teach—and this tale is a moral one—has more to do with the ramifications of a society that has lost its ability to trust those who deserve power and position.

Chapter 9 focuses on Faulkner's imaginary solutions to the real problems of history. Immersed in working through various aspects of the conflict itself, in letting characters work out their own destinies, Faulkner's texts do not generally offer answers to the conflict because it is essentially unresolvable: paternalism and liberalism are mutually exclusive and antagonistic. Literature, though, is not bound by the limits of history. On one hand, citing Fredric Jameson (1981), literature can be said to embody utopian yearnings that become revealed through unconscious solutions to the real problems of history. On the other hand, fiction can free itself from the constraints of historical drama and can attempt to present, directly, visions of resolution, alternative visions of reality. Faulkner's conscious resolution is developed in what I call the fairy tale of *The Reivers*. Here, Faulkner's resolution to the real problems of history parallels the answer that some before him articulated—he put his faith in a naturally aristocratic character who could balance opposing forces and guide society into a nonviolent and productive future. Faulkner was thus left where essentially we are still left as a nation: How does a nation fulfill the promises of equality and opportunity when it clings to certain beliefs that some people are inherently better and more deserving than others?

In-depth investigations into Faulkner's complicated relation to history and ideology have been relatively unexplored, primarily, I suspect, because seeing literature as a symbolic social and political narrative requires the acceptance of certain assumptions contrary to those guiding much Faulkner scholarship. Nonetheless, my study sees Faulkner's novels as deeply significant because they illuminate, from a particular Faulknerian perspective, a decisive historical process in the formation of modern America: the struggle between a fading ideological formation—paternalism—and an emerging one—liberalism—as the country consolidated a fully capitalist economy justified by a bourgeois ethos.[1] Necessarily confronting the problems of an incipient democracy, this process was further complicated for Faulkner by the legacy of Southern and American race relations. My account of Faulkner's career argues that he emerged from an intense attachment to a paternalist ideology into this bourgeois environment, and it encourages us to see Faulkner's career as an intellectual and historical drama of more general significance than has been discussed previously.

Acknowledgments

This project has been long in the making. It would not have come to fruition at all if not for the support of certain individuals. I would like to thank Michael Sprinker, professor at SUNY/Stony Brook, for his support of the original project that led to this book. I would also like to thank John Matthews, who has been indirectly supportive of my work in his roles as reader for and editor of literary journals. He has provided inspiration at key moments, and his work has always served as a model for me.

Two colleagues, Dana Nelson and Patrick McHugh, have been instrumental in helping me produce this book. Without their conversations, comments, and intellectual camaraderie this book would not be in the form it is now. Thank you.

Permissions

Permission to quote from the works of William Faulkner is gratefully acknowledged as follows:

From *The Sound and the Fury* by William Faulkner. Copyright 1929 and renewed 1957 by William Faulkner. Reprinted by permission of Random House, Inc.

From *As I Lay Dying* by William Faulkner. Copyright 1930 and renewed 1958 by William Faulkner. Reprinted by permission of Random House, Inc.

From *Light in August* by William Faulkner. Copyright 1932 and renewed 1960 by William Faulkner. Reprinted by permission of Random House, Inc.

From *Sanctuary* by William Faulkner. Copyright 1931 and renewed 1959 by William Faulkner. Reprinted by permission of Random House, Inc.

From *Sanctuary: The Original Text* by William Faulkner, edited with an Afterword and Notes by Noel Polk. Copyright © 1981 by Jill Faulkner Summers. Reprinted by permission of Random House, Inc.

From *Absalom, Absalom!* by William Faulkner. Copyright 1936 by William Faulkner and renewed 1964 by Estelle Faulkner and Jill Faulkner Summers. Reprinted by permission of Random House, Inc.

From *The Hamlet* by William Faulkner. Copyright 1940 by William Faulkner and renewed 1968 by Estelle Faulkner and Jill Faulkner Summers. Reprinted by permission of Random House, Inc.

From *The Town* by William Faulkner. Copyright © 1957 by William Faulkner. Copyright © 1957 by Curtis Publishing Company. Reprinted by permission of Random House, Inc.

From *The Mansion* by William Faulkner. Copyright © 1955, 1959 by William Faulkner. Reprinted by permission of Random House, Inc.

Part of chapter 3 appeared originally as "Cavalier Ideology and History: The Significance of Quentin's Section in *The Sound and the Fury*" in *Arizona Quarterly*. Reprinted from *Arizona Quarterly* 48.3 (1992), by permission of the Regents of The University of Arizona.

A version of chapter 4 appeared in *Faulkner in Cultural Context: Proceedings of the Twenty-second Annual Faulkner and Yoknapatawpha Conference* (Jackson: University Press of Mississippi, 1997). Reprinted by permission of the University Press of Mississippi.

A version of chapter 6 appeared in *The Faulkner Journal* VII: 1 and 2 (Fall/ Spring 1992). Copyright 1992 by The University of Akron. Reprinted by permission of the Author and the University of Central Florida.

I am grateful to the editors for permission to reprint this material and for their support of my work over the years.

Part One • History, Ideology, Subjectivity

1 • Faulkner's Mississippi

Ideology and Southern History

The textual real should be conceived as the product of signifying practices whose source is history itself.

—Ramon Saldivar, *Chicano Narrative*

The past is not dead. The past is not even past.

—Faulkner, *The Unvanquished*

The word *ideology* has a complicated history. In *Ideology* (1991), Terry Eagleton traces and describes six different origins and uses of the term. Although a comprehensive review is not needed here, a brief explanation of how this concept will be understood is necessary because it has come into such wide, and in many ways such indiscriminate, use. Two of Eagleton's six definitions are relevant to my purposes. One is sociological, concerned with the function of ideas within social life; Eagleton labels it the affective account of ideology. The affective account confronts the significant question of subject formation, and Faulkner's subject formation will be the focus of the next chapter. A second definition concerns epistemological questions, notions of true and false cognition, which Eagleton calls the rationalist account of ideology. The rationalist account is concerned with the relationship between ideas/values and class structure as well as with the power and influence of ideas and values within a given society; these will be the focus here.

The rationalist account of ideology stems originally from the contrast between ideology and science, or ideology and truth. Marx defined ideology as the system of ideas and representations that dominate the mind of a social group. For Marx, those whose thinking was affected by ideology—bourgeois intellectuals—believed in falsehood or illusion, while those agents of historical materialism—the proletariat—were able to see truth. Since this early formula-tion there has been much heated debate about historical materialism as a science and about the distinction between ideology and science; most important, Marx's early belief in the ability of human subjects to think in nonideological terms has been discredited. Nonetheless, this rationalist account has led Marxist thinkers to articulate nuanced and careful descriptions of the relationship between ideas/values and social class and the ways in which ideologies come to have power over people's thinking. This account has led, in the work of Raymond Williams (1977), to the concepts of dominant, residual, and emergent ideologies, and, in the work of Antonio Gramsci (1988), to the concept of hegemony.

Briefly, a dominant ideology is that relatively organized system of values and representations that upholds and maintains a social system beneficial to the rul-ing class. This dominant ideology, if effective, persuades, convinces, and seduces people from all classes in society to ascribe to its values, to identify with its representations of how the world should and does function. (The divine right of kings and equal pay for equal work are two examples of assertions about reality, though they stem from different ideological perspectives.) The subtle and intri-cate means through which this ideology gets produced and distributed involve what Althusser (1971) has labeled ideological state apparatuses: religion, educa-tional systems, family, laws and law enforcement, media, culture—all the ways in which ideas and values get promulgated and distributed throughout a society.

The concept of hegemony relates both to the ways in which an ideology be-comes a dominant influence on people's thinking—the whole social process in-volved in an ideology's dissemination and maintenance—and to the degree of success a dominant class has in persuading others in society to see the world its way. If a society is wrought with tension, conflict, and violence, the dominant ideology has not established hegemony; in short, people question its truth and its validity, and its dominant status is in jeopardy. If, however, the day-to-day life of a society proceeds relatively uninterrupted, and people do not vociferously question or rebel against the principles on which the society rests, a dominant class and its ideology can be said to have achieved hegemonic status. People have, in essence, accepted this ideology as their own. The bourgeois class and its ideology of equal rights and opportunities and reward based on merit have ob-viously enjoyed a hegemonic status in America for some time.

Ideology is a productive force in society; upholders of the dominant class work to develop and maintain hegemony constantly. Thus, history and class structure are not static; they are in constant motion. A dominant class's hold on hegemony is always in flux, and at various historical moments there is no dominant class and no hegemonic ideological formation. In these societies there is more tension than consensus. Also, opposing forces to dominant classes can be chaotic and random, very small minority voices that are almost unheard in public debate, or they can be relatively unified and consistent, demanding attention from figures in power. The two notions, residual and emergent ideology, attempt to describe these other relatively unified but nondominant systems of values and representations.

A residual ideology derives from past social formations, from a previously dominant class whose values still have influence on the way some people think. Many, especially those who resist a newly dominant ideology, who feel left behind, may identify with another time and its values and cling to a residual ideology. (My claim will be that Faulkner experienced this phenomenon.) An emergent ideology, on the other hand, denotes a set of values and beliefs that does not serve as a haven for the alienated but one that actively pushes for change in the present system. An emergent ideology seeks to define a future based on a different social vision than the one in dominance. Whether it will have its desired effect or be co-opted into the dominant order is always an open question, but there is generally more active tension between an emergent and a dominant ideology than between a dominant and a residual one. (The present push for a multicultural perspective within the definition of America is an example of an emergent ideological formation.) Moreover, all of these ideologies exist simultaneously in any given society, competing for people's allegiances.

As Jonathan Wiener has indicated: "There are periods in history when fundamental issues of class relations do not arise, but the immediate post [Civil] war South was not such a 'hegemonic' epoch. Social conflict was explicit and often intense" (1978, 5). In the following discussion I seek to delineate these social conflicts and to elucidate the ideologies that supported people's actions in the development of Mississippi society after the Civil War.

Faulkner lived in Lafayette County, Mississippi, for most of his life. This county overlaps both the North Central Hills section of poor soil and the Brown Loam and Loess Hills section of very good soil and stands between areas that then possessed the largest and lowest percentages of black Americans in Mississippi. Faulkner's map of Yoknapatawpha County, his fictional county, gives only one reference to actual Mississippi geography—the Tallahatchie River. This reference would make it appear that Yoknapatawpha overlaps sections of Panola and Yalobusha counties, with sixty-five percent black population, Lafayette County itself, and Pontotoc and Calhoun counties, with less than thirty-five percent black population. The geographical links between Mississippi and Yoknapatawpha parallel those between the sociological composition of each as well—populations of both ranging from planters, merchants, bankers, and lawyers through independent farmers, small shopkeepers, and businessmen to tenant farmers, both white and black. The materials of Faulkner's fiction thus connect very much to his historical environment. Although Faulkner wrote through the 1950s, the artistic depiction of ideological formations within his work derives from the formations that existed during this time period, roughly from 1870 to 1930.[1]

Conflicts and struggles in Mississippi had particularly acute manifestations exactly because of the state's geography and social composition. The southwestern sections of Mississippi consisted of some of the richest soil in the entire South. These lands, referred to as both the Delta and the Black counties, were the location of very wealthy plantations before the Civil War, and the potential wealth from cotton crops remained immense after the war. Other sections of the state, tilled by smaller landowners who had maintained, before the war, a yeomanlike existence with few slaves, were never as productive nor did they have the potential to bring prosperity to the state. The people there, however, had been an essential part of the South's heritage from Jefferson to Jackson and would continue to be so—unlike the very poor subsistence farmers of the hill counties who were never an active part of Southern life. Connected to these features has been Mississippi's racial mix: more populated by blacks than whites, with the counties in the southwestern sections, especially after the war, containing the vast majority of the blacks in the state. There, blacks outnumbered whites by as much as 15 to 1, whereas in northeastern and southeastern counties whites always outnumbered blacks. As Kirwan (1951) has noted, there were rich and poor, educated and uneducated, cultured and uncultured in all regions of Mississippi; the state was not simply divided between the large landowners of the Delta with their black populations and the small landowners of the hill country who were exclusively white; nonetheless, these two classes did exist, and the directions Mississippi would take in its process of rebuilding was influenced by both groups (41–42).

This social and geographical composition relates closely to ideological formations. At the heart of Southern ideological history during most of the nineteenth and early twentieth centuries was the conflict between two opposing ideologies—paternalism and liberalism. Although these two words have come to be used in various, general ways, I use them to describe very specific conceptions of distinct and coherent world views. Adopting James Oakes's formulations (1982), I view paternalism as a social order that is stable, hierarchical, consciously elitist, and therefore fundamentally antithetical to liberalism. A paternalist assumes an inherent inequality of men; some are born to rule, others to obey. A liberal espouses a far different social fiction: all men are created equal. A paternalist stresses the organic unity born of each individual's acceptance of his or her place in a stable, stratified social order. A liberal stresses individualism, social mobility, and economic fluidity within a society that promotes equal opportunity. Whereas paternalism takes as its model the extended, patriarchal household, liberal societies move more and more toward the private, nuclear family. Paternalism establishes men as moral examples, and paternalists hold a sense of honor in their dealings with others, even those they consider below them, and feel a sense of responsibility toward society. Liberalism encourages men to strive for profit in the marketplace and places women in the role of moral exemplars. Responsibility here is to the development of oneself. Thus, paternalism and liberalism are intrinsically antagonistic. (Oakes 1982, xi–xii.)

Different sections of Mississippi were relatively unified by one or the other of these ideologies. Rooted in a tradition of slavery and plantation building, the Black counties were affiliated with a paternalist social vision in which poor whites were only a bit above black slaves. Powerful, upper-class plantocrats firmly held that they were indeed better men who deserved their social position and wealth due to inherent qualities and more sophisticated abilities. As Michael Wayne explains, "many members of the planting elite . . . had developed a decided class consciousness and a belief in the superiority of their own lineage and way of life" (1983, 2). During the nineteenth century, these plantocrats were the ruling class in Mississippi. Although their hold on hegemony may have been tenuous, they maintained a social order that served their interests. They did this by pitting poor white against black and by aligning poor whites with themselves. They placated poor whites in various ways, mainly by offering them some social and political freedom, but only under extreme conditions did this entail social mobility on a grand scale—the social order was fairly static. Thus, their paternalism had both a class-based and a race-based element, but racial paternalism was heightened by an allegiance among all white men. In this atmosphere, though the ruling class had a self-consciousness about its attitudes toward both poor whites and blacks and thus could have a wider range of feeling, pointed (and vicious) racial paternalism became more prevalent, especially among the poor white population. It certainly left its mark more deeply on Southern society than class-based paternalism.[2]

Not all people in Mississippi identified with the plantocrats and their belief systems, however, and other sections of Mississippi were unified by a liberalism that led men to believe they had a right to equality and opportunity—that they deserved an even chance in the marketplace. These two ideological belief-systems were able to coexist for many years because agricultural and economic conditions allowed most to feed and house their families and to maintain a degree of independence. There were also some examples of poor whites who moved to the frontier and became successful: opportunity, people on both sides could argue, was there. And planters granted whites various freedoms that they did not grant to black slaves. Nonetheless, this coexistence was fragile. When conditions changed after the Civil War and the precarious balance of ideological forces tilted, the opposing views influenced social conflict in definitive and different ways.

The first group able to re-form itself after the war was the planters. Though not easily or smoothly, planters in the Delta were generally able to keep their social and political power because of the congressional decision against land confiscation, and they began to make moves toward determining Mississippi's future.[3] They recognized the need both for capital investment in their land and for cheap labor and tried to get Reconstruction governments to establish policies that would encourage investment in their lands. These were slow in coming because of the generally bankrupt condition of the state, the efforts toward reform, and the taxation policies of Mississippi's second Reconstruction government.[4] What were not slow in coming were efforts to expand the pool of cheap labor.

Planters immediately recognized the need to develop working relationships with the newly freed black Americans; without the technology for large-scale machinery, cheap labor was essential to the planters' rebuilding efforts. They also wanted to establish arrangements that kept control in their hands. Soon after the end of the war, planters attempted to hire blacks to work plantations in labor-gangs and planned to pay them in cash. Although this situation would have changed the South in some definite though unpredictable ways, it never developed. Planters could not get the necessary cash, and blacks, although poor and uneducated for the most part, knew they had been freed and refused these efforts to reinstitute a new kind of slavery.

Ideally, black Americans wanted to own land, and their best chance to accomplish this was through renting at a fixed price and marketing cotton themselves. Whatever profit was made could then be saved to buy their own land. This goal was sternly looked down upon by most whites, and although a few planters rented land to blacks, the practice did not become widespread or popular. At times, planters who rented land to blacks would find their barns or houses burned to the ground.

Nevertheless, black Americans refused simply to work for wages because in that scenario they had little control over their time, over their way of life. They wanted land and some semblance of family life and independence. The result was that sharecropping was established: planters would rent blacks a certain amount of land and supply them with food and tools in exchange for a share in the crop. Freed slaves would obtain a degree of independence unknown to them before and a degree of power to determine how their families would work and be organized. Planters would be relatively assured that the sharecroppers would grow cotton because they had incentive to be as productive as possible. Sharecropping, then, became the most widespread arrangement for blacks in the Delta for some time.

The success of this compromise greatly depended on the relations paternalism had encouraged and developed. Planters still felt they had certain responsibilities to the black Americans who worked and lived on their land, but they expected strict obedience and loyalty in return. The freedmen felt they had certain rights as long as they held to their side of the bargain. Although one cannot say that freed blacks accepted the attitudes of paternalism or deny that in sharecropping they had achieved a kind of compromise with whites, sharecropping enabled planters to perpetuate their paternalistic sense of themselves, and it helped them redevelop their wealth and maintain their power in Mississippi politics. (See Wiener 1979.)

Mississippi planters also encouraged black migration to their lands during this period: the more labor they could attract, the more money they could make. They promised blacks better conditions than could be found elsewhere in the South; due to the intense fertility of the alluvial land in the Delta, these promises could generally be fulfilled, and blacks went there in large numbers. Eventually, though, Mississippi planters helped forge new laws that tried to force blacks to remain on the land they tilled. They also instituted enticement statutes that forbade planters (in any state) from hiring blacks from another man's land and vagrancy laws that made it illegal for blacks not to be employed. Though unevenly enforced, these laws reveal the attitude of the planter elite toward their workers: free black Americans were *given* certain limited freedoms out of economic necessity, but planters took it upon themselves to police the black population. Arrangements might have been changing, but the planters' sense of themselves as superior was not. Moreover, sharecropping was made more difficult for farmers, due to huge price markups and the fact that the system remained primarily based on barter, not cash. All of these forces worked against the full exercise of personal and economic freedom by sharecroppers. True, conditions were better for the freedmen in the Delta, but once they arrived there in large numbers, they were virtually forced to stay.

These policies were not seen to be contradictory by the paternalists who instituted them. Their social contract implied certain gestures on their part reciprocated by certain very specific obligations on the part of the black sharecroppers: loyalty was essential to their social vision, even if they had to enforce it. (See Wiener 1979.)

The exact balance of this uneasy compromise is hard to determine, but the efforts of the freedmen cannot be overlooked. They were not simply pawns in the game. Inspired by their new freedom, black Americans were quick to identify with all of the features of liberalism. They began to exercise their rights to life, liberty, and the pursuit of happiness in a market that needed their labor rather desperately. In fact, because the planters definitely needed their labor, black Americans claimed leverage and power in ways completely unknown to them before the Civil War. The planters found themselves competing for labor and dealing with former slaves on terms they never could have imagined. Blacks sought the best deal, pitting planter against planter. Although they clung to vestiges of paternalism, planters were now forced to confront liberalism and the market economy.[5]

This uneasy and unstable balance of forces and ideologies also manifested itself in the political arena. Very few white Mississippians favored the extension of voting rights to blacks; the vote obviously gave blacks unprecedented power in Mississippi. This power was especially evident in the Delta, where blacks substantially outnumbered whites. More than other places in the state, white planters worked with blacks interested in holding political office and were willing to extend a degree of power to the freedmen in exchange for a degree of labor stability. As occurred with new economic arrangements, white planters were forced to confront the emergence of new behaviors. The political world during Reconstruction saw the emergence of a liberal ideology of equal rights and opportunities; based on self-interest planters worked in this environment for some time. Ultimately, however, planters lost only their sense of responsibility to those who were lower on the economic ladder; they did not lose their sense of superiority. As we will see, when it became clear that black Mississippians were gaining too much political power—overstepping their bounds, as it were—planters formed new allegiances with other groups in the state and helped prohibit the black vote.

These developments in the Black counties served other Southern purposes well. Without consistent access to money, blacks could hardly achieve social mobility—something most white Southerners considered a freedom reserved only for themselves anyway. Sharecropping kept blacks in the country and on the farms, exactly where most whites wanted them. Although sharecropping might have been better than slavery, it remained the only work blacks could find in Mississippi, and it perpetuated a static social structure based on social hierarchies similar to those of the Old South. The system was being infused with the exertions of the freedmen, but it was maintaining a strong resistance to them as well. Ultimately, the system successfully kept blacks from complete access to the market mentality and the bourgeois ethos.

Overall, economic and political arrangements during Reconstruction perpetuated paternalism as an active force in Mississippi society. Though liberalism was emerging even in the most stratified social arena in Mississippi and was affecting the social bonds of paternalism, race-based paternalism was still a dominant influence on the ruling ideology.[6]

Although large-scale investment in their lands was impossible, Delta planters were constantly able to obtain credit for supplies for themselves and their tenants. This was not an easy task: until 1870, there were no national banks and only two state banks in all of Mississippi, and these state banks were savings institutions, not lenders (Ransom and Sutch 1977, 110–16). Local, rural banks and northern investors supplied local credit, though they were careful about extending themselves. Large Delta landowners with stable populations of black sharecroppers were the safest risk; their lands virtually always returned a profit because of the quality of the soil. Unlike other areas where credit became a severe problem for most small farmers, Delta landowners were almost guaranteed the ability to begin operation. These developments in the traditional Black Counties worked to maintain antebellum social and economic relations too. Though planters had lost a degree of power and much of their wealth during the Civil War, after the war they were able to maintain positions of economic influence because of their large tracts of fertile soil. They were able to maintain strong political influence because of their coalitions with the black vote, which constituted a majority in Mississippi and kept planters in powerful political positions for a long time. These positions of power were also indirectly supported by the growing middle class and poor white populations because they saw the planters as serving a socially necessary function of policing the freed blacks. Though, too, not a unified group, plantocrats were not actively challenged to forsake their notions of inherent superiority, and they saw themselves as continuing to exercise their social responsibilities to re-create the South.

The relative isolation of the planter class would not continue in this new world, however. Planters and planters' sons (or other relatives) were able to operate merchant stores in both the Black Counties and other places, using the planter's lands and crops as collateral, and thus were able to spread their influence in other ways and in other areas. In other instances, when the planter could not maintain or improve his land, he would sell the land to an outside investor and keep the store for himself. At this socioeconomic juncture, the history of the planter class began to blend actively with the history of other elements in Southern society. The upper class in Mississippi was thus in the process of becoming even more diverse in its various self-conceptions. (See Woodward 1951, chap. 1; Ransom and Sutch 1977, chap. 7; Wayne 1983, chap. 6.)

In areas of Mississippi outside the Delta the local country store was "the sole survivor of the general collapse of the elaborate system of market intermediation" that enabled the middle-class white farmer to farm, gin, ship and sell his crop (Ransom and Sutch 1977, 117). Thus, as white farmers returned from the war destitute, with little chance of starting over, the local furnishing merchants became the major supplier not only of food and materials but of credit as well. As merchants made profits, they would buy more and more land and would establish tenant-farming and sharecropping arrangements with various types of men. This kind of financing was the only option for the mass of once middle-class farmers who needed to survive from January, when land preparation would begin, to November, when the crop would reach market. This process kept a major portion of the poor white population from engaging in social mobility, and the ownership of land even outside the Delta areas was becoming concentrated into fewer and fewer hands. Whether these store-owners were originally from the planter class or from the middle class, the developments served the same purpose: they diversified the upper class and united the interests of the planters with other, more strictly business-oriented, liberal-minded elements in the state. (See Ransom and Sutch 1977.)

A plantation-type system was instituted in these areas as well, with merchants making the various arrangements with different farmers and their families. As this process grew, merchants themselves sought to maintain or to increase the distance between themselves and the sharecroppers and tenants who tilled their land. In order to achieve this distance, these merchants would adopt the pose, tone, and attitude of paternalism: "Every form of labor was accompanied by landlord paternalism. More than a romantic residue left over from antebellum times, paternalism was an important feature of life in the New South. . . . But paternalism was indulged in not so much because it eased the conditions of the labor contract as because it was a means which emphasized the social gulf between planters and poorer white men" (Brandfon 1967, 133–34). In essence, simply the ownership of land became a means to identify with an important image in the Southern mind. This particular identification with paternalism, however, served more as a badge of social status and was based solely on the cash-nexus. It did not include commitment to social responsibility and leadership, avowed aspects of the earlier ideological formation; it did not include attitudes of inherent superiority; and it did not include any self-consciousness about ruling ideas or race. As planters and their sons moved increasingly into the class of merchants and merchants increasingly made money and bought lands, these two groups grew closer economically and politically, yet they did not unify into a class with consistent values.

Developments in other parts of Mississippi were not exactly the same as those in the Black counties, and there would be a backlash against the political control exercised by the planters during the 1880s; however, these developments emphasize the subtly complicated economic and ideological environment of post–Civil War Mississippi. Economically, severe conditions were leading to a shift in the composition of the upper class. More men were able to establish businesses connected to cotton farming, and these men were able to acquire wealth comparable to that of many planters: "The increasing tendency for merchants to hold on to their stores as they acquired land had major implications for the economic structure of the merchant class. . . . It meant that there now existed a segment of that class at the highest levels of the planting hierarchy" (Wayne 1983, 193). The blending of different men into the upper class led to an intersection of economic interests between the planters and those who controlled other business interests in the state—that group which eventually became the Redeemers. These shared economic interests united planter and Redeemer against the masses and enabled the wealthy to dominate the Democratic party for years. In this development, whether the wealthy were planters or railroad magnates, they felt they were above the masses, the dangerous classes. These developments only drew the merchants' and planters' interests further away from those of farmers, both black and white. (See Wayne 1983, chap. 6.)

At the same time, the new group of wealthy landowners and businessmen had a set of values more closely akin to liberalism than paternalism. They had taken advantage of opportunities open to them and identified with that value system, and they saw the large population of black tenant farmers on planter lands as a threat to their own wealth and future opportunities. This lack of ideological unity was also revealed in different attitudes toward blacks and poor whites, and it eventually influenced the refusal to follow through with the logic of paternalism. This logic would have/could have joined planters, merchants, and businessman in attitudes of elitism and could have established permanently hierarchical social arrangements, with blacks *and* poor whites on the bottom and themselves on top. This logic was not followed in part because these new wealthy landowners did not identify with class-based paternalism at all. On one hand, they did not totally believe in paternalism as a set prescription for behavior; they identified with it because of the powerful social position it offered them. They believed in opportunity and to some degree in social mobility—since they had benefited from them, how could they not? On the other hand, the paternalism they did believe in was the race-based paternalism handed down to them from their own poor-white fathers. They felt that they, and their white brothers (only), should be granted the promise of future reward. The Redeemers, then, as those who had taken advantage of whatever social mobility Mississippi had offered and who were not part of the self-conscious ruling elite, brought a different set of values and beliefs into the upper class. At the center of the first major conflict in Mississippi after the Civil War was this struggle for power *within* the upper class itself. Who would dominate—the Plantocrats or the Redeemers?[7]

The agricultural sector was the major way through which Northern and foreign capital began entering the South, but it was not the only way, and these other developments helped push the balance in favor of the Redeemers. No massive industrial development occurred in Mississippi because it did not have the necessary potential, but both railroad and timber interests began to enter the state during Reconstruction. The Reconstruction constitution placed a ban on pledging state funds to private corporations, but the leaders of Reconstruction also recognized the need for various forms of capital investment and development. These came with offers to railroad investors and sales to timber companies, both of which were connected to the cotton business. River travel had become more difficult since the Civil War when many ships were sunk in local rivers, and railroads became especially needed to transport cotton and supplies. The state also encouraged timber companies to buy land, hoping that after these lands were cleared they could be used to produce cotton, thereby increasing the state's prosperity. These developments required all kinds of middlemen, and a new class of professionals began to grow. Here, again, money was entering the South on an investment level, and business, as opposed to agricultural, interests were unifying the moneyed classes.

While this money was entering the South, both the plantocrats and the Redeemers benefited, and the new group of middlemen became increasingly successful. Meanwhile, farmers grew poorer, and their dissatisfaction with Reconstruction policies grew more intense. Rooted in a liberalism that believed in independence and opportunity for those who worked hard, these farmers were more and more frequently unable to experience success or social mobility, no matter how hard they worked. In the wake of the depression of 1873 many middle-class and poor farmers found themselves in even more desperate straits, having to sell land and enter sharecropping arrangements of various sorts, losing whatever shred of independence and hopes for brighter futures they had. This situation put them into an economic situation similar to that of the freed blacks. They placed blame for their condition on the inimical Reconstruction government, controlled by the union of wealthy white planters and blacks. These whites now wanted to destroy the Republican party in Mississippi, and they found powerful allies in the Redeemers who wanted to take power away from the planters and take more control of political and investment decisions than the second Reconstruction government had given them. This union of forces laid the groundwork for the Mississippi Plan, the political plan that "redeemed" the South from Northern rule and made the Democratic party the white man's party—the only party with any power in the state.[8]

Much of the political fight against the planters, blacks and carpetbaggers of Reconstruction was fought by the masses of whites; however, the political leaders of Redemption in Mississippi were not farmers, but lawyers and businessmen. These men had taken advantage of the opportunities opened during Reconstruction, and their distance from the people was usually great. L. Q. C. Lamar and Edward C. Walthall, powerful senators in the late 1870s and 1880s, were corporation lawyers with considerable wealth. They were avowed friends of the railroad. Though he had worked his way up from the ranks and had the sympathy of the small-farmer elements, J. Z. George, the chairman of the Democratic party who managed the Mississippi Plan, had the largest corporate law practice in the state. He consistently sided with Lamar and Walthall on issues of financial policy. The only two governors for two decades after Redemption—John M. Stone and Robert Lowry—were both conservative railroad lawyers who resisted regulatory legislation and conformed to generous policies to northern capital and corporate interests. (See Woodward 1951, esp. 17–19.)

The Redeemers' campaign attempted to convince the federal government to withdraw the Reconstruction governments and to persuade Southerners to develop a more diversified economy. Their primary purposes, however, had more to do with their hidden agenda: the intense desire to reestablish white superiority, to reinstitute the social control that Reconstruction threatened through Radical reform, and to form a new ruling class in the South, one not dominated by the old planters. (See Gaston 1970, "Prologue" and chap. 1.) And, indeed, it was the Redeemers "who laid the lasting foundations in matters of race, politics, economics, and law for the modern South" (Woodward 1951, 22).

In part, the appeal and strength of the Redeemers came from their ability to connect their values to long-standing Southern traditions as well as to speak to new conditions. If slavery had repressed blacks, as it did, it also repressed overt racist acts by poor whites. During Reconstruction these functions were served by wealthy landowners and federal troops. But the freedom of thousands of blacks struck fear into most, and the Redeemers spoke directly to it. Their rallying cries were the threats of black domination, social amalgamation, and miscegenation. These threats played off the long-standing ideals created around the Southern lady and virtually equated Southern civilization with the sanctity of white women; these women and this civilization needed to be protected—by white men. Thus, the Redeemers exaggerated, with a vengeance, repressive attitudes toward blacks and white women. (These developments reveal just how ideologies—usually seen as value systems justifying class power—always include definitions of gender and race identity.) Now, even more than at an earlier period, white men had little moral responsibility for the well-being of either white women or blacks; their major role became one of control and punishment, not edification and concern. White women became the most potent symbol of white male supremacy, and their protection became a potent rationalization and justification for the continued, vicious repression of blacks. (See Jones 1981 and

Scott 1970.) Redeemers' rhetoric claimed that all white men should be united; it sought to encourage white men to see themselves as patriarchs ruling over white women and blacks. The differences between wealthy and poor white men were glossed over by the Redeemers, and the formula made easy targets of the coalition between planters and black sharecroppers.

The Redeemers of the New South Creed spoke to the South's desperate need to justify its part in the Civil War and to return to the position of power and influence it had before the war. They used the notions embedded in the myth of the lost cause as an ideological weapon to re-form Southern ideals. This New South Creed pictured the prewar South as an idyllic, agricultural, and paternalistic land; it spoke to Southerners' need to believe they fought for more than simply slavery and allowed them to believe they had fought for a way of life.[9] During the decade or so after Redemption, the aristocratic paternalism of the Cavaliers became completely idealized; it acquired a tragic association with glory and all that was Southern, and Redeemers constantly identified themselves with this Cavalier paternalism. As Wayne comments, "The old planting aristocracy gave way to an elite dominated by merchants, financiers, and industrialists, aggressive, materialistic in the extreme, cloaking their behavior in 'a cult of archaism, a nostalgic vision of the past,' but otherwise conspicuously bourgeois [or liberal]" (1983, 197–98). These Redeemers also emphasized a social hierarchy and believed in the inherent superiority of the upper classes; however, for them, paternalism became a much more contrived position—justifying their positions of superiority and power while relinquishing them from responsibility. Those below had to make it completely on their own. This move proved most unfortunate for most identifying with these ideas, for these new Cavaliers had few pretensions of interest in the people whom they ruled.

The ideological position of the Redeemers sought in a way to wed images of the Old South, aspects of race-based paternalism, and capitalism. They maintained that whatever industry came to Mississippi—timber, railroads, cotton factories—would benefit all Mississippians, as would the growing of cotton. They stressed that as long as people stood by their captains and protected the solidarity of white superiority, all would be well. Their position was connected to the Jeffersonian as well as the Methodist sense that people's efforts brought them what they deserved, and these long-standing Southern beliefs served as potent ideological weapons solidifying the Redeemer position and weakening the plantocrats. From this perspective, they could (and did) argue that their abilities, education, and social refinement enabled and justified their roles as leaders. Representing a coalition of moneyed interests, these men were deeply invested in the stable and hierarchical social relations that had their roots in Whig ideologies, Jeffersonian notions of social deference, and paternalism. At the same time, they emphasized individual enterprise, self-help, familial responsibility, and local governance rather than social reforms and state intervention. Despite grumblings from various factions of poor farmers throughout the 1880s, the union of planter-merchant-businessman held that the intelligence and wealth of the South would govern in the interest of all classes, and it remained ensconced in political power.[10]

The victory of the Mississippi Plan was primarily a victory of certain factions within Mississippi's upper class over other factions within this same class. The Redeemers had won, temporarily, control of political and economic positions of power. At the same time, their ideological position was based on a delicate balance of opposing forces; in their victory were also the seeds of their demise. In general, Redeemers had experienced opportunity in their lives, and most held more strongly to beliefs in liberalism than did their plantocrat rivals. In their platforms these men directly appealed to the masses of white men who felt as if their own opportunities had been blocked by the union between planters and blacks; Redeemers promised opportunities to these whites and directly attacked opportunities for blacks. At the same time, Redeemers were not populists with strong democratic inclinations. They were businessmen and elitists. In their attempts to maintain their positions of power they purposely and consciously furthered race-based paternalism, which had strong roots in the South and Mississippi. At first, this move won them the votes and the allegiance of the mass of white voters. However, though generally white men felt better about the likelihood of opportunity under the Redeemers, and in general they were happy not to be threatened by a strong black labor force able to exercise social mobility, these same men did expect their lives to change. When opportunities did not increase during the Redeemers' rule, the contradictions in the Redeemers' position became more and more obvious. The Redeemers made it clear they believed in opportunity for all white men and that enabled them to become powerful. When opportunity actualized for only certain white men, it was only a matter of time before the Redeemers' balancing act would tumble. The mass of white Mississippians, united in strong beliefs in liberalism, would make it clear that elitism—except of course racial elitism—could no longer stand in the way of their advancement.

The Redeemers' precarious ideological position could not last when economic conditions were not changing and opportunities were not forthcoming for the mass of once-middle-class white farmers. On one level, the South was becoming more and more entwined in the nation's economic system: business, manufacturing, and industrial capitalism were making inroads into the South; Southern towns and cities grew because a need existed for middlemen of all sorts; and manufacturing and industry increased—not amazingly, but noticeably. The capitalist developments enabled the middle class to expand, and a capitalist ethos was growing.

These changes, though, had little if any impact on the mass of poor Southerners who tilled the land. More and more, tillers of the land did not own the land they worked. In general, agricultural interests came to be dominated by big business and relatively absent owners—those only interested in private profits. Agriculture was becoming less important as a basis for society and a social vision and more important as a business. Sadly for the mass of Southerners, as the South became more integrated in the nation, the South's prosperity did not increase. The Redeemers glorified paternalism, noblesse oblige, and Southern glory; however, as sharecropping, tenant farming, and the convict lease system revealed, benevolent paternalism itself was becoming the myth of the lost cause. Slowly, signs began to indicate that the Redeemers' position would face a challenge, and they sought to preserve their interests. The 1890 Constitutional Convention passed electoral laws that not only effectively stopped blacks from voting completely but also cut the white voting population by sixty percent. Sensing perhaps that popular will would resist, the convention ratified these changes without the consent of a popular election (Woodward 1951, 340–41). The 1890s would reveal what they had been afraid of as well as how effective their machinations were.

The traditions of the South and its race-based paternalism helped the Redeemers gain, keep, and believe they deserved their power. The opposition between poor white and black, formed in the early stages of Southern ruling-class ideology, also effectively closed off any possible union of white and black against the wealthy.[11] Nonetheless, the different interests of Redeemers and poor whites were not as easy to escape anymore. Mississippi was definitely changing. The general poverty of the South affected the farmer deeply and directly. Throughout the decade of the 1880s, the poor whites of Mississippi began to realize that their interests were not always considered in state conventions. They began to voice their complaints, to organize and to try to change the way government operated. The Farmers' Alliance and the Knights of Labor were early expressions of the agrarian unrest of the small farmers, and they had their impact in Mississippi. These movements clearly recognized the ideological union between planter and Redeemer that supported the exploitation of the farmers. The 1880s saw high and stable cotton prices, however; these calmed unrest for the most part. Nonetheless, the foundations for coalitions based on different sets of values—different ideological positions—had been laid. When cotton prices fell drastically in the 1890s, the Populist movement challenged the New South Redeemers head on.

Populists attacked the large plantation owners, whether corporate or individual, but they knew that their enemies consisted of more than the planters: railroad owners avoided taxes, bought legislatures, and charged high rates; manufacturers charged high tariffs; and Wall Street speculators gambled on cotton futures (Kirwan 1951, 93). Populists recognized the union of moneyed interests, whether agricultural or industrial, Northern or Southern. They wished to change all of these practices and unite workers of all kinds—their ideas were specifically related to class. They believed that the powers of government should be expanded at the expense of paternal, corporate interests, especially in regard to money, transportation, and land. Some of their specific programs called for fair elections, a national graduated income tax, extension of the public school system, lien laws to protect laborers and mechanics instead of only landlords and merchants, expansion of the currency, and the enlargement of the powers of railroad commissions. Populists also sought woman suffrage and equal rights for black workers who "were in the ditch with us." In short, as Woodward explains, "The political strategy of Southern Populists was based on combinations and alliances along regional, class and racial lines. . . . Every phase of this strategy was a challenge to the New South system, which had sought to divide all the elements Populists were trying to unite" (1951, 252).

In one sense, Populists resurrected the battle fought between Jacksonians and Whigs during the 1820s and expanded its scope. They stressed that those who tilled the land and worked for their bread should enjoy the fruits of their labor— that those people indeed were the foundation of the whole national edifice. Populists had, in essence, a completely different vision from the Redeemers— one that did not include monopoly capitalism, rabid individualism, and acquisitiveness. Their vision included small farmers and businessmen earning their keep through their efforts, not their chicanery, and not based on the surplus value created by the labor of others. The movement had some roots in Jeffersonian notions about the value of labor and the dangers of an aristocracy based on wealth. It sought an active role for government as a regulator of big business and wanted to break the cycle of exploitation inflicted on those who worked with their hands. It was different from the struggles of the 1820s in that it sought to unify all those who did not have control over their means of production—whites and blacks, men and women. In this manner Populism was truly a radical movement, a powerful emergent ideological formation that cut to the core of the Redeemer ideological position because it sought to undermine the very vision of social hierarchy embedded in this ideology. (See Woodward 1951, chap. 9; Clark and Kirwan 1967, chap. 3; Goodwyn 1976; Ayers 1992, chaps. 9, 10, and 11.)

Although it was true that Populist ideology was founded on a traditional vision of America rooted somewhat in the ideals of Jefferson and Jackson, it also threatened the allegiance of the Mississippi masses to the Redeemers' position—opportunity for all whites. Populism not only fought the ideology of social hierarchies, it also threatened the belief in individual effort and reward as well as the belief in white supremacy. For many, its vision remained primarily utopian. People who had for decades prided themselves in their righteous independence and who had believed that work would lead to financial and social improvement found it difficult to adopt the attitude of communal solidarity. The South's ideal of culture was not one based on the communal life of its citizens but on the individual acquisition of education, refinement, wealth, and the signs of wealth. Acceptance into the realm of materialist culture based on individual effort was the American ideal, which had, along with paternalism, been operating in the South for some time. (See Trachtenberg 1982, chaps. 4 and 5.) Populist ideology opposed that ideal with another and proposed a virtual revolution. It struggled in a world populated by people who did not want to change America but share in its promises. Farmers and laborers did not want their independence curtailed by responsibilities to political coalitions; they wanted to be able to exert it. Culture and wealth were still seen to be attainable by those who deserved them if they were just given the chance. Populism seemed to want to open doors to all, even the "lowest sort of people," who might not even deserve the opportunity, especially blacks. In short, the problem for most Mississippians was not the Redeemers' ideological position but that what it promised was not occurring for them. Meanwhile, Populism simply went too far.

For Mississippians, with their strong Jacksonian roots, Populism was tempting; however, for the 48,000 to 58,000 voters, out of a potential adult male electorate of 120,000, it was not tempting enough. It tried to shatter the very cornerstones that unified Southerners—white superiority and social hierarchy, with men active in the political sphere and women in the domestic. Many Democrats who by and large actually preferred Populist principles feared dividing the white vote by having two parties: they preferred "ring control" by moneyed interests to "negro domination" (Kirwan 1951, chap. 9). The old cry of white supremacy rallied Mississippi voters—those who were left—and the Populist program did not sweep the state.

Here we see just how effective the 1890 Constitutional Convention had been in curtailing the white vote. Those men who kept the franchise after 1890 were those who could read and pay their poll tax—that is, those who had some money and education and were not in the lowest class. This limited white franchise had always shared certain values with the Redeemers: a strong streak of romantic individualism and a belief in a kind of social hierarchy that able and hardworking people could climb. This heritage, however, was also shaped by the distinct history of race relations. Thus, though the 1890 election was a sign of the rise to dominance of a liberal ethos in Mississippi, this liberalism was combined with, and even built upon, an intense racism. Liberal values extended only to whites. In reductive through accurate terms, this combination summarizes the position of the Progressive party in Mississippi.

The voters of 1890 did want social reform, yes; they wanted their lot improved. But they did not want to undermine their whole social world. They did not want the doors of opportunity pushed wildly and suddenly open. At this juncture, Mississippi's middle and upper classes joined to protect what they had come to consider civilization against the rise of the lower classes. Unified by their beliefs in equal opportunity, achievement based on merit, and hard work, these groups were solidifying the dominance of a liberal ideology. Likewise, a class structure typical of bourgeois society was forming, with the distinctive feature that, according to the parameters of race-based paternalism, blacks occupied the lower class.

This alliance—middle-class whites and Redeemers opposed on one side by plantocrats and on the other by blacks—would become more pronounced during the rise of James K. Vardaman in the early part of the twentieth century. Vardaman's Progressivism adopted almost all the reforms of the Populists and brought Mississippi into the national mainstream as it were, but it did so in a way that did not clash with Mississippi's ideological heritage. An emergent ideology, Populism, was co-opted by Progressivism, the local embodiment of the dominant ideology of liberalism.

Although Populist candidates lost in the state elections of 1892 and 1896 and the party was pretty much extinct in Mississippi by 1900, Populism left its mark in two distinct ways: it trained the population in independent thinking and acting and it enabled people to realize that their government could help them. (See Kirwan 1951, chap. 9; Tindall 1967, chap. 1.) As Woodward puts it: "[Southern] progressivism . . . sprouted in the soil that had nourished Populism, but it lacked the agrarian cast and the radical edge that had frightened the middle class away from the earlier movement" (1951, 371). And, as Tindall explains, Progressivism was founded "chiefly on the aspirations of the middle-income groups to own and develop productive property, [and] drew strength from merchants, mechanics, farmers, small manufacturers, and the brokers and factors who serviced the farm economy"; [it was] "traditionalistic, individualistic, and set in a socially conservative milieu" (1967, 6–7).

Indeed, part of the success of the "revolution" that began with the election of Vardaman to governor in 1903 derives from his recognition that Mississippians considered reform and change to mean the threat of black domination and/or social amalgamation. His vicious attacks on blacks assured everyone—rich and poor alike—that the changes he wanted to institute would not lead to social upheaval. Although rival politicians did not like Vardaman personally, the difference between them was a "cleavage between respectability and audacity rather than a fundamental division on program" (Tindall 1967, 20–21). For the most part, "In their zeal for efficiency and the rationalization of state taxes and finances the progressives manifested important features of business development itself" (Tindall 1967, 18). Thus, though taking more of a percentage of the profits of the wealthy, Vardaman, and his successor, Bilbo, also helped stabilize the environment in which business was conducted, and they accepted the capitalist system. While keeping connections to the upper elements of the Redeemers in these ways, Vardaman also spoke directly to the fears and hopes of the mass of people who could vote. He assured them that he wanted to improve their lot without improving the lot of blacks or drastically changing the social structure. The Progressives, then, extended the Redeemers' policies and attitudes; the once self-conscious ruling-class ideology of Southern planters was effectively erased and replaced by a complete immersion in liberal and racist values that are the legacy of Mississippi.

The revolt that Vardaman did lead, however, was one directed specifically against the richest planters, corporations, and trusts who had long been granted the kind of absolute privilege only laissez-faire attitudes develop. These plans and policies also reveal his identification with liberalism in that now the duly elected representatives of the state would take care of its citizens rather than leave this care to the so-called wisdom of the elites. Vardaman made the government into as much of a regulatory agency as he could, attempting to pump money back into the state rather than into private hands. He ended convict leasing and improved prison conditions, developing cotton farms out of state lands that brought in huge profits; increased common-school appropriations for white schools almost twenty percent and teachers' salaries almost thirty percent; created a state textbook commission that broke the monopoly of the American Book Company; and regulated insurance companies, railroads, utilities, banks, manufacturers, and trusts. (See Kirwan 1951, chap. 14.) Although the plight of the farmer changed little in the first fifteen years of the twentieth century, when Vardaman's power was at its peak, the governor instituted many programs that supplied services to all Mississippians and used the government's power to benefit more than the rich. In effect, political and economic power was no longer in the hands of elitists but in the hands of the duly elected representatives of the voters, and this power was used to benefit the mass of Mississippians. These are basic liberal political policies, and their existence reveals how paternalism was indeed becoming a residual ideology.

Vardaman was succeeded by Theodore Bilbo, who continued on the same path. Bilbo created a central board of equalization that had the power to revise tax assessments on property values and corporations. As Kirwan details, "Railroad and public service corporation assessments were increased $40,000,000. Assessments in sixty-five of the poor counties were generally reduced. On the other hand, assessments in . . . three of the richest counties, were increased 463.7 per cent, 433.5 per cent and 234 per cent, respectively. . . . Writing in 1930, the outstanding authority on the subject called [this change] 'the very cornerstone' of Mississippi's fiscal machinery" (1951, 263–64). In 1919, when Bilbo left office, he had already contributed greatly to the establishment of the following: a State Tax Commission, a state tubercular sanatorium, a state charity hospital at Laurel, a statewide law for the eradication of cattle ticks, a hog vaccination law for the elimination of cholera, a highway commission with projected plans for a network of modern highways, the abolition of the fee system in county offices, the enactment of a law preventing the marketing of worthless stocks, the establishment of two lime-crushing plants where farmers could get lime crushed at cost, the enactment of an anti-lobbying law, and the abolition of public hangings. (See Kirwan 1951, chap. 20.)

In one very definite sense, the Progressives built on the foundation laid by Populism: they increased the administrative power of government, especially in the executive branch. Government leaders and the people at large came more and more to see government as an organized bureaucracy that would stand between paternal, corporate interests and the people. Programs instituted by the state and federal government came to replace the traditional paternalistic functions of local town officials, private charities, and families. Helping government officials make these changes was a new class of experts and professionals who served on regulatory and educational commissions, supervised improvements to public buildings and public services, and staffed charity institutions for the disabled and elderly. The emphasis in these new developments was not on family background, social refinement, and higher learning—as would have been the case under paternalism—but on professionalism, where one would fit in this new order. (See Wiebe 1967, chaps. 6 and 7; Tindall 1967, chap. 1.)

The radical shift in the structure and feeling of Mississippi society was founded on the principles and values of liberalism—at least as applied to whites. Nonetheless, paternalism did not totally disappear. Some resisted the changes and hated both Vardaman and Bilbo (whose career was filled with scandals). As evidenced by their comments about Bilbo—he was called, among other things, "a pert little monster, glib and shameless, with a sort of cunning common to criminals which passes for intelligence"—many in the old guard felt betrayed by developments in Mississippi (Percy 1941, 148). Their opinion of Bilbo highlights the gap between those adhering to paternalist, gentlemanly values and the new leaders. These paternalists persistently held to their values, but Mississippi kept marching into the twentieth century.

Progressivism's identification with liberalism also manifested itself in the ways the Progressives fought labor unions and resisted social legislation. Social programs seemed alien to the issues to be fought out, primarily because the belief in private property, competition, and profit had not been undermined. Men—white men—could make it on their own. Tindall summarizes these beliefs: "Shopkeepers and farmers generally held the accepted view that working men, thrifty and honest, could in due course acquire the ownership of productive property," and arguments for workmen's compensation, regulation of hours and wages, and child labor laws did not move them (1967, 6). Parental and property rights were still more important than social justice and human rights. Traditional Southern values often encouraged resistance to the more socially minded Progressive movements because social legislation and regulation reminded many of Reconstruction, when programs were instituted to help blacks. Whites often did not want to accept this help. Moreover, throughout the second decade of the twentieth century, the South experienced a wartime boom in which even tenant farmers came to know the feel of money. Their beliefs seemed to be proving true.

During the twenties, these liberal, Progressive beliefs in individual effort and reward proved just as ingrained, even in the face of adversity. After the wartime boom, cotton prices plummeted. During the flush times many had bought new land and mortgaged themselves to the maximum. Now, they were desperate for cash. The American Cotton Association was formed by the Progressive government of Woodrow Wilson to look into the matter and offer assistance. Mississippi farmers resisted the help. They continued to identify with the Jeffersonian ideal of the independent yeomanry in spite of their desperate condition, and a strong belief in God and judgment made them feel as if they deserved their punishment. Many farmers saw the advent of the boll weevil as a judgment from God and were slow to adopt scientific farming methods, including crop diversification, due to a near religious belief in King Cotton. (See Tindall 1967, chap. 4.) Farmers felt that "Heaven apportions its reward in exact relationship to the merit and goodness of the recipient" (Cash 1969, 359). Of course, "Most comforting to those who regard[ed] themselves as the leaders in the South" was the view that "the Old Testament law of retribution, of reward and punishment on earth, still prevails," and no legislation was passed during the twenties to help the conditions of the farmers (Kerr 1969, 176).

Thus, the conditions of black and white tenant farmers and sharecroppers did not change much as they were generally left out of Progressive developments. Necessary for the maintenance of social stability and their contribution to large profits, and rooted in Southern traditions that ran deep in Southern history, these classes persisted. One could still hear at times paeans to the beauty and glory of agrarian life, perpetuating visions both of noble Cavaliers ruling with care and concern, and of yeoman farmers tilling their soil with rustic independence and honor; however, though 67.9 percent of Mississippians were still engaged in rural occupations in 1930, both Cavaliers and yeoman farmers were myths of the past.

As in all societies, a definite class structure continued to exist. Once the middle rungs had achieved a modicum of improvement and success, they were as interested in maintaining a class structure beneficial to them as the upper classes were in keeping as much as they could. The defeat of the Populists proved fruitful for both groups, whose position and status were continually supported by large numbers of both industrial and agricultural laborers. Finance capitalism was no longer threatened from any quarter. The upper classes had had to sacrifice somewhat, but the ensuing stability enabled them to go about their business much as they did before, perhaps a little more quietly. The Progressives, meanwhile, were tightening the bonds of society and respectability. After World War I, the South's savage ideal, a fear and hatred of all that was not white and Protestant, became even more of a repressive force: "When the postwar South of the 1920's surged into a strange new world of urban booms and farm distress, it entered an unfamiliar terrain of diversity and change in which there lurked a thousand threats to older orthodoxies. . . . There was little freedom of feeling and little freedom of speech in matters relating to religion, race, industry or several social and moral sanctions . . . [and] there had been a growing tendency to associate American nationalism with nativism, Anglo-Saxon racism, and militant Protestantism" (Tindall 1967, 184). The savage ideal was against shifting moral standards, the declining influence of the churches, and the broadmindedness of cities and colleges. The middle classes forgot about their struggles with corporations and established themselves as models against the lower classes and arbiters of public morality. Traditions of the common man who worked for his bread had succumbed to a middle-class vision of respectability. Manners were the indication of character. Everyone was expected to go about his business, and he would be rewarded if he deserved to be.

The savage ideal can be seen to be the way Mississippi society squared its desire for liberal values of opportunity and mobility with its particularly vitriolic race-based paternalism. Opportunity and mobility remained open only to some, and those who supposedly deserved these freedoms had to reveal their identification with others in the dominant social world. Moreover, once there were no longer formal social control mechanisms—that is, in theory mobility was opened to all—the rules of social respectability and acceptance had to become more strict and had to be backed by informal means of violent social control. As mentioned earlier, a strict social order, like a plantocracy, not only repressed blacks but also repressed the fears of whites. Now, both mobile blacks and white fears were potentially everywhere; both had lives of their own.

The rise of the Progressive movement was the consolidation of a fully capitalist economy and a liberal ethos. In Mississippi, however, this ascendance had a peculiar development that was influenced by the racism stemming from pre–Civil War social formations. Liberalism did not immediately win over everyone in the state—Progressives were often considered parvenus and pretenders by the old paternalists who clung to so-called gentlemanly virtues and noblesse oblige. Nonetheless, whatever stability the society experienced during William Faulkner's lifetime came from its adherence to liberalism and its local manifestation—the progressivism of Vardaman and Bilbo. Although the Mississippi to which Faulkner was heir was filled with tumult, conflict, and struggle, and all the scars and memories of these battles lingered in the air he breathed, he could not change history. When he was born, paternalism had already become mostly a residual ideology, liberalism was well on its way to rising to dominance, and populism was in the process of being co-opted by the forces of liberalism and progressivism. The specific ways in which Faulkner himself was influenced by this general historical process can be further explored by looking closely at his family's insertions into these processes—the purpose of the next chapter. But in one regard Faulkner had no choice: he had to confront the two, strong ideological formations of his Mississippi—paternalism and liberalism.

2 • Faulkner's Ideology

Ideology and Subjectivity

Penetrated through and through by the history of his region and his family, Faulkner outran none of it.

—Philip Weinstein, *Faulkner's Subject*

You get born and you try this and you don't know why only you keep trying it and you are born at the same time with a lot of other people, all mixed up with them, like trying to, having to, move your arms and legs with strings only the same strings are hitched to all the other arms and legs and the others all trying and they dont know why either.

—Faulkner, *Absalom, Absalom!*

In what ways did material and social reality help produce William Faulkner? After detailing in chapter 1 the historical-ideological environment in which Faulkner and his family lived, here I will explain the specific forces that were internally persuasive in Faulkner's growth and development, as well as those he resisted and those he rejected.[1] I want to analyze the way in which he was embedded *within* his sociohistorical environment and how his subjectivity was dependent on it. A brief discussion of the affective account of ideology is necessary to explain the principles of my analysis.

The affective account of ideology is concerned with the function of ideas within social life, how ideas are lived on a day-to-day basis. Ideology in this sense stems from the more current assumption that *thinking* is ideological, that interests are constitutive of knowledge. In this account, no distinction exists between ideology and truth, for understanding occurs *through* ideologies—the organizing structures of society. In other words, "If men make history, ideologies make men."[2] This account comes in large part from the work of Althusser, who developed a theory about the dialectical nature of ideology.

For Althusser, ideology is not a thing or a set body of ideas but a type of relation. This relation concerns the intersection between individual psyches and external social conditions. External conditions necessarily impinge upon individuals; the process through which these necessary effects occur is "interpellation." At the same time, any individual interacts with the surrounding conditions in particular ways, and this interaction determines an ideological position. Ideology, then, "represents the imaginary relationship of individuals to their real conditions of existence" (1971, 162). This definition points to the internal component of the dialectic.

Deriving from the legal term meaning the process in a courtroom in which one is recognized to speak, interpellation rests on Althusser's distinction between individuals and subjects: ideology "interpellates concrete individuals as concrete subjects" (173). Individuals only become recognizable as human subjects by identifying with and becoming identified by aspects of the surrounding ideological milieu. Althusser stresses that to become a subject—someone about whom others can speak—individuals need to be given a name, an identity of some sort. Individuals can only become recognized by others when their actions and words become identifiable by some meaningful structure, when they enact some ideology. Ideologies, the set of meaningful structures through which our social milieu gets organized, outline our identities and form our configurations; they allow us to place each other into some overall understanding of the world.

This aspect of Althusser's theory emphasizes how external reality necessarily impinges upon individuals. In simple terms, this process says that if I refuse to perform those activities that define me as a professor, a doctor, an accountant, a father, then people will have difficulty identifying me as such, and I too will have difficulty identifying myself. The same for writers: if writers do not perform in such a way as to be considered writers, they will not get published, will not be identified as writers, and will have difficulty continuing to believe they are indeed writers. Our own identities are thus deeply interwoven with their recognition by others. One can indeed refuse to become identified by the sociohistorical ideologies of one's time; however, then one will have extreme difficulty attaining any identity at all. One will essentially be invisible, as a subject, to others. We generally label these individuals as psychotics or perhaps bums (a name given to Faulkner by his uncle and father), which means we do not have any place within our structures of meaning for them. As Eagleton claims, "What persuades men and women to mistake each other from time to time for gods or vermin is ideology" (1991, xiii).

The other aspect of Althusser's theory deals less with the ways we come to be recognized by others and more with how we come to recognize or "live with" ourselves. We do this by forming a representation of our imaginary relationship to the real conditions of our existence. For Althusser, individuals do not admit that they are indeed determined or produced to a great extent by their material conditions, by their places within the subtle network of interlocking forces and practices. Instead, people develop an imaginary representation of themselves, a self-identity they can accept and live with, which satisfies an unconscious need for coherence. Ideology offers the subject an imaginary, compelling sense of reality in which contradictions between self and social order appear resolved.[3] This image is not an illusion; it is an image of one's self to one's self in positively valued symbols and language. It is the way we wish, consciously or unconsciously, to be identified.

Althusser's theory has weaknesses, and Eagleton (1991) discusses various problems with it. In brief, Althusser's theory includes all lived experience within the realm of ideology when in fact lived experience is more of a boiling cauldron than ideology can contain. Althusser's theory of ideology is really a theory about the ideology of the ego—in the Freudian sense—rather than about the whole individual or mind. (See Eagleton 1991, 143–51.) Nonetheless, Althusser's account gives us the framework within which to see how an individual's interaction with and insertion into ideology necessarily occurs. "Ideology is now not just a distortion . . . a screen which intervenes between ourselves and reality. . . . It is an indispensable medium for the production of human subjects. Among the various modes of production in any society, there is one whose task is the production of forms of subjectivity" (Eagleton 1991, 148). With this framework in mind I want to investigate the formation of Faulkner's subjectivity, the dialectical relationship between the historical-ideological milieu and Faulkner himself. In keeping with Eagleton's critique of Althusser, my discussion will concern what can be called the manifest content of Faulkner's ideological position. Any ideological position will contain both a manifest and a latent (or repressed) content. Choosing to identify with some values and aspirations necessarily precludes identifying with others, and our choices can be seen to indicate the values that most influence our conscious or manifest image of ourselves—as conflicted as this image might be and despite the fact that we might feel we are choosing between two bad options. The latent content of an ideological position relates to values with which we do not identify and may be associated with other aspects of the sociohistorical milieu that we repress or wish to repress from our concern.

Faulkner, of course, experienced some severe conflicts in his life because his cauldron of lived experience could not always be peaceably contained in an ideological position. Still, he made decisions and choices through a system of values and beliefs and because of an image he had or wanted to have of himself. Without denying the possibility of discovering and analyzing the latent or repressed aspects of Faulkner's ideological position, possibilities to which I will point at times, it is that manifest image I try to decipher here by determining Faulkner's relation to his family's identifications and to his ideological milieu.[4]

Faulkner's great-grandfather, William Clark Falkner (writer of *The White Rose of Memphis*) has received much attention from Faulkner biographical scholars. He has come to be seen as a symbol of origin for Faulkner's own sense of who he was and what he wanted to accomplish in life because Faulkner reportedly said he wanted to be a writer like his great-grandaddy. Although undoubtedly he was a looming figure, William Clark has in my view received too much credit for his influence on his great-grandson. The truly influential figure, personally and ideologically, was Faulkner's grandfather, John Wesley Thompson Falkner.

William Clark Falkner came from a very poor background, and he made his way in nineteenth-century America very much on the strength of his own abilities and the degree to which he took advantage of the opportunities opened to him. Though he received a position in a law practice from a wealthy and respected relative, John Wesley Thompson, his first real financial coup was based on exploitation for personal gain: he interviewed a man about to be hanged, then wrote and sold the man's story for a profit. Later, he married into the planter class—much to his wife's relatives' dismay—receiving slaves as part of his wife's dowry and attaining some stability as a member of the upper class of Mississippi. By supplying contraband goods to Memphis during the Civil War—a profitable but not exactly noble practice—he was one of the rare few who returned from the Civil War with money to invest, and he quickly reestablished the Falkner Farms.[5]

Farming was not the life for W. C. Falkner, however, and he quickly turned to railroads and lumber and to reestablishing his public eminence. He claimed to be working for all of Mississippi when he built his railroad; in the meantime, he bullied people, pilfered their pockets to his own advantage, and made outrageous promises he never kept. He managed to donate money for a school in Ripley, but he did so more for what it would bring him than for altruistic purposes, for he was trying to erase the memories of his involvement in those less than honorable activities during the Civil War. Although he failed in one venture, eventually he was successful because he coerced towns desperate for transportation into contributing to his railroad by threatening not to run the tracks through them.

He was staunchly Democratic, avidly white supremacist, and he supported the policies of the Redeemers when they rose to power against the Republican/Plantocrats. Indeed, he can be seen to be the epitome of the Redeemer, voicing the rhetoric of an idealized paternalist while attempting to manipulate people for personal gain. He possessed a notorious vainglory, even commissioning his own statue, and had more personal ambition than familial or public responsibility. After his first wife's death, he gave away his son, Faulkner's grandfather, John Wesley Thompson Falkner, to his uncle—the wealthy relative who had given him a position in his law firm. He often fought with his aunt and uncle about how much money he should give to support his son. When he was killed by his one-time partner, people supposedly were not very upset.

W. C. Falkner gained a degree of social respectability through his marriage into the planter class; nonetheless, he remained a member of the upper class in Mississippi simply because he was wealthy (and white). Most of his energy was directed toward making money in one way or another. Remembering the descriptions of paternalism and liberalism offered in chapter 1, it should be quite clear that W. C. Falkner's life was primarily motivated by a liberal ethos. He clearly took advantage of whatever opportunities were opened to him to make money, and his life was a constant quest for social and financial upward mobility—at whatever cost. These quests were rarely if ever deterred by paternalist feelings of responsibility to his society, or even to his family. Whatever family responsibilities he felt were focused on his immediate, nuclear family, not on any notion of an extended family that he could easily have claimed. His social position and even the image he had of himself were based on wealth and possessions, not on a sense of refinement, manners, wisdom, or responsible leadership. He also did not feel as if his wealth and position were deserved due to his birth or to any notion of a natural superiority he possessed through character. The world, for him, was not a stratified and static organization. If asked, he would have proudly asserted he earned his wealth and deserved the mobility he experienced due to his own individual efforts. He was, indeed, a fairly brazen capitalist with few pretensions to paternalist benevolences, obligations to community, or visions of a social order where all had a natural and predetermined place.[6]

The life of Faulkner's grandfather, J. W. T. Falkner, is definitely and distinctly different from his father's. In fact, it will come as no surprise to learn that J. W. T. was not raised by his biological father, but by another family altogether, the Thompsons. The Thompsons were the very family that helped W. C. Falkner when he was a youth, and they did so out of a sense of paternalistic responsibility to an extended family member, a child of whom they otherwise knew nothing and did not at all have to help. Although not born into the planter class, this couple seemed to have identified with a different set of beliefs than William Clark; at least, this conclusion seems justified when we compare the behavior of their adopted son, J. W. T., to his father.

There is no scholarly discussion of the lasting influence of the Thompsons on the Falkner family; nonetheless, it seems clear that they had a deep effect on Faulkner's grandfather, and their influence was manifest in the ways in which he became a very different kind of man than his biological father. J. W. T. Falkner enjoyed the fruits of the Redeemers' economic policies. He was involved in many businesses that made him extremely wealthy, and he held political office at various intervals between 1886 and 1903; nonetheless, he never considered personal ambition his only driving force. As a public leader, he worked to modernize sewage systems and install electric lights, and he sometimes installed public improvements, like sidewalks, at his own expense. He offered a young "redneck," Lee Russell, the opportunity to join his law firm, mirroring the act of his foster father, John Wesley Thompson, toward W. C. Falkner, opening an economic door on his own initiative and from a feeling of social duty. Moreover, he watched over his sons' careers carefully, supplying them with every chance for success; he financed the education of two sons-in-law, took in and supported various members of the extended family at different times, and also played an active part in his grandsons' lives and careers, especially William Faulkner's.

In all these behaviors J. W. T. Falkner exhibited a strong attachment to paternalism. On one hand, he took his social and familial responsibilities and duties seriously, caring for an extended family and showing concern for social stability and improvement (cornerstones of paternalist ideology). On the other hand, though he did become law partners with Lee Russell, he would not allow this man into his home, claiming that their acquaintance was business-related, not social; in this he revealed his belief in the natural inequality of men and the stratification of society. He was, he believed, simply in a different class than Lee Russell, due to refinement and character. Meanwhile, Faulkner's grandmothers and his mother shared J. W. T.'s values. Both grandmothers were active members of the Women's Christian Temperance Union and the United Daughters of the Confederacy—organizations that helped keep alive memories of the Old South, perpetuating the myth of the lost cause—and his paternal grandmother, Sallie Murray, often sponsored the group's gatherings. Paternalism, its values and modes of behavior, was a strong influence in the Falkner family.

Dressing in white suits and often entertaining ex-Confederate officers, J. W. T. Falkner identified with a different set of values than his own biological father. Although both men were from the same class and the same family, the contrast between them highlights the behavioral differences between men in the upper class, some of whom identified with paternalist values, others with liberal ones. The Falkner family history almost directly parallels Mississippi history in other ways as well. In 1903 J. W. T. lost a bid for political office to a man he considered a redneck; his power and influence was waning as a new South was forming. At this point, he swore he would never run again; he felt that Mississippi was changing and that it did not appreciate his kind anymore. As we have seen, Mississippi was indeed changing, and the old regime and its values were being replaced by members of a new generation and a new class of men.

His own sons, in fact, verified this phenomenon. Both sons, Murry, Faulkner's father, and John, Faulkner's uncle, were more a part of the new world than their father. Though J. W. T. supported Vardaman and helped his campaign, he would not support Bilbo. He simply could not identify with the values and agenda that were becoming so prominent—those of the new ruling middle class identifying with liberalism. John became a lawyer and was active in the careers of both Bilbo and Lee Russell, the same man J. W. T. had accepted into his law firm but with whom he refused to socialize. Murry Falkner also supported both candidates. J. W. T.'s identification with paternalism made him condemn the actions of Bilbo, while his two sons could identify him as a self-made man who had risen from the ranks to achieve success. The different perceptions stemmed from ideological differences and the shift in power in Mississippi from the plantocrat/Redeemer coalition to the Redeemer/Progressive coalition, and these were formed by varying degrees of commitment either to paternalism or liberalism.

Though Faulkner's family was never part of the clique of Delta planters who had held political power and social influence for so long in Mississippi, parts of his family, through the Thompsons, J. W. T. Falkner, and certain female family members, were deeply affected by paternalism. Other members of Faulkner's family were identified by their allegiance to liberalism. Faulkner was thus in a specific historical and personal position that enabled him to see and to feel this historical conflict in detailed and multiple ways.

Looking at this personal history from the other end of the ideological spectrum, none of Faulkner's family had come from the small farming community. None had participated in the Farmer's Alliances, the Knights of Labor, or the Populist movement. Though Faulkner portrayed people from this class, at times—most significantly in *As I Lay Dying* and *The Hamlet*—his portrayals, as we will see, were not exactly sympathetic or widespread. These concerns were simply not his.

Of course, Faulkner had a unique position in his nuclear family. He seemed to be dissatisfied with his surroundings, both familial and social, never quite feeling completely at home in his world. Many critics have been influenced by the young Faulkner's statement that he wanted to be a writer like his great-grandaddy. This drive hints at his own conception of himself, which needs to be digested and explored. Yet, the strongest influence on Faulkner's early life was not his great-grandfather, nor was it his father or uncle. His grandfather, J. W. T. Falkner, and his mother were clearly the strongest influences on the young William Faulkner. Steeped in the romantic heroism of the Old South, capitalist in his economic pursuits but paternalist in his social and family values, J. W. T. Falkner was the man who mesmerized William with tales of the Old South, and at whose knee William often sat. He was also the man, rather than his own father, to whom William went to ask permission to marry Estelle Oldham. Faulkner's mother, of course, inclined Faulkner to the artistic world, and helped him envision it as a haven from the materialistic environment of the New South (and his father). She was also fiercely independent and had an unswerving commitment to individualism. Like most influenced by paternalism, though, she was more concerned with liberty and freedom than with equality and democracy. Remembering now that Bakhtin has claimed that a writer, *by necessity*, must interact with the sociohistorical voices operative in his surrounding milieu, it makes perfect sense that Faulkner had to contend with the voices and values of paternalism, in his own way. If paternalism was not in Faulkner's blood, it certainly was in the language in his head, and it certainly influenced, deeply, his views of himself and the world.

In fact, as revealed in the various biographies of Faulkner, his attachment to the values and beliefs of paternalism was perhaps the strongest early ideological influence on the development of his subjectivity. His early life clearly contained two major motivations: the desire for heroic action, and a definite alienation from the New South, which he did not consider the South at all.[7] This alienation from his surrounding society, dominated by a liberal, capitalist value-system, stemmed primarily from the identification with paternalism—its sense of honor, its romanticism, its glorification of the image of woman, as well as the social prestige it conferred on certain men. This identification also disallowed him from seeing how any behavior or activity within capitalism could satisfy his heroic yearnings. This affiliation to paternalism was also manifest in Faulkner's identification with the Oldhams, a family much more closely aligned with the upper crust of Southern society, and with Phil Stone, who too had aristocratic credentials.[8] It only heightened his sense of displacement: a dramatic theme in the lives of those identifying with a residual ideology.

Faulkner's attachment to paternalism was for a while so intense that he remained a mystery to his contemporaries. Most of those around him were unable to give him any recognizable, acceptable identity. Friends knew his name, and students at the University of Mississippi knew him, but they never knew what to make of him, how to understand him, how to relate themselves to him. His classmates at the university called him "Count No Count"; for every story and poem Faulkner wrote for the school newspaper there was a spoof of its style and values. Meanwhile, his father and uncle thought simply that he was a bum. All of these people were unable to confer upon him a viable social identity, especially one that would satisfy his desire for a position of social eminence. His own image of himself was not being mirrored back to him. Thus, interpellated by the strain of paternalism deriving from his grandfather's Old South, Faulkner was affected in two ways: he was unable to recognize how any pursuit within capitalism was worthy of his time and effort (his refusal to work at any job is well known), and, because of this, he was unable to acquire the prestige and position necessary to be a respected, revered paternalist figure—something he always wanted. If Faulkner needed any proof of his social status, he need only to understand why both his grandfather and Mr. Oldham, men whose opinions he respected, refused his request to marry Estelle: love, ideals, dreams, and poetry were not enough. Faulkner simply had no money or social position—for all intents and purposes he was invisible as a prospective husband, a respected and successful gentleman.

My account of Faulkner is indirectly supported by other discussions of this time in Faulkner's early life (the 1920s). Judith Sensibar (1984) argues that his public masquerading was symptomatic of a profound psychological disturbance, that Faulkner displayed the distinguishing features of an impostor, a psychotic personality lacking a central identity. Ilse Lind (1986) discusses how these actions may have been connected to his fragile sense of himself as a male in the South. These discussions reveal that Faulkner's major problem at this point in his life was indeed one of identity—he had no clear idea of how to portray his sense of himself to others. Their claim that this concern was a psychological disturbance, however, rests on the assumption that one might indeed have a sense of identity that is separate from the social world. Moreover, these psychological theories cannot explain how Faulkner was cured through the process of writing successful novels, or how, despite the problems Lind describes, which persisted his entire life, he was able to move forward in his life as a man and a writer. There just does not seem to be anything wrong with Faulkner's mind, or anything chaotic about his sense of himself. Yes, he was masquerading, but his problem had more to do with meshing his conception of himself with the world's conception of him; it was the problem of becoming a recognizable human subject. His problem was not his lack of understanding himself, was not in his mind, but existed in the difficulty he had finding some way to get the world to appreciate his actions and beliefs that were based on completely different values than those the people around him held. The world, so to speak, wanted Faulkner to prove his talent and worth on its terms before it would acknowledge him; he felt his rightful position was being denied. Once he found a means through which to be both true to himself and understandable to others, once he was able to develop a positively laden identity through which some relation to the outside world could be maintained, his problem disappeared. If Faulkner's struggle here in the twenties had a psychological component, it connects more to the social psychology involved in forming an identity by affirming certain acceptable aspects of one's social milieu.[9]

This search for a positive and affirming relation to the outside world was also complicated in specific ways by one of Southern paternalism's major components: honor. As I have already shown, identity is intimately connected to one's sense of self as it is reflected back by the surrounding society. Many writers attain the sense of themselves they desire by leaving their hometowns to live among more artistic and intellectual people. Faulkner did go to New Orleans briefly and did receive more recognition there than in Oxford, yet he did not stay, nor did he ever call anywhere but Oxford his home (until he moved to Charlottesville). One explanation for this decision comes from his sense of Southern honor.

As Bertram Wyatt-Brown explains, one element of honor, as it was understood in the South, has to do with the assessment of one's own self-assessment by one's environment: "Honor resides in the individual as his understanding of who he is and where he belongs in the ordered ranks of his society" (1982, 14). For Faulkner to be valued and recognized by the artists in New Orleans was not enough—as his actions and decisions clearly reveal. He needed the recognition of those from his own world, from his own environment, and he didn't rest until he received it. He needed the community to recognize his deserved place in the order of things. Moreover, the ideological determinants of an honorable man forbid his retreat into some isolated, private haven away from community; an honorable man must confront the world on its own terms, must hold his position despite the odds and the circumstances. To leave Oxford was obviously an option for Faulkner. That he chose not to do so reveals how powerful the paternalistic forces that formed notions of Southern honor were for him. He needed others to recognize the position with which he identified.

The beginning of the change in the relation between Faulkner and the public world began in the twenties. But this development was not an organic, mysterious one without choices and without strong influences from the outside. As Bleikasten claims, Faulkner *"perhaps would not even have become a writer,* if by the time he was in search of an identity and a destiny, the ambitions and claims of literature had not grown so inordinately as to make writing a possible substitute for heroic action" (1983, 37; my emphasis). Deeply entrenched in notions of Southern paternalism gleaned from his grandfather, grandmothers, and mother and from various aspects of the world around him, Faulkner's choice to become a writer can be directly linked with the cultural prestige literature was coming to have in the early twentieth century and with the role it came more and more to play in the modernist period—as well as with the ways in which this understanding satisfied Faulkner's desired relation to the outside world. It certainly did not hurt that Faulkner's choice was encouraged by both an artistic paternalist figure, Sherwood Anderson, and a social paternalist figure, Phil Stone, and Faulkner's decisions can be seen to be greatly influenced by these men's understanding of the role and function of literature.

That writers were envisioned to be the seers of humanity, able to give voice to needed but neglected values, was obviously appealing to a young Faulkner. That literary modernists such as Anderson, T. S. Eliot, and James Joyce were opposed to the same society from which Faulkner felt alienated and envisioned themselves as cultural heroes holding up the very tenets of civilization against superficial and materialistic hordes clearly attracted Faulkner. That writers were seen to have unique powers of insight and wisdom, as well as gifts uncommon among men would also naturally entice a man striving for a special place within the social order. Finally, writing was also a means through which Faulkner could participate in capitalism without having to do so directly. Certainly, both his heroic desires and his alienation from capitalism influenced his pursuit of the craft of writing: Faulkner's early interpellation by the ideology of paternalism deeply affected his choice of writing as a means to acquire an identity in the world. Using Althusser's terms, one could say that Faulkner's imaginary relationship to his real conditions of existence was a picture of himself as a natural, artistic aristocrat and that writing became the means he chose to reveal that picture to the world.

Through writing, writers, mentors, and critics, Faulkner received the first signs of recognition that squared with his sense of himself. As he claimed: "those shady but ingenious shapes" gave him a means to "reaffirm the impulses of my ego in this actual world" (Blotner 1973, 124). This initial encouragement outweighed comments from his father and uncle about him being a bum because it supported his own view of himself.

But with writing an obvious paradox ensued. Literature only becomes such through the recognition of its worth and quality by others, and Faulkner's relationship with those others was still a troubling one for much of the 1920s. *Soldier's Pay* was a start, but it had been helped along by Anderson and certainly did not give Faulkner the status he desired—which was to be seen as the best, a heroic writer.[10] *Mosquitoes* was disappointing, and then came *Flags in the Dust*. As is widely known, the rejection of *Flags in the Dust* was a painful experience for Faulkner. He had poured his artistic and paternalistic heart and soul into that book, which was to be a touchstone of his forefathers' South; its rejection was exactly like a rejection of himself. Faulkner was at a crossroads.

When *Flags* was rejected, Faulkner could have reverted back to some earlier, more alienated, stage in which he had achieved virtually no identity; his nostalgia for the past, even for a past that possibly did not exist, could have led him into a life of interminable melancholy. He could have blamed the rejection on the changed and fallen world and retreated further into isolation. He could have even become a post office worker writing romantic poems late into the night. But he didn't.

Like many Faulkner critics, I see the turning point of Faulkner's career in this crucial stage between the rejection of *Flags* and the acceptance of *The Sound and the Fury*. I read this transition as one in which changes in literature mirror developments in life and argue that Faulkner was able to move into the future because he was able, to some extent, to let go of the past and of paternalism and to begin to participate in this new world, identified as it was by liberalism. My contention is that at this point Faulkner changed both the writing and his image of himself—that the mature Faulkner, both personally and artistically, emerged during this period.

As it is understood here, ideology involves the essentially narrative, or fabulous, attempt of the subject to inscribe a place for itself in a collective and his torical process. My contention is that after the rejection of *Flags*, Faulkner began this process in a successful manner; he began to accept the real existence of "other voices" and to recognize that in order to be remembered he would have to attend to them—contend with them—on their terms. With *The Sound and the Fury*, Faulkner began to break away from paternalism: the portrayal of Quentin Compson, as will be discussed in the next chapter, is certainly an acknowledgment of the ineffectiveness and virtual invisibility of a young paternalist in a liberal, bourgeois world. Moreover, the narrative form of *The Sound and the Fury* omits the possibility of shared values voiced through an omniscient narrator, as embodied in *Flags*, and purposely follows the form considered to be the highest in modernist/bourgeois art at the time. Faulkner's artistic choices indicate an exploration of more than the paternalistic or mythological worlds explored in his earlier works. We see individuals voicing their isolated psyches and coming to terms with themselves—aspects of a capitalist world and liberalism. Although Faulkner certainly does not celebrate this new world, this new South, these signs indicate that he was indeed questioning his paternalist ideology, which had not been able to satisfy his own vision of himself, and that he was beginning to confront his own more liberal sociohistorical milieu. In the development of his ideological consciousness, these signs indicated Faulkner's ability and willingness to use the languages in his sociohistorical world for his own purposes. He began, that is, to write his way into this historical environment by shaping his materials, rather than by being exclusively shaped by them.

This development is also indicated by Faulkner's decision to marry Estelle (around the same time he wrote *The Sound and the Fury*). On one level, the marriage satisfied some need within Faulkner; it fulfilled a sense of himself as a gentleman and to some extent as someone who belonged in the upper classes. Yet, Faulkner knew that he would have to provide for Estelle and her children, and he was obviously ready to do what it took to fulfill that obligation. Only after his marriage did he begin to become almost manic about selling his stories, packaging them for market value; and, of course, he also decided to go to Hollywood. This period of his life, then, entailed a major turning point, one that did not sever Faulkner completely from the past but moved him into a new future. In fact, during this period the paradox of Faulkner's entire life and the major tension of his fiction becomes created: the ever-running conflict between two mutually exclusive value systems. The decision to marry Estelle indicated both that his identity was still very much connected to a sense of himself as a paternalist—as he was able now to fulfill the role denied him at a younger age—and that he was prepared to participate in the liberal, bourgeois world in order to achieve that identity. In short, both the man and the artist were changing.

Although Faulkner was not conscious of this process, it should come as no surprise that the conflict at the heart of his fiction mirrors the conflict at the heart of the upper class of Southern society. The raw material from which Faulkner had to work—the world in which he lived and from which he drew his narratives—was identified by two antagonistic ideologies that clashed and interacted in many ways. His own family embodied these forces. Thus, since Faulkner necessarily had to confront these ideologies, his fiction did as well. It should also be no surprise that Faulkner's mature fiction emerged just as it began to relinquish a direct identification with the past, as it began to treat the emergent and central tension existing at the heart of the South and, perhaps, at the heart of America still. For, although there is no question about the dominance of liberalism in America, questions about the world liberalism has created do exist, and these questions exist at the heart of Faulkner's social vision.

As many of his comments about democracy and capitalism reveal, Faulkner was never completely at home in a world dominated by liberalism, and his fiction constantly explores his doubts and fears. Do the Jason Compsons overthrow the Quentins? Do the Anse and Cash Bundrens lead to the deaths of Addies and Darls? Do the Jody and Will Varners lead to Flem Snopes? Do the

DeSpains lead to the selling of the South and the deaths of Eula Varners? Do Ike McCaslin and Gavin Stevens lead nowhere? Ultimately, Faulkner was afraid of liberalism and its effects on the direction of the South and the country, and he was afraid that the death of all of paternalism's values would allow the hordes to sweep away all that was sacred. Thus, his ideological struggles with the world were situated within history. His eventual relation to this ideological environment was, however, his own.

Faulkner's own emergence into the bourgeois world and his experience with increasing success in this world seem to have allowed him to accept certain tenets of liberal ideology, namely reward based on merit and the content of one's achievement. Those on top of the social hierarchy should get there, he seems to come to believe, through their talents, abilities, and character. This hierarchical social structure would not be based on blood and family and refinement, as it was within traditional aristocracies, nor on wealth, as can be seen within capitalism. At the same time, Faulkner holds fast to a belief in the possibility of a naturally ordered society whose most powerful figures are men who are, in theory, naturally better and more superior than others. This natural order would prohibit chaos from destroying society, and these natural leaders would assure that deserving folks would get their reward. Without discussing here the obvious problems in this social vision, I believe the attempt to combine elements from both liberalism and paternalism becomes Faulkner's authorial ideology, the work he exerts on the general ideological formations, the representation of his imaginary relation to the real conditions of his existence. What emerges as the central value system of Faulkner's life and art is an ideology resembling the sense of natural aristocracy first articulated in the United States by Thomas Jefferson.[11]

This ideological position, this imaginary representation of himself in positively valued terms, resolved, on one level, the conflicts and contradictions under which Faulkner lived, giving him a coherent picture of the way in which the world could and should work, and a coherent vision of where he fit into it. That this vision deeply affected his personal life seems clear. As Karl Zender comments on Faulkner's behavior in the 1930s: "he was actualizing a deeply cherished vision of his proper role in the world . . . something he evidently very deeply needed to be: a paterfamilias" (1989, 69). And he was accomplishing this goal by interacting directly with the world of Hollywood, publishing, investment in property, and so on.

This vision also points to new ways to understand Faulkner's later life and art—subjects that often seem disconnected from discussions of Faulkner the artist. Faulkner's decision to become an emissary for the U.S. government came after he had achieved a position of renown and respect—after he had won the Pulitzer Prize for *A Fable* and had been awarded the Nobel Prize. Only then, it can be argued, after he had, in his own eyes, indeed become a natural aristocrat, did he begin to feel a certain responsibility to perform a role that seems very out of character.[12] This image of himself as a natural aristocrat can also be seen to coincide with Faulkner's sense that he needed to become more of a teacher, as Zender claims, in both his life and his fiction. It also, obviously, helps us understand why he always decided to stay with Estelle even though he was clearly miserable at times, and why he so enjoyed the cultural elite in Charlottesville. As Williamson claims, "What Faulkner was doing in those Virginia years . . . was constructing yet another persona . . . [whose] essence [is] aristocratic, and it carries intimations of the cavalier riding loyally for the Stuart kings" (1993, 328). What I, too, am implying is that Faulkner's career had really only one motivation right from the beginning—the desire and the drive to be a natural aristocrat both in terms of art and life.

This Faulknerian authorial ideology serves primarily as an overall rhetoric that gives form and meaning to specific characters and narratives. Since all ideologies are narrative in function, serving to help us order (or write) the real of history, Faulkner's serves to explain the way his Yoknapatawpha County functions and the way the world as a whole should function. Faulkner's fiction does not represent reality; it represents signifying practices that conceive of the world in distinct ways. These, in turn, reveal Faulkner's own relation to the larger ideological environment around him. Many of his characters can be understood within these values and put into some overall context of Faulkner's canon as well.

Faulkner had an affinity for the powerful man, especially the powerful white man—the best examples perhaps being Bayard Sartoris, General Compson, and Lucius Priest—but he was hard on those who denied or refused their seemingly inherent social responsibilities—Ike McCaslin, Gavin Stevens, Major DeSpain. He also had deep sympathy for the poor and the powerless, both white and black—the Bundruns, Dilsey, Lena Grove, Mink Snopes, Lucas Beauchamp, Thomas Sutpen—unless or when they attempted to step out of their so-called proper places in society undeservedly—Anse Bundren, Mink and Flem Snopes, Thomas Sutpen. He also granted a great deal of power to women—Lena Grove, Eula Varner, Addie Bundren—however, this power was only justified or productive when it related to the domestic sphere, where it (naturally) belonged within any paternalist ideology. When women stepped out of that sphere, they were hurt or punished—Charlotte Rittenmeyer, Linda Snopes Kohl, Caddy Compson.

Although this brief description is admittedly reductive, it points to a somewhat unified set of values and representations that exist throughout Faulkner's canon, both before and after the supposed big break in his career so often discussed in Faulkner scholarship. Even *A Fable* shares the quest for reconciliation between two antagonistic value systems comparable to paternalism and liberalism. The tension between these two polarities operates in different ways in many Faulkner novels.

Depending upon one's own ideological position, Faulkner's authorial ideology can be deeply criticized as being reactionary and chauvinistic, even racist, or it can be valorized as an attempt to maintain the best values from directly contradictory ideologies. What is certain is that Faulkner's attempt to combine contradictory ideologies underscores a utopian yearning for an imaginary world. On one hand, this quest has a productive critical function, pointing to the failings of the ideological solutions determined by real human agents in history. Fiction has the power to present alternate visions of ways the world perhaps could and might work at some other juncture in history. On the other hand, Faulkner's political unconscious, in the last instance, posits simply an impossible world, and it thus elides the very systems of domination and oppression with which Yoknapatawpha is so enmeshed. Faulkner can never, it seems, break from a deep allegiance to paternalism and the social stratification it requires; from this perspective his social vision remains deeply conservative. For me, this conclusion is an accurate description, not a condemnation of a great artist.

The desire to be recognized as a natural aristocrat can be seen to be a central concern of Faulkner's life and art, his "lived relation" to his conditions of existence, around which many seemingly unrelated elements cohere. I do not want to imply Faulkner's life and/or fiction are unified and consistent; they are not. They are filled with conflicts, contradictions, repressions, and yearnings, which critics have discussed and will continue to discuss. His Yoknapatawpha is filled with dominant, residual, and emergent ideologies, in tension and conflict at each and every turn. Nonetheless, just as a society can cohere while still being filled with contradictory voices, forces of legitimation and repression, "Faulkner" and his Yoknapatawpha cohere around this system of values with its own specific voices of legitimation and repression. Like his description of Quentin Compson,

Faulkner too is a commonwealth of voices, whose dominant ideology can be labeled natural aristocracy.

This position is the *manifest* content of Faulkner's authorial ideology, and I wish to stress again that I do not investigate the various repressed aspects and significances inherent therein to any great extent. Working with some of the elements surrounding him, Faulkner created a lived relation to his world with which he could identify and by which he desired to become identifiable to others. He also, through much conflict and struggle, was successful in his task. Faulkner became a natural aristocrat. This ideology is not an illusion; it is the relation Faulkner established and formed with the world. Moreover, his sensitivity to all aspects of this ideological position—both its manifest and latent elements, its sense and its possible non-sense—allowed him to depict the broadest panorama of America yet created. In these two successful accomplishments, I would argue, lies Faulkner's achievement.

Nonetheless, Faulkner's limitations stem from the fact that his life did indeed always affect his art. His sociohistorical world and his relation to that world indelibly stamped his Yoknapatawpha. Faulkner's imaginary relationship to his world was dependent upon the ways in which his ideological milieu interpellated him, and his authorial ideology supports the very foundations of Yoknapatawpha. As is usually the case, it is not people's consciousness that creates the world, but the world that creates people's consciousness—and in this case, the parameters of an artistic creation as well.

Part Two • Faulkner, Paternalism, Liberalism

3 • *The Sound and the Fury*

Faulkner's Birth into History

Faulkner seems anxious to reach a fuller understanding of the relation between life and art . . . his quest for a workable aesthetic went along with a
search for identity . . . and his ruling concern was one of self-definition in
terms of life and art.

— Andre Bleikasten, *The Most Splendid Failure*

[He] had been born too late for the old time and too soon for the new.

— Faulkner, *Go Down, Moses*

As almost every Faulkner critic has claimed, when Faulkner approached the
writing of *The Sound and the Fury*, he experienced a dramatic change in perspective and ability. The usual explanation for this shift derives from a romantic, organic sense of the way artistic genius develops: it emerges, springing forth
mysteriously from deep within the artist's soul and psyche. This perspective is
less an explanation than a testament to the writer's achievement, and to move in
the direction I want to push our understanding we must resist Faulkner's own
statement that when he sat down to write this novel about the Compson family he shut the door on all those voices raging outside the quiet of his room. He
did not.

Myra Jehlen was the first to claim that Faulkner drew "characters whose inner lives are essentially linings for selves tailored to unalterable social patterns" (1976, 1), and Noel Polk (1985) has indicated that the writings of this
period are "close" to Faulkner. I want to pursue these insights in order to understand Faulkner's work as being connected to social patterns and to his sense
of himself and his world. A different explanation for the developments during
this period can be discovered if we examine them from a materialist sense of

consciousness—how Faulkner existed in and interacted with a specific place and time, and how he, like all writers, developed a degree of ideological independence from his surrounding world—that is, how Faulkner began to write himself into history.

Bakhtin explains how a writer discovers and grows into a mature voice. For writers, the process of self-definition, of coming to ideological consciousness, always entails an active struggle with the voices of their surrounding milieu. Bakhtin states, "consciousness awakens to independent ideological life precisely in a world of alien discourses . . . from which it cannot initially separate itself; the process of distinguishing between one's own and another's discourse, between one's own and another's thought, is activated rather late in development . . . [w]hen thought begins to work in an independent, experimenting and discriminating way" (1981, 345). It seems clear that, despite any one critic's assessment of Faulkner's early poems and pre-Yoknapatawpha novels, during this time Faulkner was deeply attached to "other voices." Significantly, those to which he was most attached were those that also had resisted the increasingly powerful forces of bourgeois society—the verse of decadent poets including Swinburne, Housman, and Beardsley, and those who identified with an aristocratic tradition of honor and heroism (like his grandfather).

His first Yoknapatawpha novel, *Flags in the Dust,* certainly differs from the earlier work. Faulkner was claiming, as he described it, his little postage stamp of native soil, and he utilized his personal past to develop in some detail a lexicon of social types that would serve him for the rest of his career. At the same time, *Flags* remains deeply connected to the past, entwined in both historical echoes of family and local tales and literary echoes of Keats, Tennyson, Shakespeare, Joyce, and Hugh Wiley (even Conrad and Hardy). Applying the Bakhtinian perspective to Faulkner's novels, we can understand how *Flags in the Dust* is "half someone else's" in that Faulkner had not gained complete independence from material to which he had been intensely attached—mainly paternalistic and romantic influences. Simply, the Yoknapatawpha County in *Flags* is not the world Faulkner would create; it is much more the world that created him. *Flags* is a paean to a life that had come to Faulkner through the ideologically laden words of other people told in a language filled with literary echoes of other writers of a premodernist generation. Not until *The Reivers* would Faulkner again depict such a romanticized picture of the South, and never again would he use such derivative language.

The struggle with language and the past evidenced in *Flags in the Dust,* however, was a necessary step in the development of Faulkner's independent (and artistic) consciousness. As Bakhtin again explains: "The importance of struggling with another's discourse, its influence in the history of an individual's coming to ideological consciousness, is enormous . . . *[it] creates fertile soil for experimentally objectifying another's discourse* (1981, 348; my emphasis). Clearly, the major difference between *Flags* and the novels immediately following it—*The Sound and the Fury, Sanctuary, As I Lay Dying,* and *Light in August*—is the way in which Faulkner begins to experiment with objectifying others' discourses. In the later novels Faulkner "makes use of words that are already populated with the social intentions of others [but] compels them to serve his own new intentions" (Bakhtin 1981, 299–300).

We can conclude that the intense degree to which Faulkner was connected to the paternalist aspects of his surrounding world led to his rather late separation from that world and that the objectifying of discourses found in the writings of the period from 1927 to 1932 reveals Faulkner's initial explorations of the ideological world to which he was heir. With *The Sound and the Fury,* Faulkner stands back, as it were, for the first time, from the historical world in which he had been rather unconsciously immersed and begins to reveal his own independent perspectives. Like other Faulkner novels, *The Sound and the Fury* can be seen as a symbolic narrative revealing messages about social formations, about history, but this one begins the process of revealing how Faulkner sees himself in relation to that history. It reveals the early stages of Faulkner's authorial ideology.

Faulkner opens *The Sound and the Fury* with an intricate narrative section, one told by an "idiot" in touch only with his sensory experiences. At first glance, Benjy's section seems about as far away from social history as any author could go. On one level, of course, this claim holds truth, for in writing a more or less stream-of-consciousness, sensory-oriented, time-shifting section Faulkner's clear purpose was to associate himself with the modernist writers who were becoming celebrated in the artistic world—to identify himself, that is, with ART. The aesthetic ideology identifying Faulkner's technique—what we now call modernism—is certainly the one that had moved to ascendancy in artistic circles in the 1920s, and Benjy's section holds importance, on one level, for what it tells about Faulkner: he wanted to be associated with the greats. If we have any doubt about that, his 1933 introduction to the novel should alleviate it. There he claims: "When I finished The Sound and the Fury I discovered that there is actually something to which the shabby term Art not only can, but must be applied. . . . I discovered the Flauberts and Dostoievskys and Conrads whose books I had read ten years ago."[1] In telling us about Faulkner's desire to be a great artist, Benjy's section also tells us about Faulkner's subjectivity—the vision he desired of himself. Later, after Faulkner had established his literary prowess, he would utilize a style much closer to social realism; here, he works to identify himself and his talents with the writers he considered great.

Clearly, though, Faulkner does not simply include Benjy's section for aesthetic and subjective reasons. It has a close connection to the rest of the novel and a significant place within the overall form of the narrative. In Benjy, Faulkner creates a character who closely relates to an earlier time period. In tune with sensory experience, Benjy does not possess any of the qualities and abilities so definitely valued—too valued Faulkner would say—in this twentieth-century capitalist world—those of calculation, classification, and prediction. Faulkner seems to be completely in unison with Marxist critiques of capitalist society, implying that the need to own things and the skills necessary to obtain them in this society diminish the ability to appreciate and perceive through the senses. As Edward Ahearn states, summarizing Marx's Paris manuscripts: "The system of private property and wealth is an estrangement of *all* [the] senses" (1989, 17). On a socially symbolic level, Benjy can be seen to represent aspects of precapitalist social formations, ones that have lost their value and are no longer utilized or appreciated in Faulkner's and the novel's contemporary society. Faulkner's attachment to the past is here shown to be based on a sound and thorough understanding of the personal effects of capitalist social formations on the people within it.

Important for an understanding of Faulkner's relation to social history, Benjy is also seen primarily as a positive character. The novel emphasizes this positive evaluation by offering judgments about characters via their attitude toward Benjy. Those characters who have a positive relation to him—Mr. Compson, Quentin, Caddy, Dilsey—those who in essence bring some of the older world into this new, more analytical and desensitized South, are the positive characters in the book. As the first section of a book about the transition from one kind of South to another, Benjy's section highlights the values of these two worlds and Faulkner's relation to them. Those characters associated with the old South want to keep Benjy at home, in the paternalist family structure, and care for him within a communal network. Those identifying with the new liberal world want to give responsibility for Benjy to the state, to place him in a home, and proceed on their path for individual success. Faulkner identifies with the first group.

Thus, on a subjective level, Benjy reveals Faulkner's continued resistance to capitalism; on a socially symbolic level, he symbolizes much that is fading away. Along with its literary importance, this section has historical and ideological significance. It is no mistake that Benjy's section is close to Quentin's physically, for both are closely connected to social formations that are fading from the South.

Like Benjy's section, Quentin's has been seen by many critics to be important for its artistic significance; however, even Faulkner's most literary character has ideological resonance. As *The Sound and the Fury* tells us, Quentin is "another cavalier" (171). This label highlights a historical set of values that, as I discussed earlier, was both fading from the South and strongly influential for Faulkner. As his first independent portrayal of this set of values, Faulkner's depiction and descriptions of Quentin are sympathetic and insightful: Quentin is close to Faulkner himself. Yet, Quentin's suicide comes to symbolize Faulkner's recognition of the social inadequacy of these values—a more distanced perspective from Cavalier paternalism than shown in his earlier work. With Benjy's section Faulkner purposefully wrote himself into artistic history and confronted social history only in a symbolic manner. With Quentin, Faulkner continues his artistic quest but comes into active struggle with significant ruling-class ideologies. Here, he begins to develop his independent ideological consciousness, his relation to history.[2]

Significantly, perhaps coincidentally, Faulkner dates Quentin Compson's suicide in 1910, also the final year of the slow demise of paternalist, Cavalier political influence in Mississippi. In 1910, a Delta planter, Leroy Percy, defeated James K. Vardaman in a Mississippi senatorial race, the last to be decided through secret ballot of the legislature. Percy was "a member of one of the best families of the old tradition" (Kerr 1969, 146). He would also be the last Delta planter to hold a major political office in Mississippi. In 1911, Vardaman defeated him in the general election: "The New Orleans *Picayune* regretfully observed that Mississippians were 'putting the foot down firmly on all that remains of the old aristocracy . . . and they are choosing their representatives among the new generation'" (Kirwan 1951, 230). These elections signaled that the paternalist ideology of the planter elite had lost status and thus political power, as the historical conditions within Mississippi were changing (and as coalitions between Redeemers and Progressives were becoming more prevalent). Those who continued to identify themselves with paternalist values would no longer possess social and political power; their voices would be misconstrued, misunderstood, even ridiculed. (Percy himself was later often heckled off stages, with people refusing even to listen to him.) Despite these historical developments, paternalism did not simply disappear completely—history moves more slowly than that. It continued to have a presence, for as a residual ideology it remained a force in some people's lives. Although it stemmed from the past and had little overall effect on the direction of the present, it existed within the matrix of ideologies affecting Southerners' behavior. Faulkner was one of these Southerners, and Quentin Compson serves as the literary symbol of Cavalier paternalism and its loss of status.

Late in the day of his death, when Quentin returns to his room, he sees the letter left for him by the Blands, Spoade and Shreve: "Mrs. Bland would need another Cavalier" (171). Here, as noted earlier, Quentin's affiliation becomes verified. In one subtle way, this affiliation becomes clear in Quentin's attitude about race. His comment, "a nigger is not a person so much as a form of behavior; a sort of obverse reflection of the white people he lives among" (86), and his other reflections about blacks in the South reveal a certain self-consciousness, a certain insight about blacks that, although racist, is not blindly or fanatically so. Quentin's reflections about race reveal no threat to himself, social or personal; he seems confident in his superior position, and this confidence allows him to view the black people he knows in a more objective, calm manner than others, especially Jason. His comments reveal, more than anything else, a huge distance between his consciousness and black experience, and a recognition of that distance. This kind of attitude is closely associated with the Old South paternalist ideology stemming from the plantocracy. Quentin's attitudes about race give superiority to his white status but seem to recognize that this superiority is not inherent; rather, it is a quirk of social structure and necessity. This form of thinking characterizes those in the upper class who identify with paternalism, both in history and in Faulkner's fiction.[3]

The letter left for Quentin also groups him with "another," presumably Gerald Bland, yet throughout his reveries Quentin himself rejects this association. Indeed, as Faulkner depicts them, the actions and attitudes of the two men reveal very dissimilar personalities. These differences, as well as those between

Quentin and others like Ames and Head, can be associated with those between men holding paternalist values and Redeemer values. Quentin's plight
signals a changing social reality in which men like himself were losing power
and those like Bland, Head, and Ames gaining it.

When we first hear about Gerald Bland, Quentin envisions him rowing
and remembers, "his mamma was telling us about Gerald's horses and Gerald's
niggers and Gerald's women. *Husbands and fathers* in Kentucky must have
been awful glad when she carried Gerald off to Cambridge. . . . She approved
of Gerald associating with me because I at least revealed a blundering sense
of noblesse oblige by getting myself born below Mason and Dixon" (91, my
emphasis). Immediately after these thoughts, Quentin recalls Dalton Ames,
Caddy's lover: "Dalton Ames. It just missed gentility. Theatrical fixture. Just
papier-mache, then touch. Oh. Asbestos. Not quite bronze" (92). Throughout
the day Quentin reenacts this juxtaposition: he constantly thinks of Bland and
Ames at the same time—a process of association capped by his fight with Bland
while he thinks about his fight with Ames. This association can be explained by
the fact that, for Quentin, both men are not genteel. They possess all of the
outward signs of class distinction—clothes, money, charisma, horses, even black
servants in Gerald's case—but they do not behave like "husbands and fathers"
(one might include brothers), that is, as paternalists and patriarchs. Quentin can
be said to judge them from within the Southern version of the Cavalier tradition, which projected the male as patriarch—as provider, protector, and defender
of his wife and his family as well as their respective reputations. Most people in
this society would not not condemn Bland and Ames's behaviors, but Quentin
does because he identifies with the husbands and fathers that these men have
insulted. Unlike Bland, who gains what he would call a masculine thrill from
seducing women and who mistreats his servant, Quentin seeks the role of moral
exemplar and authority figure both within his family and within society at large
precisely because he identifies with Cavalier values.[4]

According to the parameters of Cavalier ideology, boys learned early the importance of familial reputation and often enacted the paternal role toward their
sisters. As Catherine Clinton (1982) explains, "males took both a paternal interest and an active, exaggerated role in their sisters' lives. . . . [S]ensitive on
behalf of their family name, [they] monitored their sisters' every move (55–
56); and "[b]rothers might also take action against other gentlemen to protect a
sister's honor" (57). Quentin's smacking of Caddy when she undresses by the

branch, his spying on her, his challenging Ames because he slept with Caddy before marriage, and his rejection of Head because he was a cheater all reveal his connections to paternalism.

In fact, the very cornerstone of paternalist ideology was the "purity" or "honor" of white women within the upper class. In the earlier slave society, "'racial purity' was a defining characteristic of the master class," and the planter class could not be assured of absolute authority without the total control of all women, white and black alike (Clinton 1982, 6). This ruling-class ideology eventually took on a life of its own and remained an active force well into the twentieth century (Jones 1981, 15). The potential debasement of elite families through sexual or marital connections between Southern upper-class white women and blacks or lower-class whites threatened the elite's dominance of society, and men throughout the South took an active role in defending the honor of all white women. (They did this, of course, by policing their behavior.) Functioning within this ideology, Quentin Compson has actually more than just a personal stake in the honor or safety (or control) of his sister: his very status, he believes, would be threatened if he failed to protect her. In this sense, all white women become Quentin's sisters. Thus, he is indeed, as Spoade mockingly claims, "the champion of dames" (167), and his fierce question, "Did you ever have a sister?" (166), directed at both Bland and Ames, needs to be read as a rhetorical one, serving not as a sign of Quentin's personal pain but of ideological differences. It signals a last attempt to assert the power of a displaced class and its fading values.[5]

Ames, Bland, and Head embody the changes within the dominant class whose members came to reject Cavalier values for those of the Redeemer. Significantly, attitudes toward white women's sexuality did not change that drastically; there remained an emphasis on the need for white women to maintain purity before marriage. (Head's divorce of Caddy after he discovers her premarital sexual relations reveals his connection to this value.) With the instability of postbellum society came a different emphasis, however. Southern white women before the war were generally seen either as ladies or as whores. Women did play crucial roles as domestic heads of the household and as social entertainers, but their domestic roles were downplayed in the creation of the ideal of the Southern lady—an ideal that also served to separate white women from black. After the war, as power shifted away from the planters and as plantation life disappeared in the South, the possibility of social mobility grew for white women, as much as it did for others. Thus, with the Redeemers and with capitalism, white women's domestic roles became much more important, and their social roles were curtailed and redefined. (See Scott 1970.) Indeed, virtually their only function came to be that of a mother (revealed in the behavior of Bland's mother), as if white women could be only mothers (or daughters and sisters) or whores. For Quentin's adversaries, white women who were out of the home, where they did not belong, could no longer be classified as sisters who deserved respect; they became free game, so to speak, no longer protected by rules of chivalry or decent behavior. Quentin's adversaries can justify their behavior toward these women and do not feel the guilt or concern that Quentin feels. Women are "bitches" (160), as Ames says, or are "'waiting . . . [for me] to give [them] what [they] want'" (166), as Bland claims. For Quentin, in contrast, white women were "Plain girls. Remote cousins and family friends whom mere acquaintanceship invested with a sort of blood obligation noblesse oblige" (105).

This same type of conflict is restated *within* the character of Gowan Stevens in *Sanctuary*. Gowan wonders about Temple Drake: Is she or isn't she? During the course of the novel, he reveals one type of demeanor with Narcissa Benbow, much like Quentin's public behavior, and a more overtly sexist demeanor toward Temple, much like Quentin's behavior toward Natalie. This behavior, then, cannot simply be due to what some have labeled Quentin's idealism or his romanticism; it has to do with an ideological affiliation that had both social and psychological ramifications—which Faulkner knew quite well.[6]

Indeed, these values also connect Quentin directly to darker aspects of the Cavalier code. Before the Civil War, men in the planter elite were more easily able to maintain what they labeled a brotherly or fatherly attitude toward white women than after the war, primarily because of their access to and power over a large population of black women. White women could more easily be defined as ladies because black women could be coerced into sexual activity. Breaking the gentlemanly code by seducing a white woman was severely frowned upon, and nocturnal visits to the barn were not uncommon. In general, this ideology made "southern white women 'untouchable' and . . . sexual behavior toward them had to occur 'against a personal sense of guilt'" (Jones 1981, 32).[7] Quentin's situation reflects his intense guilt about sex, a guilt that forces him to remain virginal. His only sexual interaction mirrors the Cavaliers and their slaves. It occurs in a barn with Natalie, whom he calls "a dirty girl" (134), and is interrupted by a white woman, Caddy. Quentin is caught in a double-bind: he only wants to experiment with Natalie because she is "a dirty girl," but he cannot admit this fact—he denies his actions to Caddy. Many Cavaliers were caught in this same conflict and never admitted their actions; however, they were able to live with these contradictions because the socioeconomic system supported them. Quentin's would give him no such support, and he has no solution for his double-bind. Here, as elsewhere, Quentin's behaviors become understandable and identifiable when they are seen to be connected to his residual ideology.[8]

Precisely because they identify with different values, Spoade, Bland, and Ames see Quentin as Head does: as a "half-baked Galahad of a brother" (110). Head can be said to speak for all of them: "a young man gets these ideas and I'm all for them does him good while he's in school forms his character good for tradition . . . but when he gets out into the world he'll have to get his the best way he can because he'll find that everybody else is doing the same" (109). Like the Redeemers, Head thinks that the paternalist values of chivalry and responsibility are good for one's reputation but bad for business. Quentin's problem, however, is not that he is young and still in school; it is that everyone around him believes and acts differently than he does. They believe in clothes, money, horses, and strength, not character, tradition, honor, and chivalry. In this sense, because he identifies with values no one else holds, Quentin has no power—personal or social (very much like Faulkner himself through the 1920s). His interactions with Ames and Bland—his frustrated and near absurd attempts to defend women's so-called honor—reveal this powerlessness.

Finally, Quentin's displacement from the new order is demonstrated by his appearing as a misfit in the North. When he enters the jewelry store in Boston—a city symbolizing, in literature, perhaps the best of bourgeois democracy—his concerns and questions are perceived as strange by the jeweler, who believes Quentin is drunk (84). To Quentin, the clocks in the window represent a cacophony of contradiction: "There were about a dozen watches in the window, a dozen different hours and each with the same assertive and contradictory assurance that mine had, without any hands at all. Contradicting one another" (85). Later, when he listens to the boys arguing about the old fish in the stream and what they would do with the reward money for catching it, Quentin hears: "They all talked at once, their voices insistent and contradictory and impatient, making of unreality a possibility, then a probability, then an incontrovertible fact, as people will" (117). The clocks and the voices can be said to represent a time in which there exists no arbiter to end the argument and contradictions, no shared value system to adjudicate between differences: in this age "every man is the arbiter of his own virtues" (176). Like it is to Binx Bolling in Walker Percy's *The Moviegoer,* to Quentin, this age of democracy and capitalism is the "very century of merde . . . where needs are satisfied, everyone becomes an anyone" (1962, 228).

Quentin rejects the notion that men are their own arbiters and the builders of their own realities: he does not at all identify with the liberal values of his peers and the world at large. His repeated complaint about his father's advice—his father's attempts to convince him to accept the conditions of this new world—is the single word, "temporary." To him, father was teaching that man is "a stalemate of dust and desire" (124), "that all men are just accumulations dolls stuffed with sawdust swept up from the trash heaps where all previous dolls had been thrown away" (175), and that "no live or dead man is very much better than any other live or dead man" (102).

Like many, Mr. Compson sees men within capitalism as hollow. He has come to understand the displacement of Southern paternalist ideas, seeing in this motion the ultimate relativity of man's ideals. He tries to get Quentin to accept this relativity—to accept history. But Quentin refuses. He yearns for that world in which "a gentleman was known by his books" (81) and was respected for what he knew, in which no gentleman would ever be suspected of kidnapping or seducing a little girl, as the local people and the Harvard crowd suspect him of doing (144–45). He yearns for the old world of order and social hierarchy (where some men were considered better than others). Precisely because that world no longer exists and because his actions and feelings are still motivated by the ideology that organized it, Quentin's actions seem like "shadows" (170). As revealed by the attitudes of the jeweler, the local sheriff and deputy, and even most of his Harvard friends, Quentin's actions and feelings in 1910 have indeed become "antic and perverse mocking without relevance inherent themselves with the denial of the significance they should have affirmed" (170)—and this is precisely because he holds values that hardly anyone else holds. He simply does not have social credibility anymore. In essence, he is a non-entity even before he plunges into the Charles River, and his shadowy existence can be explained by historical changes within his world—changes that mirror those that were taking place in Faulkner's Mississippi.

Quentin Compson is a character for whom the residual ideology of Cavalier paternalism still has meaning. He is a social agent whose language and behavior stem from his identification with those particular historical forces. On a symbolic level, the movement toward Quentin's death mirrors the movement toward the demise of paternalism as an active social force. Although in Quentin's section Faulkner suppresses specific references to historical occurrences, except to a single date, the section does indeed intersect with the ideological milieu of Mississippi. If the year 1910 serves as a historical signal of the demise of the Cavalier ideology's power, then Quentin's suicide can be seen as a symbolic embodiment of this demise, as a place where art and history intersect.

In contrast to other characters, of course, Quentin seems a positive, at times even a noble character. This stems not from the inherent worth of paternalism, but from Faulkner's close identification with Quentin's position and his aversion to liberalism, especially to liberalism that uses paternalism as a pretence. As his sensitive, affectionate depiction of Quentin's consciousness reveals, Faulkner did not at this point in his life see anything inherently wrong with the paternalist position. Quentin's yearning for a hierarchical and stable social order was not something Faulkner was willing to condemn outright. We should not hastily conclude, as many critics have done, that Quentin's values reveal insanity or debility, since they so closely resemble Faulkner's. In order to write himself into history in a manner with which he felt comfortable, Faulkner needed to preserve something from Quentin's values. Yet, at the same time, Quentin's suicide acknowledges, for Faulkner, a more distanced perspective from paternalist values than he exhibited in his earlier poetry and novels. It initiates a dissatisfaction with the *social* powerlessness of Cavalier ideology.

For Faulkner, Quentin's biggest problem was that he could not find a social role for himself, and Faulkner's sacrifice of the ideological position Quentin holds reveals an acknowledgement of this position's limitations within the world of twentieth-century Mississippi. As a distinctly historical figure, Quentin Compson embodies an ideological orientation available to Faulkner, but one he would partially and necessarily forsake in order to attain the social eminence and the financial position he so obviously desired. By objectifying the discourse of one so close to him, Faulkner began to struggle actively with the forces affecting him so deeply. By killing off this voice, so to speak, Faulkner revealed that he, unlike Quentin, was willing to confront history, to engage it and challenge it if need be. He chose the path of Stephen Daedalus rather than Quentin Compson, the path of art over a strict adherence to dead values from the past.[9]

Faulkner's willingness to accept history left him looking onto the wasteland world he had avoided and from which he had guarded his own artistic creations. With Jason Compson, all of Faulkner's avoidance of realistic social situations came to an end—with a vengeance.[10] Jason Compson clearly indicates a new direction for Faulkner, one that directly confronted the contemporary,

Progressive/liberal world of Mississippi. The objectification of this discourse, though portrayed with a different feeling than Quentin's, demonstrates a new Faulknerian willingness to write, in a sense, about history—in doing so he would continue to write himself into history.

Similar to other Faulkner characters, such as the younger Bayard Sartoris, Horace Benbow, and even his brother Quentin, Jason Compson is someone caught in what might be described as a hinge of history—a place where society's structure and value-system is noticeably turning from one type to another. On one hand, Jason knows his family's heritage and the place it once held at the top of a stratified Southern society. On the other hand, he wants to disassociate himself from the paternalist order on which this society was based and succeed in the new South. Jason Compson finds himself in a world in which an emergent liberal ethos is in the process of becoming the dominant ideological formation, but he does not resist this process as his brother and father had. Rather, he is bound and determined to enter this newly emergent bourgeois class. Discussions of Faulkner's relationship to Southern social formations always neglect this conflict within the upper class itself, but clearly for Faulkner, there were two conflicting ideologies there. This is revealed in Jason's section, and the conflict between Quentin's section and Jason's has much to do with the historical conflict and Faulkner's attitude toward it.

Faulkner is sensitive to the ways in which the newly instituted liberal bourgeois world takes on some of the features and uses the rhetoric of paternalistic power and authority. As one reads Jason's section, there is little doubt that Jason has ascended into a position of authority in his world. In his family, he asserts this position by requiring all to be present when he eats his meals, and he is supported in this by his mother. Although not as well as his family thinks, he also manages their financial concerns. In town he claims a similar position of authority through reference to his heritage: "my people owned slaves here when you all were running little shirt tail country stores and farming land no nigger would look at on shares" (239). Yet, while Jason uses some of the language of paternalism and claims his authority through his association with it, he does not follow the dictates of the ideology. Although he makes grandiose claims that he is the man of the house, the one who keeps the flour barrel full, he steals from his sister, niece, and mother and shows no sense of responsibility or concern for them or his extended family. (He wants, after all, to place Benjy in a home, and he burns the carnival ticket wanted by Luster.) As he states elsewhere: "Blood, I says, governors and generals. It's a dam good thing we never had any kings and presidents; we'd all be down there at Jackson [in the asylum] chasing butterflies" (230). Like many in the first Redeemer/Progressive coalitions, he wishes to hold the same power as those of the old planter elite, yet he does not want to bear the same level of responsibility for social cohesion and the welfare of people in the community. Jason's values show how Southerners on the rise were redefining their existence, but for Faulkner something seems to be very much amiss.[11]

The bourgeoisie began its reassessment of aristocratic, paternalistic society through its foundation on the ideas of individual rights and equal opportunities. Those who identified with this class felt that they should be given the opportunity to achieve success through their own efforts—not on the basis of their position within a stratified social structure. In keeping with this ideology, Jason Compson develops a near hatred for his father, his older brother, and his sister for denying his rights and taking away his opportunity to succeed. On a couple of occasions he articulates this bitterness: "I never had time to go to Harvard [like Quentin] or drink myself into the ground [like Father]" (181); "I says no I never had university advantages" (196); "because Mother kept saying she [Caddy] would at least have enough regard for the family not to jeopardise my chance after she and Quentin had had theirs" (198). In turn, Jason's attitude stems from a complete lack of sympathetic comprehension for his sister's and father's actions after Caddy's husband suspects her baby is not his. Mrs. Compson had wanted Caddy and Mr. Compson to force Herbert to make some provision for the child. But, due to a sense of honor, an allegiance to a moral principle, Caddy refuses to take any money from Herbert when he decides to throw her out. In the long run, Jason sides with his mother, feeling that Caddy "beat me out of a job" (205) and "deprive[d] me out of a job was promised me" (206). What remained important for Jason was his inalienable right to have the opportunity to succeed, not the principle that influenced Caddy's and Mr. Compson's decision. As he claims: "I just want an even chance to get my money back" (264).

Jason's life also coincides with the specific aspects of Southern Progressivism. Progressivism was the product of the new middle class, whose members tended to identify themselves more by occupation and level of social respectability than by personal and family reputation. (See Wiebe 1967, pref. and chap. 5; Grantham 1983; Woodward 1951, chap. 14.) The major part of Jason's identity comes from his life in Jefferson, not his life at home, and his two major concerns are his occupation as a businessman and his social position in the eyes of the townspeople. He prides himself for being "'man enough to keep that flour barrel full'" (208) and on knowing what it takes to be successful: "Six days late. Yet [women] try to make men believe that they're capable of conducting a business. How long would a man that thought the first of the month came on the sixth last in business" (190). He has insiders in New York advising him about how to bet the cotton market, and he constantly checks the cotton broker's office to see how the market fares. He tries to manage his money efficiently and to watch over his bets carefully in order to become wealthy enough to buy his own business. Further, his concern about his niece's behavior stems from his concern for *his* position, not from any concern for her welfare. As he says, "I dont care what you do, myself. . . . But I've got a position in this town" (189).

Progressives also believed that Wall Street financiers controlled the economy to the disadvantage of the middle class. (See Tindall 1967.) Much of their sentiment for the farmers' pitiful economic plight was mere lip service in that they continued to value individual rights over communal responsibilities and considered social legislation antithetical to the rights and opportunities of individuals. They tended to feel the typical middle-class *ressentiment* toward the lower classes. Jason constantly voices this individual independence: "I guess I dont need any man's help to get along I can stand on my own feet" (206). In many places, he voices anger toward "the fellows that sit up there in New York and trim the sucker gamblers" (192). At one point he voices sympathy for the farmers, saying "Do you think the farmer gets anything out of it except a red neck and a hump in his back? You think the man that sweats to put it into the ground gets a red cent more than a bare living?" (191). Later, however, in a personal interaction with a farmer, he voices that typical *ressentiment:* "I . . . went and waited on the damn redneck while he spent fifteen minutes deciding whether he wanted a twenty cent hame string or a thirty-five cent one" (194–95).

The Progressives in the South were perhaps most notoriously associated with what W. J. Cash labeled "the savage ideal": "Tolerance, in sum, was pretty well extinguished all along the line, and conformity made a nearly universal law" (1969, 138). Here again, Jason fits the mold. He prides himself on his nationalism: "I'm an American. . . . Not many of us left" (191). He is a sexist: he calls his niece a "dam little slut" (185). In keeping with the savage ideal, he is xenophobic: "But I'll be damned if it hasn't come to a pretty pass when any dam foreigner that cant make a living in the country where God put him, can come to this one and take money right from out of an American's pockets" (192). He is also anti-Semitic: "I have nothing against Jews as an individual. . . . It's just the race. You'll admit that they produce nothing. They follow the pioneers into a new country and sell them clothes" (191). Finally, he is anti-intellectual: "Like these college professors without a whole pair of socks to his name, telling you how to make a million in ten years" (249).

As all these attitudes reveal, Jason is a very different person than Quentin even though they belong to the same family. Jason also clearly distinguishes himself from Quentin in his attitudes toward race. He is a fanatical racist, one in whom the ideology of race has taken on a life of its own. He has absolutely no sense of black people's experiences and does not recognize his own ignorance. In his comments about black labor he reveals the effects of feeling threatened by black workers: "What this country needs is white labor. Let these dam trifling niggers starve for a couple of years, then they'd see what a soft thing they have" (190–91). He goes to the extreme of essentializing race and connecting it to behavior: he claims he is "not going to have any member of [his] family going on like a nigger wench" (189), and "When people act like niggers, no matter who they are the only thing to do is treat them like a nigger" (181). Jason clearly reveals the vicious effects of Mississippi's racial paternalism (which Faulkner will further explore in *Light in August* and *Absalom, Absalom!*).

Unlike Quentin, Jason is anything but sympathetic. Faulkner may have been distancing himself from paternalism in Quentin's section, but Jason's certainly does not indicate any affiliation, on Faulkner's part, to Mississippi's form of liberalism. The significance of Jason's section for Faulkner's ideological development lies in its willing confrontation with contemporary history. Before, Faulkner simply ignored this world and wished it away; here, he actively confronts and criticizes.

The final section of the novel continues this criticism and furthers Faulkner's position in relation to Jason and to the Progressive ideology of which Jason is the symbolic representative. Earlier in the book Jason had been juxtaposed against his father, the bearer of Cavalier values, when Caddy asked, "'promise to take care of her [Ms. Quentin]. . . . She's kin to you; your own flesh and blood. Promise, Jason. You have Father's name: do you think I'd have to ask him twice? once even?'" (209). In this scene Jason clearly shows that he functions under an entirely different set of values, denying his responsibility to his family, to his flesh and blood. As he progresses into section four, Faulkner develops his commentary about Jason through Dilsey's remarks. Dilsey says about Benjy: "'de good Lawd dont keer whether he bright er not. Dont nobody but white trash keer dat'" (290). These remarks reverberate in sympathy with Caddy's— Mr. Compson loved Benjy and refused to commit him to an asylum—and in contrast to Jason's persistent negative remarks about Benjy. They imply the novel's—and Faulkner's—assessment of Jason: he is white trash. This reveals Faulkner's attitude toward the Progressives: they did not have the wisdom, vision, or character to lead effectively (a theme that is developed further in the Snopes trilogy).

Indeed, at the very end of the novel Jason asserts his authority over his black servant and his brother by redirecting the carriage, reclaiming, only through violence, some sort of authoritarian position. However, what he does, essentially, is direct Luster to guide the carriage in the direction Benjy thinks it should go. Once Luster redirects the carriage, everything flows by, "each in its ordered place" (321), and peace is restored to the village and in the novel. This peace does not stem from Jason's insight, however. Jason has been scrambling around for days without ever achieving any sense of peace, for himself or anyone else. The order established by Jason, and by implication the ideology he represents, creates a social cacophony of isolated individuals all living in their own worlds. Now, with Mr. Compson, Quentin, and Caddy gone, only Benjy knows that everything needs to have a place, that society must have order for peace to exist. At least this seems to be Faulkner's conclusion. Although historically the transition from a paternalistic social order to a liberal one was a move toward democracy, Faulkner's depiction of it in *The Sound and the Fury* demonstrates a level of chaos and a lack of wisdom in this new world. He sees no real social order or system of shared, communal values and responsibilities. Although he recognizes the ascension of Jason, indicating his acknowledgment on a symbolic level of the ascension of the Progressives, he remains uncomfortable with the historical transition.

This Faulknerian assertion of the need for order, of the need for people to know and to accept their places within a social order, leads us to understand Dilsey and the Gibson family. Although Faulkner criticism is filled with testaments to the nobility, morality, and strength of Dilsey and her family, these assessments seem one-sided precisely because they tend not to take into account the social reality of the Gibsons and what their existence means for Faulkner's own implicit social vision. Certainly, in comparison to Jason and Mrs. Compson, Dilsey can be seen to be the pillar of moral strength in the novel; however, she also willingly submits to them, and thus to the social order over which they preside. Dilsey willingly sacrifices herself, so it seems, and though this choice may be seen as noble from certain viewpoints, it certainly is not the only way to view Dilsey's behavior.

Overall, Dilsey reveals an absolutely passive resignation in the face of injustice and emotional insanity. This resignation and its fulfillment in religion implicitly admits to a social powerlessness and ultimately reveals a complete alienation from the social system and any of the rights and freedoms that this system might extend to black Americans. In effect, Dilsey prostrates herself before God and sacrifices her social agency. In contrast, her grandson Luster reveals the desire to participate in the new social order by wanting to go to the circus and by voicing a degree of rebellion when Dilsey holds him to his assigned chore of watching Benjy. This more modern rebellion is quashed by Dilsey, to whom Faulkner gives moral authority. Thadious Davis has argued that Faulkner gives Dilsey a simplicity that the Compsons lack and that therein lies her heroic vision (1983, chap. 3). However, Richard Wright's *Black Boy* reveals that this attribution of personality traits has more to do with Faulkner than with any essential traits black Mississippians might have possessed.[12]

It would seem that Faulkner values Dilsey precisely because of her passive resignation, because she accepts her place. She has accepted the insight offered by Anse Bundren in *As I Lay Dying:* "When He aims for something to be always a-moving, He makes it long ways, like a road or a horse or a wagon, but when He aims for something to stay put, He makes it up-and-down ways, like a tree or a man [or a woman]" (36). Like Benjy, she accepts that people should be in their ordered place, and in this way she too becomes associated with an earlier social formation and a romantic paternalism. These associations explain why Faulkner values her.

More directly than in his earlier novels, Faulkner confronts in *The Sound and the Fury* the voices of the changing South—a fairly modern, capitalist society in its preliminary stages of transition from an agrarian plantocracy, and characters' words and actions embody ideological orientations characteristic of this world. Faulkner saw this transition as a collapse of a social order and an incursion of the unqualified into the ruling class. The tragedy of Caddy Compson, whatever else one argues, signifies a pollution of the upper class and has direct connection to the social collapse Faulkner dreads. His portrayals reveal that though he was beginning to explore, critically, his paternalistic heritage, Faulkner still identified with and was identified by this ideology. This overall perspective would, in fact, influence Faulkner's narrative perspectives for some time even while he came more and more to probe the various nooks and crannies of its social and psychological ramifications. Meantime, Faulkner was clearly not at all enamored with the bourgeois world sprouting all around him. Though he would explore it, especially in *As I Lay Dying* and *Light in August,* his opinion of it would change little.

At this point in his career, Faulkner is alienated from the social options his world has offered—distancing himself from an increasingly residual paternalism but still disaffected by the increasingly dominant liberalism. His life and art seem to be primarily motivated by an intense yearning for a true life, but this life does not seem to exist within the confining ideological parameters of his local sociohistorical milieu. Nonetheless, Faulkner remains fascinated by and his canon continues to confront these two ideological perspectives of paternalism and liberalism. That there were other options to explore—a strong Populist, even Communist social option, examples of blacks and whites working together against the Southern ideology of race, a growing women's movement—implies that Faulkner could not move completely away from these particular ideological positions: his own struggle was in fact interpellated by these ideologies characteristic of the upper class in Mississippi. Art has given him the means to move toward independence and to resist the world he rejects, but he has yet to construct a clear space, a definite authorial ideology for himself. *The Sound and the Fury* announces the terrain on which Faulkner will tread for some time: a close and perhaps personal struggle with paternalism and a tense but realistic struggle with liberalism and a working through of various confrontations with class and gender and race. This process defines Faulkner's early period—as discussions of *Sanctuary, As I Lay Dying,* and *Light in August* will reveal.

4 • *Sanctuary*

The Social Psychology of Paternalism

Men make their own history, but they do not make it just as they please; they do not make it under circumstances chosen by themselves, but under circumstances directly found, given, and transmitted from the past. The tradition of all the dead generations weighs like a nightmare on the brain of the living.

—Karl Marx, "The Eighteenth Brumaire"

To reiterate briefly, I want to see all of Faulkner's novels written during this early period of his life as one long interwoven text that confronts and explores the sociohistorical world in an independent way for the first time. *The Sound and the Fury* begins a process that reaches no real conclusion until *Absalom, Absalom!*, but the book opens various pathways that Faulkner proceeds to explore in more detail. The depiction of Quentin Compson in *The Sound and the Fury* reveals Faulkner's objectification of and slight separation from paternalism, but it certainly does not exhaust Faulkner's involvement with this ideological perspective. The emphasis there is on the difference between Quentin and others in his social class; its effect is that of a sad farewell, but the novel also exposes certain attitudes toward women and sexuality. These become the main focus in *Sanctuary*. There, Faulkner exposes what we can call the inner workings of paternalism— its deeper effects and ramifications. Faulkner seems to know these from the inside, as it were, but he also reveals an insight into their destructive potentialities. In *As I Lay Dying* and *Light in August* Faulkner explores questions about a social world organized by liberal ideology; in *Sanctuary,* his rather intense focus is on the social psychology of Southern paternalism.

Sanctuary has frequently been discussed as an exploration of evil and more recently as a text delineating the cultural significances of the Oedipal conflict.[1] Psychoanalytical readings have in fact been the best readings of the novel and have elevated *Sanctuary* to the level of importance it now rightly holds. These readings, though, have not and will not lead to insights connecting the social world envisioned in the novel to the depictions of personal behavior characterized by that world. For these connections, we must utilize the theory of ideology.

Recognizing the function of ideology as the production of human subjectivities, as explained in chapter 2, I want to investigate how *Sanctuary*'s narrative perspective highlights the ideology that forms and guides Horace and Temple's world—namely paternalism—as well as the types of subjectivities formed by this world.[2] Through the depiction of Horace we get a close-up look at someone who is identified by paternalism, a look at the social psychology characteristic of an upper-class, aristocratic male mentality. Through the depictions of Narcissa, Temple, and Popeye we come to see how this social psychology gets projected onto others in society and how it produces subjectivities based on its sense of reality. Following his critical exploration of paternalism in *The Sound and the Fury*, Faulkner reveals that the logical pattern of evil is the logic of paternalism's social psychology.

Faulkner establishes Horace Benbow's association with paternalism by labeling him a "gentleman." Like Quentin Compson, a very similar type of character who had received the label, cavalier, Horace receives a label identifying him with the paternalist ideology stemming from old South social formations (and enjoying considerable revival during the 1920s). Horace underscores this identification when he comments, "God is foolish at times, but at least He's a gentleman," and Faulkner reiterates the association when he has Clarence Snopes call Horace and his father "southron gentlemen."[3] Furthermore, Horace's motivation for leaving his wife, Belle—the motivation for the novel itself—stems from his desire to return to his patrilineal home in order, it can be argued, to claim his father's paternalist status as well as to attain a sanctuary from the present society. What John Irwin says about various Faulkner characters is certainly true for Horace: he is "a twentieth-century male descendant of an aristocratic Southern family . . . a descendant who personified, if not the South, then the Southern ruling class at a certain point in this century" (1992, 543).

Horace seeks refuge from his society because it has become a bourgeois, middle-class world with which he feels no kinship. Faulkner clearly indicates this situation in a revealing scene in the original version of the novel. Late in the story Horace considers Temple's surprise entrance into the courtroom where she will testify: "He realised now that it was too late, that he could not have summoned her; realised again that furious homogeneity of the middle classes when opposed to the proletariat from which it so recently sprung and by which it is so often threatened" (1981, 260). Although the class-specific vocabulary, the reference to middle *classes,* and the mistaken pronoun reference all seem a little odd, these thoughts can explain some of the novel's social dynamics. First, Horace recognizes that Judge Drake, Temple's father, has cooperated with the district attorney only for the purposes of the trial; second, Horace distances himself from the kind of "low-class" legal chicanery forced on Judge Drake for the D.A.'s political purposes (that is, Horace distances himself from the lower of the middle classes); and, third, Horace senses that these two men, the D.A. and Judge Drake, are from different classes in some way—that is, Judge Drake is from the higher of the middle classes. Horace's lack of identification with these "middle classes" points to an affinity with some other class—as I suggest, the upper, aristocratic paternalist class—and he senses that Judge Drake, despite this chicanery, is closer to him than to the D.A. Faulkner at least posits this possibility. Thus, even though the Jefferson society in this book can be associated with the bourgeois, middle class, the novel's narrative perspective—Horace's perspective—has more to do with that of an aristocratic paternalist.[4]

Klaus Theweleit (1987; 1989) has analyzed in detail the fantasies of upper-class, aristocratic men in patriarchal social formations. His two volumes titled *Male Fantasies* are wide-ranging analyses of the patriarchal (paternalist) male mentality as it was exhibited in the writings of the pre-fascist *Freikorpsmen* of post–World War II Germany. However, although his specific subject is the writings of these men, he is more broadly concerned with the correlations between these extremists and patriarchy in general. In fact, a constant theme of Theweleit's books is how the fascist's psychosocial reality reveals tendencies existing in all patriarchies. Barbara Ehrenreich enumerates this point in her foreword to volume 1: "the point of understanding fascism is . . . because it is already implicit in the daily relationships of men and women. Theweleit refuses to draw a line between the fantasies of the Freikorpsmen and the psychic ramblings of the 'normal' man" (1987, xv).

Beyond this explanation that Theweleit's books put into vivid relief otherwise less extreme forms of patriarchal masculine behavior, there are some direct, general areas of connection between his subject matter and Faulkner's. The Freikorpsmen were all heirs to the European aristocratic tradition. All considered themselves part of the highest civilization; all considered themselves gentlemen. Most of them had been soldiers, and all of them felt the defeat of Germany in World War I as a crushing loss of their hopes and dreams, their pride and sense of self. Their very formation into the Freikorpsmen was dependent upon a shared sense that civilization was being threatened by unruly and chaotic forces with which it was their duty to contend. They saw themselves as defenders of culture and preservers of law and order—in the face of threats from a new class of people who wanted to take power and from the so-called lower orders of society who were trying to rise above their station.

These defining characteristics can certainly be related to the Southern paternalist tradition and its legacy. Southern paternalists held to the belief that materialistic and vulgar hordes from the North were descending upon them, ruining their civilized life in the creation of a New South that was not the South. They felt that destructive forces from the lower orders, especially from black Americans, were being unleashed, and they sought to maintain the status quo in the name of justice, law, and Southern (civilized) life. In *Sanctuary*, this fear and its realization are embodied in the way Faulkner describes the Old Frenchman's Place as being taken over by the lower elements of society, who have allowed it to revert back to a kind of jungle status. These descriptions parallel those of Horace's patrilineal home, which also lacks the hand of husbandry and has reverted to a primitive state. Horace's attempts to revive his home parallel his attempts to bring the principles of "law, justice and civilization" to bear on Lee Goodwin's trial—both are attempts to reassert paternalism. Although Theweleit analyzes extreme versions of this aristocratic mentality, comparisons between the social psychology of these men and various Faulkner characters—Quentin Compson, Gail Hightower, and here, Horace Benbow—seem not only plausible but also especially relevant in understanding the implications of the novel.[5]

Theweleit offers an avenue of departure from the Freudian analyses that have dominated discussions of *Sanctuary*. He emphasizes that what these aristocratic men seem to repress is not incestuous desire, as Freudian interpretations would have it, but desire itself. He finds ample evidence that these men never experienced warm, close relationships with their mothers. Thus they have both a desperate yearning for and a desperate dread of love and sex, of intimacy, and the fusion of human beings that intimacy entails. The combination of yearning and dread can culminate only in violence—which combines both the need and the dread in one final and explosive moment.

This lack of closeness to one's mother also leads to an inability to draw boundaries between self and other and increases the fear of dissolution of the ego when forming intimate relationships. Theweleit explains that the motivation for the patriarch's fantasies and behavior stems not so much from a wish for incestuous union with the mother but from a wish to rid himself of all those maternal qualities of warmth, intimacy, sensuality—and the deep-felt emotions they engender—which can be called mother. Because of this, the patriarch's world banishes women and all associated with women as much as possible.

As if Theweleit and Faulkner observed similar phenomena but presented their observations in different media, Faulkner identifies the origins of Horace's psychological reality in a way parallel to Theweleit's descriptions. Horace's mother "had been an invalid so long that the one picture of her he retained was two frail arms rising from a soft falling of lace" (1981, 62). Contrary to Polk's claim (1985, 27) that Horace was mothered his whole life, this memory indicates that for all intents and purposes Horace had no real relationship with his mother at all. The effects of Horace's inability to relate, to connect to all that is his mother, are recorded throughout the entire novel.

The ways in which Horace becomes affected by his non-relationship with his mother are revealed through a series of dream images that at first seem rather bizarre. In the context of Theweleit's theories, though, Horace's dream imagery reveals the foundation of the paternalist's psychosocial world. Just prior to Horace's memory of his mother he imagines the following: "After a while he could not tell whether he were awake or not . . . but he was talking to his mother too. . . . Then he saw that she wore a shapeless garment of faded calico and that Belle's rich, full mouth burned sullenly out of the halflight, and he knew that she was about to open her mouth and he tried to scream at her. . . . But it was too late. He saw her mouth open; a thick, black liquid welled in a bursting bubble . . . and he was thinking He smells black. He smells like that black stuff that ran out of Bovary's mouth when they raised her head" (1981, 60). Here, Horace's pleasant fantasies are of a prepubescent state of childhood, and these are annihilated by the black liquid erupting from the woman—who is both mother and wife.

The reference to black liquid, associated with the lower-class, sexually deviant Popeye, and the description of Belle's mouth as rich and full charge this scene with unmistakable sexual energy. This energy causes the horror Horace feels and associates it with wife and mother. Thus, this vivid and bizarre scene reveals that Horace becomes repulsed by both mother and wife because they are together associated with sexuality and the lower class. (As we will see, this repulsion is a constant in Horace's behavior.)

In other instances, Horace's less nightmarish fantasies involve prepubescent or asexual women, namely his stepdaughter, Little Belle, and his sister, Narcissa. These women do not conjure the same repulsion in Horace precisely because they are pre-sexual or asexual. Like the men Theweleit studied, Horace's lack of relationship with his mother causes a fear of fusion, of losing the boundaries of self, of intimate relationships with other people, especially women. This fear manifests itself primarily as a reaction against the supposedly innate sexuality women are seen to embody.

The psychology of paternalists, then, revolves around their fear and dread of sexuality—the act of fusion that is seen as self-destructive rather than life-affirming. Moreover, the images in this scene link mother to sexually active wife and sexually deviant Popeye; thus, like for the men Theweleit analyzes, Horace's reactions to the so-called low and base emotions are connected to his responses to supposedly low and base people—and these people are linked to liquids and the color black. Here, Horace's inner states of mind and feeling—his sense of himself—are seen to be connected to ideas and feelings about others, specifically women and those associated with being black. His social position as aristocratic paternalist relates to a particular type of psyche. An ideology, ostensibly a class-based value system, thus is seen to have within it values affecting ideas about gender and race. Horace's psychological fixations, then, connect directly to images of women and the lower class (and by extension blacks), showing how paternalist fantasies get projected outward onto society. Faulkner implies that the paternalist's psychological reality has definite social ramifications—that a paternalist ideology does not just define the behavior of paternalists but attempts to define proper behavior for all the others within the social system as well. Thus, we need to investigate how Faulkner's novel explores both the psychological root of these paternalist, masculinist fantasies and their social effects.[6]

MASCULINIST FANTASIES

Paternalism and Female Sexuality

When discussing his reasons for leaving Kinston, his wife's hometown, and returning to Jefferson—the very motivation for the plot of the novel—Horace stresses that the "flat and rich and foul" country had gotten him "upset," and he needs to get away from that feeling of emotional agitation: "I thought that maybe I would be all right if I just had a hill to lie on for a while" (1985c, 16). The specific reasons for his departure he explains as follows: "'it wasn't Little Belle that set me off. Do you know what it was? . . . It was a rag with rouge on it'" (16). A bit later, in answer to Ruby's question about why he left his wife, Horace responds: "'Because she ate shrimp. . . . And I still dont like to smell shrimp. But I wouldn't mind the carrying it home so much. I could stand that. It's because the package drips. All the way home it drips and drips'" (18).

A careful reading of this rhetoric of images reveals that Horace reacts to the reported foulness of the rich, fertile homeland of his wife—a direct association between women's bodies, the earth, and sexuality that parallels the description of Belle's mouth as rich and full. Somehow the literal threat of a flood across the Kinston plain becomes associated with a flood of emotions that he desires to escape, and this flood becomes associated with Belle. His description of the dirty handkerchief can be seen to represent menstruation, a function of the female body that disgusts him. And his odd overreaction to the dripping of the shrimp seems to indicate an aversion to getting his hands wet, here associated with Belle and indirectly to the foulness of her homeland and her sexuality. These images link in a pattern associating dirt, fluids, and female sexuality, and this sexuality, with its overwhelming emotional agitation, is something Horace wishes to avoid. His stated fear of a literal flood connects to his implied fear of a flood of emotions caused by his relationship with his wife. Thus, although critics have focused on Horace's journey *to* Narcissa, *to* his incestuous desire for Narcissa and Little Belle, and *into* evil, these particular motivations for Horace's departure seem important in terms of what he flees *from*. In fact, Horace seems to flee from evil—that is, from female sexuality as embodied by Belle.[7]

To some extent Bleikasten (1985) has noted this pattern of images in *Sanctuary;* however, he does not attempt to link the rhetoric of images to the novel's narrative perspective (see also Bleikasten 1990, sec. 3). In order to make some sense of the images in relation to the novel's sociohistorical perspective we need to turn to Theweleit, who explains the manifestations of the paternalist's psychological reality in ways corroborating Faulkner's vivid depictions. He explains that the fear paternalistic men have of sexual women often manifests itself in a dread of fluidity or motion, of anything that flows or streams. This dread manifests itself in physical ways as negative reactions to wet hands or dirtiness, to being immersed in water or wet substances; it manifests itself in psychological ways as reactions against emotion and feeling, that which flows inside. These men attempt to maintain a pose of tight, rigid control, of order and stasis; they stay erect and firm in a whirlwind of chaotic forces or put distance between themselves and impulses that lead to chaotic feelings.

Here we find a way to understand Horace's desire to reach the top of a hill, to find a distant and therefore safe spot that is dry and away from his wife. We also discover a link between the images associated with Horace and those associated with the Drakes—a link that further justifies correlations between them and the Benbows. Late in the novel, Faulkner describes Judge Drake and his sons waiting for Temple to step down from the witness stand and be returned to them: "the old man erect beside her. . . . Four younger men were standing stiffly erect. . . . They stood like soldiers" (1981, 279; 1985c, 304). These descriptions indicate a degree of sexual tension, as others have noted, but they also reveal a dread of releasing that tension, a stiffening of the defenses against the sexuality associated with Temple. Like the very "soldier-males" described by Theweleit, these men's postures reveal both desire and an intense inhibition of desire. Horace and the Drakes need somehow to protect themselves from Belle and Temple and what they represent in the novel—sexuality, intimacy, a loss of self. This can only be accomplished by remaining firm and erect or by distancing one's male self from the threat.

Nowhere is this need to avoid chaotic emotions and sexuality, as well as the loss of self they imply, more evident than in the now infamous scene where Horace falls into his bathroom and vomits his coffee. Several aspects surrounding this scene are significant for my discussion of the novel. First, Horace has just returned from Memphis, where he heard Temple's horrific tale of her rape by Popeye. That story does not make Horace feel sick, nor does it cause a sexual fantasy involving himself and Temple. Rather, Temple's tale of vicious violation causes Horace to feel a cruel pity: he thinks she would be better off dead (a point to which I will return). Indications of Horace's sexual desire for Temple, a key point in Freudian interpretations, seem nonexistent. Second, Temple's story leads Horace to think about Little Belle's sexuality and eventually her sexual initiation; these fantasies cause the reaction and the rather strange psychic interlude where Horace refers to himself as "she." Here's the interlude: "he gave over and plunged forward and struck the lavatory . . . while the shucks set up a terrific uproar beneath her thighs. Lying with her head lifted slightly . . . she watched something black and furious go roaring out of her pale body. She was bound naked on her back on a flat car moving at speed through a black tunnel, the blackness streaming in rigid threads overhead" (1981, 220).

Significantly, Horace does not imagine himself *with* Little Belle in this scene but imagines himself *to be* Little Belle during a sexual encounter. Empathizing or identifying with that plight causes a violent physical reaction. The shift in pronouns during the scene symbolizes Horace's wish to remove his male self from this scene of sexuality; the linguistic shift fulfills the function of shielding him from unwanted contact with both liquids and sexuality—as if the black liquid does not really roar out of his body. Listening to Temple's story of violent rape moves Horace little; thinking of his pre-sexual stepdaughter experiencing sex causes a violent repulsion, an experience that Horace must literally purge from his body.[8]

Moreover, Horace's other behaviors support my contention that he was re-pulsed by and wanted to avoid sexuality. He recalls trying to convince Narcissa not to get married, arguing that they both should avoid sexual relations; he also advises Little Belle, "'You don't soil your slippers'" (1985c, 15), trying to stop her from getting involved with boys; and when Miss Jenny mentions sex in ref-erence to Narcissa's marriage and Ruby mentions it in terms of payment for legal services, Horace overreacts with strong feelings of aversion and repulsion. As his slipper comment to Little Belle reveals, he also links sexual relations to im-ages of dirt and filth, and the book is filled with numerous instances of Horace removing himself from areas of dirt or dirty liquid: a couple of times he moves from a train car in which men spit; he avoids Ruby's baby, who spits up; and he avoids becoming dirty or soiled at any expense. In whatever form it erupts into his psychic ramblings and into his day-to-day life, Horace constantly seeks to avoid coming into contact with sexuality. Like that black liquid he purged from his body, Horace attempts to purge sexuality from his life.

As the very basis of the paternalist's psychic world, this aversion to sexuality comes to explain other aspects of Horace's personality: his rejection of sexuality, for him the low and base, becomes revealed through his admiration for what is considered high and lofty; his rejection of the material body is mirrored by his fascination with ideals; his rejection of manual labor is a sign of his aristocratic association. These characteristics—the enjoyment of the high and the lofty, the pursuit of ideals—show that paternalists' neuroses become socially accepted, even venerated qualities, and thus, indirectly, how the neuroses of the powerful are never simply private. We should not be persuaded by the polite front Horace shows the world, for the rejection of sexuality at the root of his character has dire consequences.

Paternalism and Masculinity

As the direct connection between the black liquid and Popeye indicates, Popeye comes to represent what Horace represses. As the opening scene of the revised version of the novel—where Horace and Popeye sit across a pond from one another for hours—reveals, they are fractured mirror images of one another. Again distancing myself from Freudian analyses, I do not want to say that Popeye enacts Horace's incestuous sexual desire. The specific way Popeye performs his violation of Temple seems anything but sexual; his behavior seems more rooted in a desire to punish than to have sexual relations. This behavior, the specific ways Popeye is described in the novel, and the juxtaposition of Popeye and Horace indicate attitudes toward manliness and sexuality as they are defined in a paternalistic version of masculinity.

The version of masculinity associated with Horace and the term *gentleman* obviously relates to the idealistic, chivalric aspect of paternalistic masculinity, which Horace epitomizes almost in caricature. This aspect of masculinity struggles with sexuality because men who are supposed to treat all women like ladies find it difficult to have sexual relations with them. Thus, in order to have sexual relations at all—something Horace (and Quentin before him) seems perfectly willing to avoid—men affected by this notion of paternalist masculinity are attracted to so-called dirty women—women who are (supposedly) inherently sexual and who are seen to bewitch men into having sexual relations with them. Even here paternalist men have to steel themselves and refuse any intimate relation or any shred of human feeling for the event or the woman.[9]

Of course, for a long time the social structure of the South allowed upper-class men to maintain this paradoxical and perverse attitude toward women and sexuality. They had their wives in the big house, safely ensconced, and their "whores" in the city or in the slave quarters, always available. As the social structure changed, however, men found it more difficult to maintain this situation, both in personal and social terms, and had more and more to face both aspects of their masculinity—their gentlemanly side and their manly side, so to speak. The social world of *Sanctuary* resembles this world; the two sides of paternalist masculinity cannot exist in the same man any longer. But, the narrative perspective itself highlights that of paternalism, and Horace and Popeye, like the fractured mirror-images they are, embody the dual aspects of paternalist masculinity.[10]

A key aspect of this version of masculinity is the objectification of women. Horace objectifies women into ladies for whom he can fight the good fight, denying their sexual presence, praising them almost as if they were goddesses or statues—ladies on the pedestal. These attitudes are revealed in the way he treats Ruby, Lee Goodwin's common-law wife, who has been a prostitute: Horace refuses to see her as anything but a damsel in distress. They are also revealed in the way he treats Narcissa, who becomes identified as "heroic statuary" (1985c, 110). Popeye's objectification, on the other hand, makes women simply into dirty objects to be used and thrown aside: to him, all women are whores. Both of these attitudes, though, derive from the same paternalist impulse to deny women flesh-and-blood status as human beings with whom the natural human drive for sexuality, intimacy, and fusion can be consummated.

Another key aspect of this version of masculinity is the objectification of men themselves. For Horace this objectification denies the close association implied by two people's entwining their lives together in marriage. Intimacy and the concomitant loss of psychological isolation cause Horace to yearn to be "counsellor, handmaiden, and friend" (1981, 19)—anything but intimate husband and lover. A platonic, idealistic relationship—that is, a non-physical one—with a woman is Horace's goal precisely because it does not involve sexuality, that "dirty business." On the other hand, as the projection of the sexual side of paternalist masculinity, Popeye's is precisely that "dirty business," and his actions reveal what that entails for him. The use of the corncob in the rape scene represents the dire need of the paternalist to remain as detached as possible from the sexual act. Paternalists never want to get themselves "dirty," and Popeye's behaviors—using a corncob and blaming Temple—symbolize this wish. Moreover, descriptions of Popeye throughout the novel indicate that he is less human than machine: "His face had a queer bloodless color . . . he had that vicious depthless quality of stamped tin" (1985c, 4); his "eyes looked like rubber knobs" and he looked "like a modernist lampshade" (1985c, 6); he also seems to be part of his car when the door opens without any movement on his part. As symbolic embodiment of the sexual side of the paternalist, Popeye comes to reveal how paternalistic men had to objectify themselves, to make themselves into inhuman machines in order to partake in sexual relations. He epitomizes the effects on men within this version of masculinity—the mechanization of the male body.[11]

Indeed, Popeye's treatment of Temple symbolizes, in an extreme and exaggerated manner, the way paternalist men approach women. Their actions have nothing to do with pleasure and fusion, but with violence and punishment. Punishment for sexual women must be enacted through violence on the female body, and men will do anything to avoid contact with this body. This aspect of Horace is not revealed for the most part because he remains so much in control, so safe from the impulses that would conjure these reactions in him. But lest we be fooled by Horace's gentlemanly exterior and think there exists no connection between Horace and Popeye, gentleman and rapist, Faulkner offers a scene where Horace's repressed true nature becomes revealed. Here we see the killer underneath, the beast in the jungle that is part of the masculine identity of paternalism. In this imagined scene in the original version of the novel, Horace's fixation about cleanliness becomes a vicious comment on women.

Horace has become sick of the trial and thinks about how he could end it and go to Europe. He explains, "The first thing would be to clean up the mess. He would sub-poena Temple; he thought in a paroxysm of raging pleasure of flinging her into the court-room, of stripping her: This is what a man has killed another over. This, the offspring of respectable people. . . . Stripping her, background, environment, all" (1981, 255). Although often read as an indication of Horace's sexual desire for Temple, this scene implies punitive, violent desires rather than sexual ones. Horace wants to clean away all that might hide what Temple truly is—a woman—to strip her down to the bare essential—her body. He wishes, that is, to reveal that her female body contains the fault, holds the blame, and certainly is not worth the killing of one man by another. Horace does not want to clean up the mess Temple has made but the mess her body is, in and of itself.

Ultimately, then, Horace and Popeye feel the same way about Temple. Any woman who behaves the way Temple does is inherently dirty and should be punished harshly. In fact, if a woman does not control herself and behave cleanly, "Better for her if she were dead" (1985c, 232), as Horace says about Temple. Popeye does indeed enact what Horace represses, and these two characters symbolize two aspects of the same ideology. As both men reveal, the consequences of this ideology are dire, for the paternalist demeanor is one of controlled violence and repression, his nature violent, even deadly. Attempting to kill off the need for sexuality, emotional involvement, and closeness to others in himself, the paternalist can become an armored death machine, enacting both suicide and murder. Needing to avoid his twisted dread of these human essentials, he becomes a repressive, control-oriented madman enjoying punishment rather than pleasure. Faulkner's novel thus becomes part of a discourse that reveals the masculinist death-vision. From locking "madwomen in the attic" to worshiping frozen images of women that they do not touch, from armoring themselves for either competitive or deadly battle with one another to using "mother earth" for their own purposes, paternalists represent a death-in-life principle—this seems to be one of Faulkner's insights.[12]

THE SOCIAL PSYCHOLOGY OF PATERNALISM

As has been indicated throughout this discussion, in a world dominated by the paternalist perspective, paternalist psychological fantasies do not simply have psychological effects. Paternalist ideology works to create a social world and individual subjects that fulfill the paternalist's psychic needs. Masculine fantasies, then, become projected outward onto social reality. Because of the way in which paternalist men need to define their relation to the world, repressing all that flows, social power becomes equated with control, cleanliness, order, stasis—a near pristine state that denies affection and intimacy, sexuality and emotion, and change, mobility, and motion. Because women become the embodiment both of the desire for and the dread of sexuality and intimacy, of fusion with others, paternalist fantasies project two different types of women. Theweleit labels the image of woman that permits the paternalist to maintain the image he has of himself and thus to maintain his social power "the white woman." The image that threatens the paternalist's need for control, stasis, and sterility and thus shakes the structure of his psychic world and threatens the social reality it upholds he has labeled "the red woman." In blunt terms, these types of women are, respectively, the lady/sister/wife, and the whore.

As Theweleit (1987) explains, the white woman is the safe woman; clothed in her white uniform or dress, seemingly already in her sepulchre, she inspires men to leave her alone and perform great deeds for her benefit—or so the men say. She is glorified and deified, always in absentia; her image looms significantly, her body is ignored completely. She helps the paternalist maintain control and calm by shunning sexually explicit clothes, language, and behavior; she mollifies his combined need for and dread of sexuality and intimacy by allowing him to play the role of counselor and friend. The red woman, on the other hand, does not accept or fulfill these roles. She shakes off the constraining white garments, in any number of ways, revealing both her own and man's need and desire for fusion. She threatens man's ability to control himself. Always in a state of constant tension due to his perpetual repression of needs and desires, he reads the red woman's behavior as a threat to his very being. As he sees it, she has "only one thing on her mind." And because this activity is dirty, as we have seen, he often punishes her.

In *Sanctuary*, Narcissa Benbow is the white woman. She lives in "the home of her husband's people" (1985c, 24), walled in and protected by their name and heritage. She always dresses in white, and she remains one of the "sheltered chaste women" (1985c, 121). She lives with no man and has only non-sexual relations with men; she is inviolable and impenetrable. She does not need control by men because she has so definitely accepted her role and therefore controls herself. She is safe: she will have no impure thoughts, and she will cause no unwanted emotions. Narcissa is indeed the idealized woman on the pedestal—statuesque, frozen in time, the proper state for a woman under paternalism.

Clearly, the most prominent aspect of Narcissa's character is the absolute quiet that surrounds her. There is never a rushed movement, never a spontaneous outburst; in all descriptions of her she retains a stillness. This state indicates, and her actions reveal, that she will never be moved from her position as the white woman. She is appalled by Horace's actions: she sees his leaving Belle as the action of "a nigger" (1985c, 112)—another correlation between being low class and being black. She refuses to allow him to offer Ruby a room in their old house: she does not see Ruby as a lady in distress but as a whore. She is also horrified by Horace's involvement in a trial for people who are "not his people," who are below him. Revealing how her subjectivity has been defined by the paternalist social order, Narcissa's reactions oppose sexuality, what she thinks are the low and base emotions, oppose associating with those she considers below her social station—the low and base people—and oppose the upheaval of the social order.[13]

These attributes are heightened by the contrast between Narcissa and the other significant female characters: Ruby and Temple. Both Ruby and Narcissa are housekeepers and mothers of children, yet, while we see Ruby cook, clean, and change her child's diapers, we never see Narcissa involved in similar activities. As an upper-class woman, Narcissa never gets her hands wet or dirty, while Ruby, who is common, so to speak, is associated with fluids, liquids, dirt, and sexuality. Within the masculinist fantasy world, and the social reality it works to create, this is as it should be. Both characters reveal female roles defined by paternalism. If these characters seem real, it is because paternalism still has influence on the ways in which American society defines roles for women according to class. Not at all connected to universal definitions of women, which do not exist, both characters embody projections of the real that paternalist ideology places onto the social definitions of women. When the novel focuses on the story of Temple Drake, however, it confronts a woman who threatens to topple these limited definitions. In her actions, Temple reveals she has not accepted the role prescribed to her by paternalist ideology. In her attempt to define herself, to define her own subjectivity, Temple is a threat to this perspective and thus becomes the perfect personification of the red woman.[14]

Although when we first meet Temple she is not associated with fluids as Belle is, she most definitely becomes associated with fluidity and motion. She has "long legs blonde with running" (1985c, 29), and throughout the novel she constantly moves, runs, darts, whirls, spins, and writhes. In fact, this fluidity of motion defines her entire subjectivity, as she hardly ever stays still: she never stays with one boy and always drives around to different places; her favorite activity is dancing. Within this narrative perspective, this "running around," Temple's mobile subjectivity comes to represent her defiance of the role of the white woman (or lady), which she is supposed to occupy by virtue of her class. Unlike Narcissa, Temple refuses to sit still and mollify the twisted forces of desire and repression charging the masculine world around her. She expects to be treated on her own terms. That, however, cannot be tolerated.

As the narrative makes clear, Temple's "running around" leads to her rape. Gowan comments, "'Look out . . . you're getting all that stuff stirred up in me again'" (1985c, 54), and Ruby reiterates, "If she'd just stopped running around where they had to look at her" (1985c, 169). Temple's constant motion leads people to think she should be manhandled, that in fact she probably wants to be. From the paternalist perspective of the novel, it does not matter that almost all of Temple's movements indicate resistance and flight; it does not matter that they indicate independence and agency rather than desire for sexuality: movement, motion, fluidity—anything that flows or streams—is read as seductive and threatening. We should not be surprised when Temple paints her mouth "boldly scarlet" (1985c, 38) or that she has red hair, for she stands in direct opposition to Narcissa and represents the image of "the red woman." By filling the expectations of that role, Temple becomes threatening; she must be punished, put down, as it were.

The first time Temple is still for any duration occurs during the rape scene itself. Finally her motion has been stilled; her identity is pinned down, importantly, *for her.* The red woman has been punished. Within the patriarchal social perspective of the novel, Temple's rape represents the culmination of a sick and perverted logic: Temple's movements defined her subjectivity while Popeye was emasculated by the social system—Faulkner takes pains in the revised version to explain his childhood—and thus feels the most pressure to exert some power over Temple. This action does serve as a punishment, of sorts, in that it curtails Temple's mobility. At the same time, this punishment is not the proper one for Temple from the perspective of the patriarchs for it only releases the wild, chaotic forces that they think always lurk in women. Temple obviously needs further treatment, from their perspective, in order to be restored to her proper place—frozen on the pedestal. Likewise, the lower class needs to be shown its proper place.

The need to return Temple to the position of lady and to punish the lower class shows how the paternalist's need to repress sexuality connects to the way he must repress all that is associated with sexuality in society. As Theweleit explains, the way in which patriarchs want to control emotions from flooding their psyches and causing whirlwinds within the order of their subjective identities parallels the way in which they wish to keep the lower elements of society from rising up and creating a threat to the social order. As they must repress what they consider low and base elements of their psyches, they must repress the same elements of society.

In *Sanctuary,* Faulkner clearly links female sexuality to the lower class. We have already seen the association of dirt and liquids with female sexuality and how all of these become related to the figure of Popeye through the one, repeated image of the black liquid. Specific images related to female sexuality are associated with the lower class in other ways as well: Pap constantly spits into a handkerchief, reminding us of Belle's handkerchief, which disgusted Horace; Popeye also has a handkerchief, a soiled one, reminding us of Horace's request that Little Belle not soil her shoes by associating with the wrong type of boys; the men at the Old Frenchman's Place always spit, reminding us of the dirty liquids with which sexual women are generally associated. The fear of the threat of female sexuality, then, becomes directly connected to the patriarch's fear of the threat from the lower class. After Temple's experiences with Popeye and Red, the patriarchal perspective of the novel demands that a supposedly foul and filthy aspect of both the personal psyche and the social order must be controlled, punished, set straight. The desired state of psychological calm demands a state of social calm.

That these two threats to patriarchal order are the significant concerns of the novel, rather than the specific events surrounding Temple's rape, becomes dramatically revealed in the trial. Ironically enough, Lee is not on trial for rape but for murder, both having been committed by Popeye. For the patriarchs, though, the point is not to find Tommy's murderer or Temple's rapist. It is, on the one hand, to punish the lower class, to set an example so that none step over the boundaries again, and, on the other, to rescue Temple from this class and from the raging demons within her. To them, the crime is not the physical attack on the individual woman: since women are seen to cause sexual feelings in men, that can scarcely be a crime at all. Rather, the crime is the threat to the dominant order. Both Lee and Popeye die, both for crimes they didn't commit; no matter, their deaths serve as reminders to others. Meanwhile, Temple is taken away from the "slimy and dirty" Popeye, away from the sexually prolific Red, and returned to "these good men, these fathers and husbands" (1985c, 299).

Short of the death Horace wished for her, Temple experiences a living death after the trial. In their cooperation with this process, the Drakes show their (class) allegiance to Horace's unspoken punitive desires. They allow Temple to be condemned publicly and to serve as an example of what happens to girls who behave as she did. Returned to the control of father and brothers for what they hope is a more long-lasting lesson in discipline, Temple's agency is voided and she is returned to her role of lady. Represented by the statues of dead queens at which she gazes at novel's end, Temple's position now is one of stasis, stillness; like Narcissa's state of heroic statuary, Temple is now back where the paternalists want her.[15]

Interestingly enough, although Temple is in the proper state of immobility and stasis at novel's end, she is not in the state of Mississippi; she is in Europe. Her physical removal seems to indicate the paternalists' lack of power over the social world of Jefferson. Although the novel's perspective has been dominated by paternalism, Horace's own failures to revive his patrilineal heritage or to bring the principles of "law, justice, civilization" to bear on Lee Goodwin's trial also point directly to an absence of paternalism's power in the current social world. These failures signal the passing of paternalism in a manner similar to the passing indicated by Quentin Compson's suicide in *The Sound and the Fury*. Thus, the perverse duality of paternalism's definition of masculinity no longer has a social structure that can support its continuation, and the novel shows that the representations of that masculinity must change: Horace returns to his sexual wife, and Popeye accepts execution. Now, the bourgeois world of Jefferson itself, represented by the district attorney, the church ladies, and the men who hang Goodwin (those like Jason Compson), will ascend, and different definitions of masculinity and femininity will develop to some extent as will different relationships to sexuality. As shown by the D.A.'s association with Judge Drake and by the attitudes of the men outside the jail, however, these different definitions will not necessarily be completely new: they certainly will maintain some definitively patriarchal attitudes. Attitudes toward female sexuality might become less conflicted and perverse, but they will not exactly allow for female subjectivity and independence, except to some extent under the cover of motherhood. Attitudes toward the low and the base, whether psychologically or socially, will continue to affect Yoknapatawpha society dramatically, especially when Faulkner turns to explore the charged terrain of race and sexuality.

Sanctuary also demonstrates Faulkner's acknowledgement that paternalism was fading as a socially viable, comprehensible ideological formation: to most people in Jefferson, Horace's quest seemed absurd right from the start. In his exposure of the rather bizarre and twisted web of desire and depravity, idealism and sexuality, though, Faulkner reveals none of the affection for this ideological position shown in his depictions of Quentin. True, Faulkner seems close to this novel. The exact line between Faulkner's sense of what is real and a paternalist's sense of what is real, as represented by Horace, seems very hard to draw; Faulkner, clearly, knows these characters and these perspectives well, perhaps even inside and out. Nonetheless, Faulkner's revelations about paternalism here indicate a rather intense critique of its effects on male behavior and psychology. Unlike Horace, who could not decipher the logical pattern of evil because he was so immersed in its tangled strands, Faulkner seems able to depict both the inner psychological root of paternalism as well as its dire consequences and social ramifications. Ultimately, Sanctuary indicates that the only embrace left for people within paternalism is "the embrace of the season of rain and death" (1985c, 333) into which Temple falls at novel's end—that one's only sanctuary lies in the past, and that the past, unfortunately, is not everything it has been made out to be.

Reading Sanctuary from a perspective that seeks to integrate psychological fixations with social reality and that recognizes ideological formations as the link between the subjective and the social allows us to understand it as part of the ideological, cultural history with which Faulkner was intricately involved— the intensely complicated transition from one kind of South to another. Sanctu-

ary reveals in vivid detail the ways in which this transition touched even the most personal aspect of people's lives, how attitudes toward sexuality and intimacy were linked to the ideological formation by which characters were identified, and how the ideological perspective guiding this world was rooted in a twisted web of desire, fear, and dread, all of which affected attitudes toward gender, class, and (implicitly in this novel) race. This kind of indictment could only cause Faulkner, its seer, to yearn for and to be open to and curious about other forms of behavior, other values, other ideological formations. Faulkner was beginning to explore these other values and perspectives—as my discussions of *As I Lay Dying* and *Light in August* will reveal.

5 • *As I Lay Dying* and *Light in August*
The Social Realities of Liberalism

The polarities that shape and animate the culture of modernism [capitalism] . . . are the theme of insatiable desires and drives . . . and its radical antithesis, the theme of nihilism, insatiable destruction.
—Marshall Berman, *Everything Solid Melts into Air*

Although critics who focus on the question of race see *Light in August* as a significant novel, most critics do not see it or *As I Lay Dying* as central texts in Faulkner's canon. Never are they seen to be related to each other in any significant manner. I would like to move in another direction by investigating what I consider to be the primary, underlying focus of both novels: the question of mobility in a liberal society. From the sociohistorical perspective both novels fit into this early period of Faulkner's career where he began to explore the social terrain by which he was surrounded.

Both *As I Lay Dying* and *Light in August*, like *Sanctuary*, focus on the world of Jefferson and the surrounding area in the 1920s. In *Sanctuary*, Temple Drake epitomized the most modern, contemporary character, and it was her mobility that both defined her and made her threatening to the paternalists' desire for stasis and rigid order. Following *Sanctuary*, as if Faulkner became intrigued by the question and ramifications of mobility itself, *As I Lay Dying* has as its basic metaphor, the journey, and its most significant symbol, the road. Likewise, opening with Lena Grove traveling the open road and describing Joe Christmas's frantic search for that identity which always eludes him, *Light in August* also concerns itself with mobility—both geographical and psychological. Both books, in fact, are centrally concerned with the process of subject or identity formation in a socially mobile society.

Faulkner's insights into and assessments of capitalist society—defined by constant and continual mobility—in these two books parallel the best critic of capitalism, Marx, and the two men share many insights. Marshall Berman explains one of these: "In order for people . . . to survive in modern society, their personalities must take on the fluid and open form of this society. Modern men and women must learn to yearn for change . . . to delight in mobility" (1982, 95–96). Faulkner makes this assessment, but he is not always comfortable with it. Those characters who identify with mobility do survive in Faulkner's New South; those who do not suffer painful and tragic fates. Importantly, however, those who do not are the more noble. In *As I Lay Dying* Faulkner explores the way liberalism legitimizes identity, and the novel reveals his discomfort with the ways and means people achieve bourgeois social mobility. This discomfort leads him to explore a natural form of legitimation for people's place within a social order in *Light in August*.

More than any other Faulkner novel, *As I Lay Dying* focuses directly on life in farming country. It depicts a section of the South and a social group with which Faulkner's fiction in general remained only tangentially concerned. The Bundren family clearly is overshadowed in the Faulkner canon by other families—Sartoris, Compson, McCaslin, and Snopes—who return again and again. This contrast highlights the fact that Faulkner's interest in the Populist farmers of Mississippi was rather slight. *As I Lay Dying* does not treat the full range of subjectivities of poor white farmers, especially the historical consciousness to which some came within the Populist movement.[1] Rather, the novel focuses on the consciousness of those poor, working-rural-class whites who came to identify with the ideology of the middle class in Mississippi, Progressivism, supported as it was, especially in rural sections, by Protestantism. Although to some extent Faulkner's depiction is historically accurate in that this process is one aspect of what did occur in Mississippi, it also reminds us that *As I Lay Dying* is a symbolic history told from a particular standpoint. That standpoint is more closely connected to the dominant ideological formations—liberalism and paternalism—than it is to the nondominant one that motivated some among the working class. This observation does not take anything away from Faulkner's critique; it does, however, help explain the solutions to historical conflicts to which Faulkner comes in later works. Affected by the dominant ideologies as he was, Faulkner was not open to the working-class responses to the crises of his time.

This story is a symbolic history, then, in the way it indicates the main directions of Mississippi society. If depictions of Quentin Compson's and Horace Benbow's world revealed the lineaments of a paternalist social order and its fading status, depictions of the Bundrens reveal the lineaments of the New South world and the ascendant status of the new ideological formation—liberalism. The Bundrens have long been country folk, yeoman farmers who have had little chance of social mobility. For them, farming the land has been an endless ritual seemingly with no beginning and no end. Now, however, they live in the same hinge of history that affected Jason Compson. They find themselves in a world in which an emergent liberal ethos is in the process of becoming the dominant ideological formation, and most of them do not resist this process (though Addie and Darl do). Rather, like Jason Compson, they are bound and determined to enter this newly emergent middle class.

In a discussion of Faulkner's novel *Sanctuary,* Sundquist discusses a Theodore Dreiser story by the same title and comments that, in Dreiser, "characters . . . succeed or fail . . . because they desire exactly what the machinery of their society offers" (1983, 45). To my mind this insight applies quite directly to the characters in *As I Lay Dying.* Anse Bundren and his family, except Addie and Darl, identify with middle-class values even though they have not achieved middle-class status. At this moment in their lives and in the history of Southern society, the solidification of liberalism and capitalism meant, as it has always meant for this process, the separation of the country from the city; the two were, in fact, set in opposition to one another. Being in the country and identifying with country ways meant isolation and separation—virtual nonexistence; to become part of society as full-fledged citizens, people, the Bundrens included, had to adopt city ways.[2] And, in fact, the entire point of their journey, for everyone but Darl, is exactly to attain this middle-class identity.

The Bundrens (except Darl and Addie) reveal their acceptance of middle-class values throughout the book. What this acceptance means for them as Mississippi farmers is an identification with the values of the Protestant middle class—independence, individuality, and reward based on merit—which were buttressed by religious beliefs. Throughout the novel, and seemingly for his entire life, Anse is caught between expressing his independence and revealing his need for help. Many men in the novel admit they have helped Anse many times; indeed, he has been offered assistance constantly throughout his life: "'I reckon [God's] like everybody else around here. . . . He's done it [taken care of Anse] so long now He cant quit'" (89). Nonetheless, Anse refuses to ask for help, and the assistance he does accept comes in the form of neighborly labor, never in the form of borrowing another man's property. When Tull offers his wagon to Anse so he can immediately move Addie's dead body, Anse replies, "'We'll wait for ourn'" (92), even though he will have to wait three days with his wife's corpse in the coffin. When Tull offers his team, a faster and stronger one, Anse again replies, "'We'll wait for ourn'" (92). Later, when Samson offers the Bundrens dinner while they rest for the night, Anse refuses, saying, "'I thank you. . . . We wouldn't discommode you. We got a little something in the basket. We can make out'" (115). To offers of feed for Jewel's horse and beds for the children, the response of both Jewel and Anse is "'We wouldn't be beholden'" (117). The desire to avoid indebtedness and a strong need to express their independence motivate the Bundrens, especially Anse—even when it means slowing down their mission to bury Addie's body in Jefferson, forty miles away, even when that body stinks and attracts buzzards. They reveal their desire to remain affiliated with middle-class independence even when their cause would have been greatly aided by accepting other people's help. This inability to accept help with gratitude follows the Bundrens much like the bad smell of Addie's rotting corpse.

Connected to their assertion of economic independence and their identity as yeoman farmers is a deep belief in the religious nature of farming and the awareness of God's judgment, as exemplified by the conversation of Cash, Tull, and Peabody:

> "'It's the cotton and corn I mind.'"
>
> "'Washed clean outen the ground it will be. Seems like something is always happening to it.'"
>
> "'Course it does. That's why it's worth anything. If nothing didn't happen and everybody made a big crop, do you reckon it would be worth the raising?'"
>
> "'Ay. The Lord made it to grow. It's Hisn to wash up if He sees it fitten so.'"
>
> (90–91)

The essentially bourgeois, liberal belief in equal rights and opportunities combined with the Protestant belief in reward and punishment identifies this farming community.[3] These beliefs about the plight of the farmer serve also to replace human agency with divine law, and Faulkner seems to imply that part of the explanation for the farmers not coming to historical consciousness as a group united by a Populist ideology lies with their explanations of their life, which place responsibility for their fate with God rather than with themselves. This rhetoric of divine and natural law denies the circumscription of subjectivity by economic exploitation. Thus, *As I Lay Dying* reveals how the farmers, by identifying with an ideological formation that justified their own poverty, participated in their own exploitation. Anse becomes a symbol of the Mississippi farmer who aids his own exploitation by rationalizing his economic plight through religious beliefs characteristic of a middle class that did not really serve his interests. Historically, these beliefs separated some farmers from others, notably independent farmers from tenant farmers, both white and black, even though the interests of all farmers were more similar to one another's than to those of merchants, townsfolk, and industrialists.

The novel makes clear as well, however, that, for the Bundrens, religious and natural justifications of poverty have begun to wear thin. Cash has branched out from farming and learned carpentry and also does odd-jobs for people; Jewel works for another farmer to earn the cash to buy a horse; and even Anse, by the time the events of the novel begin, feels a certain dissatisfaction with his plight, one not explained by religious and divine law: "'Nowhere in this sinful world can a honest, hardworking man profit. It takes them that runs the stores in the towns, doing no sweating, living off of them that sweats. It aint the hardworking man, the farmer. Sometimes I wonder why we keep at it'" (110). These actions and comments point to the historical tension occurring in the larger setting of the novel—the historical turning point where urban, town interests were coming to outweigh rural, country ones. This juncture is indicated by the coming of the road into their small community and the subsequent taxation to pay for it—events that change their lives forever. This conflict is mentioned throughout the novel, with almost every character experiencing it. Besides Anse's comments about this conflict, Dewey Dell thinks, "I dont see why he didn't stay in town. We are country people, not as good as town people" (60); Vardaman wonders, "'Why aint I a town boy'" (59); and Jewel strikes out violently at the man who comments on Addie's corpse, saying, "'Thinks because he's a goddamn town fellow'" (230). All these comments point to the conflict between town and country underlying the novel's plot. This conflict and the anger and malaise felt by the Bundrens do not get resolved by rebellion or political agitation for the farmers' cause. The Bundrens take another direction, and their geographical journey to bury Addie's corpse serves really as the means through which they will mitigate their historical plight. Their sense of feeling unimportant and detached from the ongoing world gets resolved through a closer affiliation with the newly forming middle class. In effect, Anse has chosen not "to keep at it," but to change with the changing times.

Despite the fact that the Bundrens, as farmers, have been relatively excluded from the material developments sponsored by the middle class, their quest in this novel is to gain access to bourgeois subjectivity. Disguised by the trappings of loss and bereavement, the journey serves to fulfill each one's secret, selfish, and individual desire: Anse will get his set of teeth, his new wife, and her money; Dewey Dell wants her abortion in order to maintain her value as a marriage-able woman and her association with morality; Cash wants his gramophone; Vardaman moves closer to his train and his bananas. Rather than see their economic plight as one in conflict with those in town—an insight at least plausible based on their observations—the Bundrens maintain their identification with the middle-class ideology of liberalism and seek to gain the material appearances necessary for identification with this class. Anse's new teeth, in fact, wipe away the past and grant him a brand new subjectivity: "It made him look a foot taller, kind of holding his head up" (260).

In order to become part of that larger community of the town, the Bundrens, with the exception of Darl, reject their potentially subversive position in relation to liberal ideology. They choose to replace Addie with material objects—commodities—in order to achieve social status as members of this new middle class. The replacement of Addie makes perfect sense, of course, because it has been Addie all along who has been intensely aware of the effects of liberal ideology and capitalist society. Addie's comments about the children she teaches—"Now you are aware of me!" (170)—and her remarks about words—"I would think how words go straight up in a thin line . . . and how terribly doing goes along" (173)—reveal the two greatest effects of capitalism on the people within it: isolation and alienation. Moreover, Addie reveals that she has not been affected by the capitalist ideology surrounding her. Her deeply human desire, a universal one, to be united with another person and to resist cosmic loneliness has not been perverted into the pursuit of material objects, a quest that will never satisfy human desire for intimacy. Although her relationship with Whitfield remains a secret, wordless as it were, her actions are directly connected to her desires; thus, she remains a nonalienated character. Addie's insights into the world around her indicate that the reality of living in a capitalist society means living in a world where "all that is solid melts into air" (Marx 1972, 476). Moreover, much like

Darl, she resists this world. For these reasons she is noble and tragic, the heroine of the novel.

Of course, Darl's plight serves to reiterate both the parodic nature of the Bundren's journey and that at its center is indeed the quest to attain bourgeois subjectivity. On one hand, Darl's constant laughter emphasizes his ability to see through the appearances of the journey; he sees the trip as a parody of sorrow and bereavement. (And, of course, Darl is shown to be the one who can see beyond the surface all throughout the book.) When ideologically laden discourse substantiates and approves of this quest, laughter is indeed an appropriate reaction and commentary. Darl's laughter also shows how he stands outside the signifying practices that organize and justify this journey and this society. He is not concerned with attaining bourgeois subjectivity. He has always been the son least concerned about work; he has been the only one who has constantly attempted to subvert the trip; and he rebels against the cornerstone of bourgeois ideology, private property. In fact, this act secures his banishment from the society as it convinces Cash that "[t]his world is not [Darl's] world; this life not his life" (261) because "nothing excuses setting fire to a man's barn and endangering his stock and destroying his property" (233). Darl's tragic-comic laughter serves as judgment upon his family's drive to attain bourgeois status. Darl is crazy only in the sense that he identifies with a completely different set of values (much like Quentin Compson). For Faulkner, his laughter is moral judgment, not psychic gibberish.

Of course, Darl stands in direct opposition to Anse, and another aspect of the parody in this novel has to do with Anse's extremely specious claims to his position of authority. Like Jason Compson, Anse asserts power and position through his manipulation of the rhetoric of paternalism, but his actions reveal no real affiliation with the expectations of this ideology.[4] As we have seen, the edifice of paternalism founds itself on the avowed protection of and the self-serving devotion to white women. The very authority of the patriarch stems from his control over the woman, couched in terms of devotion to her, and from a sense of responsibility to his dependents that justifies their obedience. A number of times during the novel, Anse states that the quest to bring Addie's decaying corpse to Jefferson is motivated by her last request and his promise to fulfill it.[5]

We also learn that each of his older sons has disappointed him by not working hard enough on the farm: Jewel had worked secretly through the nights in order to buy a horse; Cash had gone to carpentry school when there was plenty of work for him at home; and Darl short-hands Anse "just because he tends to his own business" (36). Anse stresses these points when he says, "I have raised such a durn passel of boys, and when you fixes it so folks can say such about you, it's a reflection on your ma . . . it's on your womenfolks, your ma and your sister that you should care for" (106). Centered ostensibly on the wishes of the women, Anse gets his boys to do as he wishes only by manipulating them to think they owe something to Addie. Anse's acquisition of new teeth and a new wife places his devotion to Addie into serious doubt, however. His own secret selfish agenda really motivates the journey, and the boys, knowingly or unknowingly, assist their father in reasserting his patriarchal position as head of the family. Meanwhile, Anse's selfish motives have also caused Jewel to sacrifice the horse he loves, Cash to break his leg, and Dewey Dell to sacrifice the only money she has. Indeed, Anse's behavior seems a near-perfect caricature of paternalism—claiming all the authority with absolutely none of the responsibility. Faulkner's depictions of Anse's paternalist authority reveals how some can use its rhetoric to manipulate others. Like Jason Compson, Anse is not at all identified by this ideology in the way Quentin Compson or Horace Benbow is; he simply wants the power and authority to help him get his own way. This type of behavior was particularly repugnant for Faulkner as he felt it had deep consequences for the South (and he would turn to these issues in the Snopes trilogy).

Riding into Jefferson with a rotting corpse, harassed each step of the way by law-abiding citizens, embarrassed and insecure, the Bundrens ride out as solid citizens, with all the appearance of a solid nuclear family intact. Although many have read the Bundrens' quest as a mythic journey of heroic proportions, I find it hard not to see the parody here.[6] Characters in *As I Lay Dying* have been affected by the historical changes elevating town/city values and forms of citizenship over country values; they see themselves, as their world does, as second-class citizens and want a different life. From Faulkner's perspective, though, this society enforces a trivialization of human desire, allowing people to become fully enfranchised only if they attain material appearances that make them just like everyone else.[7] Capitalism, as Faulkner understands and portrays it, encourages, even forces, self-development, constant motion and movement; however, as Addie and Darl come to realize and as Anse, Jewel, Cash, Dewey Dell, and Vardaman epitomize, people in this society can only develop in distorted and limited ways. In this world, much of what lives inside human beings never has the chance to come to active life at all—the best of Addie and Darl dies with their departure from the social order. For Faulkner, people in *As I Lay Dying* "go on, with a motion so soporific, so dreamlike as to be uninferant of progress" (107–8). That is to say, despite the fact that the Bundrens get to Jefferson and bury Addie, their accomplishments do not indicate progress. For Faulkner, life in this new liberal, capitalistic, materialistic South, defined by social mobility, leaves much to be desired.

Precisely what separates this newly formed society and its ideology from the aristocratic paternalism Faulkner explores in other places is that, on one hand, it will allow anyone who acquires the necessary material signs of class affiliation to join, and, on the other hand, it creates a social order in which people have no relation to others. The quest of each character in *As I Lay Dying*, in fact, is to discover the answer to a complex question: "How can I, whose self has depended upon, and been defined in relation to another self, now understand the integrity of my own identity?" (Sundquist 1983, 32). Faulkner's answer is that they cannot: as *Light in August* shows, people who live with no relation to others do not really live at all. A world consisting of isolated individuals with no stable identity creates no real life at all for Faulkner. Some kind of social cohesion, some form of relationship among people as citizens is necessary.

Although *The Sound and the Fury* and *Sanctuary* began to question a society structured by paternalism, *As I Lay Dying* reveals that a society which promoted opportunity and advancement based on acquisition of the material signs of citizenship also had, for Faulkner, some glaring failures. One of these was the lack of guidelines for people to follow. After all, Tull had taken and cut down for money the two big white oaks that would have guided the Bundrens where to cross the river successfully (142). Like Addie Bundren and Caddy Compson, who see through the words structuring their worlds, Faulkner recognizes that capitalism does create a world where everything solid melts into air, where people are left to identify themselves only with material signs of success. At this point in his career Faulkner yearns for some other form of legitimation. His novels during this period do not depict any alternate subjectivity, at any length, but the yearning remains. If Faulkner had not been so interpellated by the dominant ideological formations, so deeply identified by them psychologically and by what they expected socially, he might have been able to pursue a more adequate accounting of the subjectivity of the poor whites, or of either Caddie or Addie. If he could have, he might have given a fuller account of the subversive capabilities of these positions vis-à-vis the ideologies of his historical moment. The signs of these alternative forms of subjectivity are there, certainly, and they will reappear in later novels, but here they appear only in repressed or latent form.

The questions Faulkner explores in *As I Lay Dying* focus on social mobility as a means to attain identity and on the formation of this identity by channeling human desire into a quest for material objects. Faulkner acknowledges the rise of the middle class, sees its lineaments and determinations, and presents and implicitly criticizes the ways in which one becomes a full citizen in a bourgeois social order. Nonetheless, this particular social order seems to have become a given by this time, and in *Light in August* Faulkner becomes concerned with how one can find some order in the face of unwarranted or illegitimate social mobility. The state of affairs is summarized by Byron Bunch, whose insight into the world resembles Addie's: "it was like me, and her [Lena Grove], and all the other folks that I had to get mixed up in it, were just a lot of words that never stood for anything, were not even us, while all the time what was us was going on and going on without even missing the lack of words" (401–2). With Lena's pointless perambulations, Lucas Burch's amoral anomie, and Joe Christmas's confused wanderings, the world of *Light in August* certainly represents a society where mobility can be seen to threaten social cohesion and communal stability. On the other hand, as Percy Grimm reveals, this mobility has also created a backlash: some people will do much to enforce their vision. Thus, the backdrop for the novel is a social world in which people do not share beliefs and values or an understanding of their world.[8] When a social order does not offer these, another way to find them is through a vision of a natural order to the world, where everything and everyone has a prescribed place. It is precisely this sense that society should have some order with which Faulkner himself is primarily concerned in *Light in August*—he wants to know, that is, what is this "us" that keeps going and going despite the words. This concern leads him to explore the relationship between biology/genetic makeup and identity. In *Light in August*, to a very large degree, biology is identity, and identity defines one's prescribed place.

Before moving ahead, I think it imperative to discuss the sensitive issue of race. Unlike others, I do not think this issue is the main concern of this novel. I do not because distinct and limited definitions of racial identity establish the entire context in which the narrative unfolds and because questions of race are only one of a number of ways in which the book explores essentialist explanations for people's behavior.[9]

Joe Christmas wonders whether he is "black" or "white" as if those terms have definite referents in material reality, that is, in biology. His question only exists because he has already accepted the terms of a strict ideology of race as they have been established by the majority white population of Yoknapatawpha County (and Mississippi). Critics have claimed that *Light in August* investigates this very social structuring. I disagree. The whole novel operates from within the basic premises of what has been labeled the psychocultural school of thought about race relations.

As will be explained in detail in chapter 7, the psychocultural school claims that it is human nature to be prejudiced against those who are different and that racism and white supremacy were foreordained before English settlers sailed into the James River. The so-called natural tension and animosity *between* the races becomes manifest *in* Joe Christmas's subjectivity, and his internal conflicts exist because of the essentialist assumptions and ideologically laden constructs guiding Yoknapatawpha. Although critics demonize the remarks of Gavin Stevens, they define the narrative's context: "Because the black blood drove him first to the negro cabin. And then the white blood drove him out of there, as it was the black blood which snatched up the pistol and the white blood which would not let him fire it" (449). Clearly racist, these remarks cannot be put aside simply as indicators of Stevens's character since they serve as a valid explanation within the scope of the novel. Joe Christmas has very much accepted Jefferson's psychocultural theories about race, thinking that to have "black blood" makes you black, and that black and white are definitely two different and separate modes of existence. He clearly believes that if he can discover whether he is black or white (as if that quest has any meaning at all!), he will know how to behave, where he fits, who he is. With this quest accomplished, he will find, finally, the peace he has sought for thirty years. In short, his genetic makeup is the map that will lead to self-knowledge and awareness of his social position. He and Gavin Stevens think exactly the same way on the issue, and Stevens voices the overall community's idea.[10]

Christmas allows the past, an uncertain and unsubstantiated past, to hang over his head like a guillotine. He allows a paranoid dietician and a perverted maniac, Doc Hines, to define his identity and destiny for him. Importantly, he sees no possibility of admitting a mixed-race heritage, accepting it as perfectly fine, and moving forward with his life. This thinking highlights the parameters of the rigid and strictly defined ideology of race so prevalent and pervasive in Jefferson and Faulkner's Mississippi, determined as it is/was by white-supremacist thinking. I contend that Faulkner does not question and criticize this ideology here, as he will in *Absalom, Absalom!*, but that he explores race as one essentialist means through which to seek order in a chaotic world.

Despite Faulkner's later explorations, I do think it important to assert that much of Christmas's tragedy stems from the fact that there is no social space for mixed blood people in the white society of Jefferson or within the imaginary (white) space of this novel. Many discussions about Faulkner elide and detour around this difficult subject, and many adopt the psychocultural theories about race and the relation between black and white people these theories purport.[11] Even many sensitive to and concerned about issues of race understand Joe's quest as one that entails a necessary decision: whether he is black or white. He is both, for these critics, only in the sense that these two bloods are (and seemingly will always be) antagonistic. This line of thought only replicates the ideology of race guiding the novel itself and does not open the possibility that there are societies where this decision would simply be absurd because it would not matter one way or the other. As Faulkner's story "Delta Autumn" reveals, however, this type of world does exist for Faulkner's so-called black characters (who later in Faulkner's canon often think differently than whites on the subject of racial identity). The question that Joe Christmas asks, "When do men who have different blood in them stop hating one another?" (249), remains essentially a rhetorical question for most of *Light in August*. The answer, "When people stop seeing themselves as having different blood," the very answer Jim Beauchamp's granddaughter offers to Ike McCaslin in "Delta Autumn," is not voiced at this point in Faulkner's career.

Another argument against race being the novel's main concern emerges when we investigate how Christmas's story relates to the rest of the novel. Joe's internalization of essentialist thinking about race is only one instance of the general mode of the novel, where we see instance after instance of essentialist thinking. Faulkner fills the book, in fact, with set definitions of race and gender. The narration constantly explains people and actions in these terms. These explanations assume a natural order against which behavior can be judged. The characters, and Faulkner himself, are searching for systems of legitimation based on universally recognized values and the absolute truth of natural law. Thus, the novel's main concerns are, I believe, identity and community: finding stable means through which to define oneself and understand others and to know how everyone joins together in a structured society.

Besides Joe, there are other characters who reveal essentialist thinking throughout the book. When Byron Bunch remembers a conversation about Joe, he links Joe's name to his racial identity and to an explanation of behavior. He remembers the foreman saying, "'Did you ever hear of a white man named Christmas?'" (33), and then the narrator comments: "And that was the first time Byron remembered that he had ever thought how a man's name . . . can be somehow an augur of what he will do" (33). Here, Joe's murder of Joanna Burden is explained, in Byron's mind, by his racial heritage. Later, a local resident discusses Christmas' behavior: "He never acted like either a nigger or a white man. That was it. That was what made the folks so mad" (350). Here, the ways in which people understand the world around them through essentialist categories is made clear; they expect a certain order and need that order to be enforced.

This thinking is supported by the narrator of the novel and to some extent by Faulkner. At one point the narrator describes Joe: "He had grown to manhood in the country, where like the unswimming sailor his physical shape and his thought had been molded by its compulsions without his learning anything about its actual shape and feel . . . he remained a foreigner to the very immutable laws which earth must obey" (338). Joe's confusion seems not only to be about his own identity but about "immutable" laws which people must follow—such as the difference between black and white. At least at some points in his life Faulkner supported this kind of thinking; in an interview he commented that when it came to black and white in the South it had to be all one way or the other.[12] In this novel Faulkner certainly explores essentialist categories as a response to the alternative of chaotic mobility.

The essentialist thinking explored in the novel is revealed in other ways as well. At one point Hightower listens to Bunch and the Hines couple, and "It is as though he were listening to the doings of people of a different race" (81). The whole town, in fact, understands the Hines couple this way: "The town looked upon them both as being a little touched—lonely, gray in color, a little smaller than most other men and women, as if they belonged to a different race" (341). The narrator even describes Joanna's relatives in these terms: "the tall, gaunt, Nordic man, and the small, dark, vivid child who had inherited his mother's build and coloring, like people of two different races" (242). Finally, even Joanna Burden falls prey to this rigid form of thinking in one place, when she attempts to explain why her father did not kill Colonel Sartoris: "I think that it was because of his French blood. . . . he was French. . . . Enough French to respect anybody's love for the land where he and his people were born and to understand that a man would have to act as the land where he was born had trained him to act" (254–55). In all of these cases, characters and narrator are searching for ways to understand other people and they utilize essentialist categories to explain behavior. Their interpretations are all based on the assumption that people, underneath all the trappings of society, are something solid; that race and nationality determine and therefore explain behavior. In short, in this novel, blood tells.

These examples lead us to recognize another Faulkner reaction to the social reality of liberalism. He explores ways to identify people, to characterize them, that will hold no matter where the person moves within society. He searches for means of adjudication that are internal to the person/character, not ones based on material acquisition. These, he hopes, will help people understand each other as well as their relation to others.

These explorations about blood are not the only instance of the linkage between behavior and essentialist categories. Another way Faulkner explores this linkage is through gender. Joe learns early, from the dietician and from the McEacherns, about the "difference" between men and women: "Perhaps he was thinking then how he and the man could always count on one another, depend upon one another; that it was the woman alone who was unpredictable" (159). In another place, Armstid thinks about Lena's actions and thinks: "right then and there is where she secedes from the woman race and species and spends the balance of her life trying to get joined up with the man race" (15). In both instances, men and women are seen to have definite and different modes of existence—immutable laws guide their behavior as well it seems and those who do not know or follow these do not fit the definition. Through this lens, Hightower is seen to be an unnatural man. People comment: "About how he had made his wife go bad and commit suicide because he was not a natural husband, a natural man" (71), and he himself realizes later that perhaps he was not indeed (488). Finally, this relation between gender and natural behavior extends outward to link physical form to the state of one's spiritual existence. The narrator comments about Bobbie, Joe's girlfriend, that her smallness was "not due to any natural slenderness but to some inner corruption of the spirit itself" (172), and after her plunge into intense sexuality, Joanna is described in similar terms: "She had begun to get fat" (261). In both cases the physical state of these women indicates their spiritual and moral corruption. In other words, their perversion of the assumed natural moral order has caused ramifications in the natural physical order.

Finally, Faulkner also links the essentialist, natural categories to a stable, social order in the way he extends this overall mode of exploration by linking certain characters' banishment from the social order with a commentary on the way he/she subverts a natural order as well. In Joanna Burden's case, she had always been ostracized by the townspeople because she did not accept certain definitions of people, did not accept the strict order ratified by those around her. As Bunch reveals, "'Folks say she claims that niggers are the same as white folks'" (53). Joanna's assertion reveals her rejection of the society around her, and it forces her exclusion from the social world of Jefferson. She is also excluded from the natural order the novel assumes.

In all of his interactions with Joanna, Joe Christmas seeks to understand her in prescribed terms of female behavior, assuming that because she is a woman she will behave in certain ways. He is, however, constantly amazed that these categories do not hold: "There was no feminine vacillation, no coyness of obvious desire and intention to succumb at last. It was as if he struggled physically with another man for an object of no actual value to either, and for which they struggled on principle alone" (235). Later, the narrator comments: "And by day he [Joe] would see the calm, coldfaced, almost manlike, almost middleaged woman who had lived for twenty years alone, without any feminine fears at all" (258). Joanna's isolation from the social world of Jefferson becomes mirrored by her implicit isolation from the natural order supporting the novel's assessments of characters. The overall sense readers receive about Joanna is that there is something wrong with her: she is not natural. The novel, thus, seems to accede to her exclusion from the social order. Similarly, Hightower is excluded, justifiably it seems, because he is an unnatural man, and Joe's story is tragic it seems because readers cannot come to any satisfactory conclusion—based on the novel's premises—whether his self-destruction is justifiable or not.

Rather than race, Faulkner's major concern here is the conflict between the almost rebellious openness of a socially mobile world and the need for social cohesion and personal identity (knowing who one is offers instructions about where one fits). For Faulkner, the liberal society of Jefferson in the 1920s allowed for so much movement that personal identity itself was hard to determine. What we learn about Faulkner through this aspect of the story highlights the authorial ideology guiding the text. As noted, Joe's plight is tragic; Faulkner presents him in sympathetic and moving terms. Not knowing where one fits in a social order means not knowing who one is, and that fate is worse than knowing that one belongs on the bottom, so to speak. Joe's desire for a place in a structured society is, in this manner, a Faulknerian desire. Faulkner creates a world in which it is important to have a place, creates a world that should have some order to it, some rules and mores upon which people can rely, and investigates the plight of one who does not know the rules as they apply to him.

What seems a given for Faulkner, stemming, I would argue, from his affiliation with a paternalist ideology, is the need, perhaps the dire need, for some kind of social order. After paternalism, where will order come from, and what are the results of a lack of order? This backdrop is what makes Joe's plight a tragedy. Beginning with the incursion of the circus into his hometown, Joe's plight is directly connected to an intensely fluid and mobile society, one in which a sense of a natural order has become even more important due to the breakdown of other forms of adjudication.

Hightower's slave's comment articulates Faulkner's own frustration with the newly formed society in which mobility has become the norm; it hints at his continued attachment to paternalism: "'Free? . . . Free? What's freedom done except git Marse Gail killed and made a bigger fool outen Pawmp den even de Lawd Hisself could do?'" (477). As is usually the case in Faulkner's work, a black character plays chorus to an authorial sentiment. Christmas himself clearly shares this attitude, as his refusal to name himself reveals. Unlike, say, a Jay Gatsby, or a Thomas Sutpen, or even a Lena Grove, Christmas refuses to delight in absolute mobility, refuses to name himself.

A liberal society demands that individuals invent, create, and define themselves. Revealing his rejection of this society, Joe refuses to participate in this process and thus inevitably slides into nihilism and self-destruction. On one hand, Joe's virtual death-wish stems from his inability to find a place for himself in this new world; on the other hand, it also derives from his refusal to see that nothing about oneself, even one's racial identity, is inherent or given but subject to self-definition, self-nomination. Joe could have been anything he wanted to be, but all he wanted was to discover what he was—as if he could—so he would know where he fit, and his refusal to accept the terms of this new capitalist world led to his own inner psychological desire for destruction. Unlike the Bundrens, he will not reap the fruits of this new society, but from Faulkner's perspective, Joe is tragic like Darl and Addie, not absurd like Anse and the others. For Faulkner, not knowing what one is leads to not knowing who one is—the most tragic condition (Gwynn and Blotner 1959, 72).

The character who does choose to name herself, the character who links both mobility and order in *Light in August*, is, of course, Lena Grove. From the very beginning Lena sets the overall tone of the novel by traveling the open road. Her motion has the overt motivation of finding the father of her unborn child, but behind it also lurks aspirations. Lena wants people to think that she is from the town (4), not from the country, and she comments on her travels: "'I et polite. . . . Like a lady I et. Like a lady travelling'" (26). These comments link Lena with the Bundrens in one regard as they all wish to be identified by town standards, but Lena seems to want to become a different kind of person, a better person.

This mobility and the aspiration that sponsors it can be supported because Lena still fits within a natural order: she is a mother; she knows the identity of the father of the child; she wishes to unite the nuclear family. Lena's actions of mobility are redeemed by the motivations behind them: to reclaim and reassert the natural bonds of people in a family. Even at the end of the novel, when Lena clearly understands that Lucas Burch is a scoundrel, she continues to say that she is seeking the father of her child because it offers her a cover to continue traveling. Lena's story winds up being another focused on identity and social position, but her secure natural identity offers her a freedom of mobility seen as justified and permitted. Other characters who defy the natural order surrounding them, on the other hand, lose any sense of identity and their right to a place in society.

Davis comments about *Light in August:* "Joe's place is settled as it is because maintaining everything in its proper, assigned place is the end of the southern code of order" (1983, 166). After looking at these other developments, we can extend her insights to recognize how this book focuses on those who in some way defy both social and natural order. Percy Grimm claims that his/their job is to preserve order (451), and though Grimm's actions are, well, grim, his words resonate with the concern underlying the entire book. Grimm rises to prominence because of the breakdown of a shared sense of the natural order of things. He plays a role here similar to the one Jason Compson plays in *The Sound and the Fury* and to the one Anse Bundren plays in *As I Lay Dying.* They all claim and gain positions of authority, but they never deserve these positions. Jason Compson is a hypocrite of the highest order; Anse Bundren's claims to paternalistic status are rhetorical ruses to cloak his trivial desires; and Percy Grimm's ascension to a position of authority stems from the lack of true authority figures who can guide society with wisdom and foresight—he gains his position by default.

The explorations of liberalism Faulkner began with Jason Compson and pursued in *As I Lay Dying* focus to some degree on how social mobility did allow undeserving people to assume positions of authority, and the depiction of Percy Grimm follows this trend. Faulkner's exploration of natural definitions here in *Light in August,* his quest for a natural order to things, can be seen to stem from his recognition that within capitalism nothing solid does exist and his discomfort with this reality. It can also be seen to stem from the vacuum of moral and community leadership Faulkner perceived to exist in a society ruled by liberalism. (Faulkner would return to this concern in the Snopes trilogy.) The demise of paternalism meant the demise of an entire class of men, and this necessitated other means of social and moral adjudication. Natural justifications were one possibility.

Within the panorama of American literature Faulkner is not alone in his quest for a social order rooted in the sense of what is natural or in the exploration of characters' destinies based on blood. A similar unfolding occurs in the work of James Fenimore Cooper, especially in *The Last of the Mohicans,* where mixed-blood characters such as Cora and Magua are seen to be tainted and corrupt to one degree or another, and where moral character is linked to blood heritage.

Cooper and Faulkner seem to be concerned with similar questions: how do we adjudicate among people in an intensely mobile, rapidly changing world where past systems of order have collapsed? Faulkner probes an extension of an ideology based on biological determinations, exploring issues of identity for many characters including Joe Christmas and in other ways besides race. Faulkner is seeking, it would appear, some means to determine legitimate and acceptable human behavior within a social order that defined itself on mobility, and he bases his determinations on universal definitions that have the weight of natural law behind them. Coming to understand that liberalism and the society it engendered were here to stay, Faulkner was seeking ways to infuse them with a sense of order and a means of adjudication.

We are left near novel's end with Hightower's vision of two faces—Joe Christmas and Percy Grimm. These faces seem to be the legacy left to this society, where any shared sense of social order has been forsaken and any shared sense of values guiding behavior has been lost. At this point, Percy Grimm alone is left to assert what the townspeople themselves want; his actions seem realistic within the scope of the novel's world, and they clearly have resonance with Mississippi history. Faulkner seems to be in touch with these realities and to understand them. These two faces represent what was left to the South from its ideological heritage. Order now, after the breakdown of older forms, would have to be imposed in near hysterical ways—unless some natural justifications could be discovered and articulated. Questions were left at the end of *Light in August:* first, how did the South get to a place that seemed so fated and so real, yet so wrong? Second, were there natural justifications to be discovered? Faulkner turns to these questions in *Absalom, Absalom!*

Part Three • Faulkner's Authorial Ideology

6 • *Absalom, Absalom!*
and Natural Aristocracy

[This novel] creatively exposes as unworkable the larger culture's ideological designs.

—Philip Weinstein, *Faulkner's Subject*

In the shady but ingenious shapes of his first mature novels—*The Sound and the Fury, Sanctuary, As I Lay Dying,* and *Light in August*—Faulkner did begin to affirm the impulses of his own ego.[1] In his creation of Yoknapatawpha County he did begin to move toward the ideological independence Bakhtin claims occurs with all great novelists. At this stage Faulkner manifested this relative independence through critiques of those social and psychological voices clamoring in Mississippi and reverberating in his head. Resolutions to the crises he experienced and depicted were nonexistent as yet; nonetheless, growth was occurring. Various incidents in his personal life indicate the changing relationship between Faulkner and the world; developments in his literary life reveal how his assessments of the ideological formations were beginning to change as well.

During this period, Faulkner's personal life changed dramatically. First, he married Estelle Oldham, who brought with her two children from her first marriage. A high school sweetheart who had married another man after her family had refused to allow her to marry Faulkner, Estelle was alone and adrift and wanted Faulkner to rescue her. Broke and uncertain about his feelings after nearly ten years, Faulkner nonetheless acceded, and soon after his marriage he bought a run-down antebellum mansion. Remember, the Oldhams were from the highest echelons of Southern society and Faulkner had always associated with them, in part, because he was attracted to this class; thus these developments were certainly connected to Faulkner's affiliations with the gentlemanly code of paternalism. He must have also felt some satisfaction in now marrying the woman whom his grandfather had once said he should not marry.[2]

Two years after the marriage, Faulkner's father died, leaving Faulkner's mother with enough money to live only for about a year. As the oldest son, Faulkner felt a deep sense of responsibility. In 1933, his daughter Jill was born. Thus, in the course of a four-year period, Faulkner had gone from a fairly isolated individual, writing and living in the home of his parents, to a virtual patriarch, overseeing an extended household. While Faulkner was still writing *Absalom, Absalom!*, his brother Dean died; Faulkner was deeply saddened, and he offered a home to Dean's wife and child, further extending the household to which he was responsible. These decisions and behaviors all reflect Faulkner's desire to model his personal life after his grandfather—to care for an extended household, to be responsible in the eyes of the community. They reveal a close affiliation with paternalism as well as his desire to be a patriarch. Despite the depictions of paternalism in his novels, Faulkner was not at all free from its influence, and his vision of himself remained very much related to it.

During this same period, Faulkner also began to taste success. Although most reviewers had severe reservations about *The Sound and the Fury* and *As I Lay Dying*, the books did receive favorable comments and were especially lauded in literary circles. When in New York, Faulkner was a celebrity whom people wanted to meet, and there was a conference held in his honor at the University of Virginia. He continued to write stories for publication, with mixed success, but he was making some very necessary money. Moreover, the revised *Sanctuary* sold extremely well and gave him a notorious reputation, and he wrote and published *Light in August*, which helped his literary reputation. Finally, on the success and notoriety of *Sanctuary*, he was offered a stint in Hollywood—more money than he had ever seen, a veritable fortune for the depression years.

Faulkner was now making money and gaining a reputation due to his ability and merit as a writer. The liberal, bourgeois world was not, he was finding, totally inimical to his talent and ability. Based on these experiences, the middle-class world he had depicted in his books did not seem to tell the complete story. Unlike Jason Compson and Anse Bundren, Faulkner's rise to a position of status and respect was based on his own hard efforts, on the merit of his achievements, on the quality of his work. Faulkner could not have helped but notice that rewards were, at times, based on talent and given to those who deserved them. After all, his acceptance into the artistic elite seemed imminent.

With these developments Faulkner's life acquired a pattern it would keep for some time; it began to run on two parallel tracks. One involved the establishment of an extended patriarchal household at Rowan Oak, and the continual purchase of farmland and woodland to increase its domain. This life was primarily funded by his stints in Hollywood. The other course involved the continued growth of his reputation through the writing of novels (and to a certain extent stories). The continual job offerings from Hollywood were indeed based on his literary reputation as well as on the respect that certain people had for his talent. From here on, the two ideological perspectives that dominated Faulkner's explorations were not totally at cross-purposes—either in his life or his art.

Faulkner's mature acceptance of history after the rejection of *Flags in the Dust,* his willingness to begin to engage his socioideological world on its own terms, to some extent had begun to move him into an active interaction with this world for the first time in his life. In the Yoknapatawpha novels, this process led, on one level, to Faulkner's serious explorations of more social issues. Although the social and the historical issues were there in the previous novels, they did not take center stage as they would in *Absalom, Absalom!,* the Snopes trilogy, or *Go Down, Moses.* As he approached this new stage of his life and career, Faulkner began to write his way into history much more actively than ever before. He was working on actualizing the subjectivity he envisioned for himself and delineating its features in his work. As he approached the writing of *Absalom, Absalom!,* Faulkner was, in essence, at a crossroads. "He [was], in many respects, . . . the man who must make a transition to another kind of America. . . . in the middle of his journey, [he] was trying for the first time to put it all in perspective" (Karl 1989, 493).

With this novel, Faulkner brings to bear the full weight of a historical imagination on his critique of society. He actively and purposely confronts Southern society's operative ideologies, placing characters identified by various versions of them side by side and exploring the values that guide their behavior. The novel implicitly posits a system of values by which characters are judged and with which Faulkner himself identifies. By first placing Thomas Sutpen's life in relation to the other "white" characters in the novel, this chapter's focus, and then placing his life in relation to larger contexts of Southern society and history, the focus of the next chapter, we can both understand Faulkner's assessments of paternalism and liberalism and determine the implicit authorial ideology around which the text coheres. This authorial position combines values from each ideological formation, paternalism and liberalism. As we will see, it is reminiscent of Thomas Jefferson's idea of natural aristocracy—an ideal that joins ideas of equal rights and opportunities with the belief in a naturally aristocratic character which would enable one to earn respect and admiration through merit and achievement.[3]

Many historians and a few literary critics have written about the South's nineteenth-century ideological milieu. Two discussions are directly relevant to my considerations of *Absalom, Absalom!*—Genovese (1969 and 1972) and Porter (1981). Genovese argues that the major ideology operative in the nineteenth-century South was paternalism and that this ideology grew out of the necessity to justify and perpetuate the plantocracy around which the South's economic system was based. True, the South was part of a global capitalist economy, he asserts, but this fact did not affect the internal relations of Southerners: "Capitalism is . . . the mode of production characterized by wage labor and the separation of the labor force from the means of production—that is, as the mode of production in which labor power itself has become a commodity" (1969, 16), but this feature never existed in the South's plantation system of agriculture—even after the Civil War and Reconstruction. Thus, the majority of Southerners never entered the capitalist economic system, never formed social relations characteristic of that system, and were never affected by the ideology supporting it—liberalism. Instead, paternalism "constituted an authentic world-view in the sense that it developed in accordance with the reality of social relations" (1972, 86)—those of the plantocracy—and it affected the minds and behaviors of many Southerners. All of the usual features of a capitalist economy, Genovese argues, did not exist for most white and all black Mississippians; therefore, these people were not affected by liberalism's values.[4]

In his discussion claiming that Thomas Sutpen was not a representative Southern planter, Brooks (1978) bases his argument on Genovese's account of the South. Porter disagrees with both. In "Faulkner's America," the best treatment of Thomas Sutpen along these lines, Porter puts to rest the assertions that nineteenth-century Southerners were completely identified by paternalist ideology and that Sutpen is a northern, Puritan character transplanted to the South. She carefully and correctly documents the strain of capitalist, Sutpen-like entrepreneurism operating in the nineteenth-century South, especially in the activities of Jacksonian democrats. She notes, as I did in chapter 2, that Faulkner's great-grandfather, William Clark Falkner, participated in these capitalistic exploits, explaining how it would have been impossible for Faulkner not to have perceived the capitalist realities of the Old South. Porter agrees that the ideology of paternalism existed but argues it did so only in name, in order to cloak exploitive capitalist activities.

My understanding of the ideological milieu of the South comes from those who have come to be called revisionist historians and from a Marxist understanding of the relationship between ideologies and class structure. Oakes (1982), from whom I take my original definitions of paternalism and liberalism, explains in *The Ruling Race* that the South was characterized by conflict and struggle for many, many years. Yes, the predominant economic formation was a plantocracy, and this plantocracy justified itself through the ideology of paternalism. On the other hand, the hegemony of paternalism was always tenuous.[5]

Many people who settled in the South left their homelands influenced by liberalism. They accepted plantocracy in the same manner in which they had accepted aristocracy in Europe—only grudgingly, and whenever they could, as the actions of Jacksonian Democrats reveal, they broke away from what they considered to be the repressive structures of plantocracy. Thus, though it never united Southern society, liberalism always had some influence on the minds and actions of some Southerners.

On the other hand, to argue that people in the South did not sincerely believe the values of a paternalist ideology, as Porter does, implies that many Southerners were simply conscious and outright hypocrites and denies the long-standing values of honor, duty, and *noblesse oblige* for which Southerners have been admired on both sides of the Mason-Dixon line.[6] Whether one views those values as a suspicious outsider or as a trusting and forgiving insider, they existed. Clearly, some people in the South (and elsewhere too) felt they were inherently superior to others, had better training in education, law, and politics, deserved high social, economic and/or political position—and tried to fulfill their obligations in good conscience. This does not mean, of course, that these people constructed an Eden or that their society was any less cruel and unjust than the one that followed.

To date, all societies have been class societies, distributing the benefits of society unevenly, disproportionately rewarding the upper class, and the dominant ideology seeks to justify those disproportionate rewards as natural phenomena. In this, plantocracies are no different than capitalist societies. What differs are the value-systems through which the justifications are made. Paternalists would, at times, make different decisions than capitalists; at other times, they might indeed make the same decisions but the degree of remorse or satisfaction would be different.

Both Genovese and Porter argue that the South identified with one ideology, but neither, ultimately, is convincing. The ideology of liberalism existed side by side with paternalism throughout the nineteenth century, constantly contradicting it and working to undermine its hegemony; nonetheless, it remained for the most part an emergent ideology, not a dominant one. And even though paternalism eventually lost its social and political power, its effects have been long-lasting. Paternalism's enforced stratification of southern society, with certain whites in power, others in the middle, and any person with as much as one-sixteenth African heritage on the bottom has left a particularly vitriolic legacy: when poor whites fought to better their economic plight, their social position, and to achieve political equality, they were as much influenced by paternalism as liberalism. On one hand, liberalism told them all were created equal and should be given the opportunity to prove themselves; on the other, Southern paternalism, in its racial cast, told them that some, particularly white men, were better and more deserving than others, namely women and African Americans.[7]

Liberalism's avowed values have continued to operate, serving eventually as justification for the political rights of women and African Americans, but this process has been slow. In fact, the South, and the United States in general, have experienced a very slow process of transition from one dominant ideology to another: the complete ramifications of liberal ideology—equal rights and opportunities for all—have as yet to occur completely.

My point here, though, is not to evaluate paternalism and liberalism, or to argue that one of their respective social structures, plantocracy or capitalism, is a good one. Rather, I claim here that the South's pre–Civil War ideological conflicts have very much to do with the ideological conflict at the heart of Faulkner's own Mississippi, and the creation of Yoknapatawpha County. Paternalism's existence for a period of time as a dominant ideology, even though only a tenuous one, has caused its legacy to have distinct effects on the South's historical development and on Faulkner himself.

In *Absalom, Absalom!*, Faulkner investigates this development, tries to understand why God let the South lose the war. The novel is definitively affected by the distinct historical situation of the South, and in writing it, Faulkner uncovers a means to write himself into that history.

Faulkner's presentation of Sutpen's origins and early life makes clear that Sutpen represents the Protestant bourgeoisie, a class that historically has organized itself around the liberal beliefs in individual rights and equal opportunities. Faulkner spends most of chapter 7 carefully recounting Sutpen's origins and how they created his thinking: "The first Sutpen had come (when the ship from the Old Bailey reached Jamestown probably)" (180), and the family settled in the mountains of what would later become West Virginia, where Sutpen was born. While growing up Sutpen experienced a world in which "everybody had just what he was strong enough or energetic enough to take and keep" (179). For him, in a world where all men were white, all men possessed equal worth, and he believed that they should have the opportunity to achieve all they were capable of achieving. Indeed, his society was organized around these shared principles. As pariahs from an aristocratic society seeking opportunities, as Protestants believing that all were equal in the eyes of the Lord, Sutpen and his family reveal their connection to the bourgeois, liberal ethos as it originally entered the South.[8]

Historically, the bourgeoisie rose in conflict with aristocratic paternalism and defined itself against the values of this order. Sutpen's experience at the front door of the Tidewater mansion represents this historical conflict. Aristocratic paternalists assumed their social power and their inherent superiority as God-given conditions passed to them through the blood of their ancestors; the bourgeoisie claimed that everyone had the right to prove their merit and worth through their actions. During the early nineteenth century, where Faulkner places Sutpen's birth and youth, the dominant system in Virginia had come to be a type of aristocratic paternalism. This system established a static social hierarchy ruled by certain white men, based on heritage and valuing educated refinement, manners, and leisure. In the middle of this hierarchy were other whites and at the bottom the black slaves.

On the way down the mountains of West Virginia into the lowlands of the Tidewater, Sutpen begins to learn how this society differentiates between black and white. In the Tidewater he is first exposed to a plantocracy supported by paternalism: he sees his father become assigned a relatively powerless place in the middle of the social order, just barely above the black slaves of the plantocrat. For the most part, Sutpen rejects this order. His reaction to his treatment at the front door of the mansion—when the planter's black servant tells him to go to the back door—and his subsequent decision to leave the Tidewater are essentially a form of rebellion for himself, his family, and his class. Through it, he defies the static social order and its aristocracy of heritage and claims his right to the opportunity to achieve what he can through his effort.[9]

Implicit in this initial conflict of Sutpen's life are Faulkner's own reassessments of liberal and paternalist ideologies at this point in his life. As Jehlen (1976) notes, "Faulkner's depiction of Sutpen's encounter with the upper class is strongly sympathetic" (63), and as Faulkner himself says, approvingly: "'[Sutpen] wanted to establish the fact that . . . man, if he is man, cannot be inferior to another man through artificial standards or circumstances'" (Gwynn and Blotner 1959, 35). Faulkner sees Sutpen's rebellion as essentially just. Sutpen has the right to rebel from a social order ready to judge and position him based on class origin and his family.[10] Unlike his depictions of Jason Compson and Anse Bundren, neither of whom receive any sympathetic treatment for identifying with aspects of a liberal ethos, Faulkner gives Sutpen's rebellion a social context that explains and justifies it. Sutpen's quest does not originate from some personal anger and resentment, like Jason's, or from the desire to gain meaning through material objects, like Anse's. Its origin (not its eventual design) lies in social injustice. For Faulkner, part of this assessment stems from Sutpen's ideological perspective, part from the faults of this particular paternalist system.

Faulkner depicts those in the upper class of the Tidewater in distinct and definitive ways. In his depiction of the man in the hammock, Faulkner stresses the leisure and laziness of the upper class: "And the man who owned all the land . . . spent most of the afternoon . . . in a barrel stave hammock between two trees, with his shoes off and a nigger . . . who did nothing else but fan him and bring him drinks" (184). This man "owned all the land and the niggers and apparently the white men who superintended the work" (184). This ownership of people, as if they were just another breed of animal, causes an intense devaluation of work and labor: watching his sister, Sutpen muses, "her back toward him, shapeless in a calico dress . . . and broad in the beam as a cow, the very labor she was doing brutish and stupidly out of all proportion to its reward: the very primary essence of labor, toil, reduced to its crude absolute which only a beast could and would endure" (191).

These depictions of those in the Tidewater plantocracy reveal the ways in which these men had relinquished their responsibility to the social order over which they ruled. The effects their system has on people in it point to its weaknesses: autocratic power, idleness of character, and corruption of labor. Faulkner's depictions implicitly label this class the "pseudo-aristoi." The claims to authority and power come to mirror Anse Bundren's own: the man in the hammock is not shown as doing anything to deserve his status and wealth, his position of power. His laziness is also out of all proportion to its reward. Although placing poor whites on a higher level than black slaves, the static social order of the Tidewater offered neither a venue for the aspirations of lower class whites (or blacks, of course) nor much respect for them as individuals.

The depictions of this class of men, though brief, reveal Faulkner's more involved investigation of the men in the South's upper class who made claims to paternalism, and they indicate how Faulkner was coming to be deeply concerned with the means through which people gained status, power, and reputation. More than any other Faulkner characters, these men resemble Horace Benbow in their effete ineffectuality. As leaders, Faulkner implies, these men had formed a society with deep-rooted problems. His depictions of the problems lead one to infer that he was coming to value a fluid social order in which able and deserving people would be able to change their status and gain respect for their efforts. Here, for the first time, Faulkner's fiction identifies with some features of liberalism.

As Faulkner depicts it, Sutpen's rebellion and his success are caused by his liberal values of equal rights and opportunities based on his strength and merit; this rebellion and the values that inspire it are supported by Faulkner, in contrast to lazy autocratic refinement that does not earn its social power. But, as hardly needs reiteration here, Faulkner does not approve of Sutpen's entire life or the consequences of an unchecked liberal ideology. Almost exactly like Jason Compson and Anse Bundren, Sutpen comes to guide his quest solely by his drive for the possession of material objects, which he attains through his strength—"land and niggers and a fine house" (192), "money, a house, a plantation, slaves, a family—incidentally of course, a wife" (212). His social vision involves only the ownership of these items, and it reduces people to the same level as objects. As in many capitalist social orders, Sutpen's design contains no necessary moral responsibilities or reciprocal obligations; its organizing principles are based on the separation of people and on the commodification of human relations rather than on the recognition of interdependence and collective responsibility—avowed cornerstones of paternalism.

That Faulkner does not approve of these aspects of Sutpen's design is revealed by his comments: "'He [Sutpen] said, I'm going to be the one that lives in the big house, I'm going to establish a dynasty, I don't care how, and he violated all the rules of decency and honor and pity and compassion'" (Gwynn and Blotner 1959, 35). The novel makes clear that this design is limited, for Sutpen's downfall and death are caused by aspects of his liberal orientation and his inability to adopt certain paternalist attitudes that place men within a social hierarchy.

In its exploration of the rise of Thomas Sutpen, Faulkner's novel comes to confront one of the most significant conflicts existing at the heart of America as a social and political commonwealth. This conflict is between the democratic principle of equality and social mobility, and the need for social order and cohesion, cooperation, and interdependence among its citizens. Faulkner's own resolution to the historical and personal struggles he witnessed has much to do with Thomas Jefferson's notion of natural aristocracy. I will explain this further shortly. For the moment, to illustrate how close Faulkner's questions here, in regard to Sutpen, mirror Jefferson's own concerns, consider the following. Jefferson felt that the propertied classes should not limit the legitimate ambitions of the lower classes for they would withdraw their consent to be governed. In the depiction of Sutpen's rebellion from the Tidewater plantocrat, Faulkner depicts just this phenomenon. Furthermore, Jefferson also felt that individualism carried too far could be dangerous to the nation; it could atomize the society, dissolving deference, public spirit, and patriotism in a scramble for wealth and position. Sutpen's quest certainly demonstrates this likelihood. More compellingly, Jefferson saw Andrew Jackson as this type of man from the rising class; for Thomas Jefferson, Jackson was a sinister figure (Slotkin 1985, 69, 123). Perhaps not coincidentally, for Faulkner's town of Jefferson, Sutpen is a sinister figure.

In one way, Andrew Jackson represented the achievement of the promise of American life. This promise stipulated that anyone could achieve aristocratic status, a social position so firm that its possession not only entitles one to rule, but also to conceive of oneself as possessing unique and inherent attributes of virtue and intelligence—attributes that might be inheritable by an heir. At the same time, Jackson was seen by many, including Jefferson, to be more representative of the nightmare of social mobility. Men like him, from Jefferson's viewpoint, with his lack of character and virtue and public concern, should be prohibited, somehow, from gaining positions of power and authority. In *Absalom, Absalom!* Sutpen comes to represent a similar nightmare for Faulkner.

As Faulkner develops Sutpen's story in Mississippi, Sutpen does indeed become representative of a group of men who possessed a specific ideological heritage and who struggled for power within the upper class of the South. That Faulkner places Sutpen's arrival in Mississippi in 1833, the date coinciding with the historical period during which Jacksonian democracy spread throughout the South, hardly seems accidental, especially considering Faulkner's obsession with history. Moreover, this period was characterized by the acquisition of land and the establishment of plantations by previously poor white men—as is Sutpen's design. Faulkner's depiction of Sutpen's arrival and acceptance in Mississippi mirrors the rise of Jacksonians into the class of wealthy plantation owners. These occurrences were essentially an outbreak of liberal capitalism within a relatively static social world. The Jacksonians did advocate equal rights and opportunities, yet when they became powerful, some began to see the advantages of a stable social order, and they developed the image of the Cavalier as a conscious symbol of emulation. Although it recognized the ideology of equal rights and opportunities, and was thus forced to develop elaborate ruses for the continued justification of slavery, Cavalier ideology attempted to compensate for the ruthlessness behind the drive for financial success by offering to kneel down before the altar of femininity and familial benevolence. In this manner, it sought to maintain a vision of society bonded by relations similar to those of a patriarchal family.

Despite the attempt to justify actions through this consciously developed ideological position, Jacksonians on the rise were anything but a unified group and were seen by others in many different ways. Some saw this development as the natural product of American social opportunity; others saw it as an invasion of the hordes into the sanctity of culture and society. How Faulkner felt about this phenomena becomes embodied in the interactions among Sutpen, the townspeople, General Compson, and Goodhue Coldfield. These interactions explore various responses to the conflicts at the heart of America.

When Sutpen arrives in Jefferson, Mississippi, he buys land, and with the men he has brought with him from Haiti he builds his mansion.[11] When he rolls into town with four wagonloads of furnishings, the townspeople feel they need to halt his actions, and Sutpen is arrested. As General Compson explains it, the arrest is due more to Sutpen's denial of certain responsibilities he might have to the townspeople, of the bonds between himself and his community, than any actual crime: "'it was a little more involved than the sheer value of his chandeliers and mahogany and rugs. I think that the affront was born of the town's realization that he [Sutpen] was getting it involved with himself; that whatever the felony which produced the mahogany and crystal, he was forcing the town to compound it'" (33) by sanctioning it. The townspeople at first resist giving this sanction; they try to deny Sutpen's "utter disregard of how his actions which the town could see might look and how the indicated ones which the town could not see must appear to it" (56). That is, people in town were acting from a set of values that expected cooperation and respect among citizens; they had formed a socially cohesive group and Sutpen acted in utter disregard of it, focused as he was on purely his individual pursuits. They want Sutpen to acknowledge his connection and responsibility to them and their mores, or, at least, to offer an explanation with which they can live. Sutpen never does this; nonetheless, he becomes accepted because General Compson and Mr. Coldfield, two established and respected men who know what Sutpen's activities involve, post his bond, and get him exonerated.

General Compson and Coldfield show their class allegiance to Sutpen in this action. They have also taken advantage of the opportunities open to all in Mississippi at one point or another; they have become powerful, and they side with Sutpen's right to gain what he can. In this, they all share some allegiance to the values of liberalism. As the novel states: "if Mr Coldfield had believed Sutpen guilty at the time of any crime, he would not have raised a finger to take Sutpen out [of jail]" (38). That he does help Sutpen reveals that Sutpen's methods may have been devious, unscrupulous, and shrewd, all of which are allowed within a system based on opportunity and strength, but that they were not illegal. This allegiance to Sutpen, however, does not indicate that the three men possess the same sense of character, the same notions of right and wrong, the same structures of feeling infusing their ideological perspective.

Goodhue Coldfield hated "his conscience and the land, the country which had created his conscience and then offered the opportunity to have made all that money to the conscience which it had created" (209). In these attributes, he highlights both the best of an equal rights and opportunities ideology as well as Puritan religious morality. He has used his own ability and the opportunity afforded him to be socially and financially mobile. At the same time, he appreciates his position within a community of Christians.

Coldfield is the only person in the novel who recognizes that the fulfillment of a liberal ethos means freedom for the black slaves. Based on his identification with this ethos he sees the moral outrage of slavery, recognizing that in the coming Civil War, "the South would realise that it was now paying the price for having erected its economic edifice not on the rock of stern morality but on the shifting sands of opportunism and moral brigandage" (209). In his personal life, he grants his slaves their freedom after they have worked long enough to pay for the money he spent to purchase them, attempting to wed capitalism with morality.

Coldfield represents the means through which most Americans resolve the conflict of living in a capitalist system based solely on concern for individuals and profit: they temper that system with some form of commitment to a vision of a spiritual community with moral rules and edicts. Although this is an attempt to balance contradictory forces, this uneasy balance envisions human relations, on both sides of the contradiction, in abstract terms; it does not offer a social vision in which people come to understand how to live with one another. As his depiction of Coldfield's demise reveals, Faulkner senses this. Coldfield realizes his resolution does not actually resolve the contradiction in which he finds himself embedded, and he chooses to dispense with his own individual existence in a way in which he sees fit.

The contrast between Sutpen and Compson, which Faulkner carefully crafts, reveals Sutpen's lack of traits characteristic of paternalist ideology as Faulkner reads it. The very real difference between these two men has been overlooked by critics. Most critics feel that both men are, or have been, Jacksonian Democrats; therefore, they are basically akin. But, as Faulkner crafts them, General Compson comes to epitomize the democratic diffusion of characteristics that are essentially those of an aristocratic class while Sutpen never seems to beat down the beast lurking within him, potentially within all members of the lower class, and remains, in essence, a white savage.

When Sutpen first comes to Jefferson, Compson befriends him and lends him cotton seed for the first crop; later, he attends Sutpen's wedding as a form of welcome to the community. These acts have been seen as traditional acts of paternalistic benevolence throughout the formation, both materially and imaginatively, of America.[12] Compson also helps Judith Sutpen buy tombstones for her relatives. To Charles Etienne Bon, Sutpen's grandson of mixed heritage, Compson shows sympathy, intercedes for him with the law, and attempts to give him advice and assistance. In these actions he shows an ability to see through Mississippi racial categorizations and to understand how these may be different from those in places like New Orleans or the North. When Sutpen tells Compson that he put his first wife aside, Compson is horrified: "'Conscience? Conscience? Good God, man . . . what conscience to trade with which would have warranted you in the belief that you could have bought immunity from her'" (213). In all of these behaviors General Compson shows his affinities with the paternalist values that the Cavaliers advocated. He recognizes his connection and responsibility to others in his community; he uses his financial resources to help those in need; he justifies the offering of moral and practical advice based on his position in the community; and he voices his respect for women (though only white women) and a certain responsibility to them and to one's commitments.

Compson's actions contrast sharply with Sutpen's. Sutpen disowns his original family and his first wife and disregards the effects of his actions; he never aids anyone or uses his social position to act as a moral guide; only at the last moment does he intercede with Henry, showing no responsibility to the situation developing between Judith and Bon at all; and he shows little respect for women throughout his life. Although Sutpen and Compson share a similar lower-class origin, Sutpen develops in a very different way than does General Compson. As Faulkner makes quite clear, especially in the way he depicts Sutpen fighting with his slaves and the way he has Sutpen treat Rosa regarding the possibility of their marriage, Sutpen remains completely low class (metaphorically speaking). Faulkner signals this when he has Mr. Compson say to Quentin: "'yes, he [Sutpen] was underbred. It showed like this always, your grandfather said'" (34). This contrast reveals that though Sutpen comes to belong to the upper class because of his wealth, his behaviors are influenced by his original ideological affiliation with liberalism, with all the emphasis on the individual, not with the values of paternalism.

In the contrast Faulkner creates between these two men, General Compson comes to be pictured as the man who has the interests of others in mind and who has a clear sense of moral principles guiding his actions. He has acquired (Faulkner does not explain how) a sense of a society bound by interdependent human relations and reciprocal obligations. He is a decent man functioning within a distinct society. Sutpen, on the other hand, is depicted to be a demon indeed, in many ways a beast. He has been unable to check that deep-seated individualism rooted in his frontier, backwoods youth; he has been unable to transcend the primitive aspects of his being to blend into a civilized and ordered social world. Although Sutpen tames the land, he does not tame either his crass materialism or his, seemingly, innate savagery.

Significantly, Sutpen also does not even recognize that he is out of place in the ruling, wealthy class. Faulkner reveals him to be a parvenu, a pretender, a man who should not have attempted to change his social status because he does not possess the moral character to merit a higher, elevated social position. This fact is highlighted in the story of Sutpen's demise at the hands of Wash Jones—one who does recognize and accept his place, his low place, in a social order.

Sutpen has always felt that he had the right to attain what his strength would allow and that ownership of possessions testified to this strength. He has never considered himself *essentially* better than Jones, only better because his strength and ambition have brought him more material success.[13] When the opportunity arises again to exert this strength and achieve his ambition, after Rosa refuses Sutpen's outrageous proposal to mate with him, he seduces Jones's granddaughter, Milly. After she has a girl, he refuses to acknowledge any connection to her, treating her worse than one of his horses. Although self-destructive, Sutpen's behavior remains consistent: he is a capitalist without the slightest shred of moral conscience or sense of responsibility; at heart, a savage. Wash Jones, of course, feels the affront and kills Sutpen, claiming: "Better if his kind and mine too had never drawn the breath of life on this earth" (233).

Jones's action reveals that he was indeed a different "kind" of man than Sutpen. He accepts the "down-looking" of Colonel Sutpen because he feels Sutpen is different and because he feels Sutpen possesses bravery and honor. As Faulkner depicts it, Jones sees Sutpen not just as a stronger man but a better one. He grants Sutpen the position of superiority: "And how could I have lived nigh to him for twenty years without being touched and changed by him? Maybe I am not as big as he is and maybe I did not do any of the galloping. But at least I was drug along where he went" (231). In this way, Jones reveals his affiliation with paternalism, based as it is on a static hierarchy of men. Despite the fact that he has never been in the upper class and does not feel he belongs at the top of the hierarchy, he has adopted the ideology that says some men are indeed better than others, and that he is not one of the better ones.[14]

In keeping with this perspective, he expects certain behaviors from Sutpen. Men at the top of the hierarchy are supposed to act like better men as well; they serve as moral exemplars. The entire time Sutpen "courts" Milly, Jones sees what is occurring. He knows Sutpen will sleep with his granddaughter. But, he thinks the Colonel will then marry her: "'And I know that whatever your hands tech, whether hit's a regiment of men or a ignorant gal . . . that you will make hit right'" (228). Jones expects Sutpen to act according to a certain code of honor, to accept responsibility for his actions and for Milly's welfare. When Sutpen shows he will not make it right, when he treats Milly just like, or worse than, any other object he owns, Jones is shocked, appalled, and driven to murder. For Jones, it *is* better for both their kinds—and, again, they are different kinds of men—never to have been born.[15] The blame for Sutpen's death lies in his inability to act, in a sense, the way General Compson would have, and though Jones too dies, the retribution he enacts is clearly justified in Faulkner's eyes.

For Faulkner, though Sutpen's initial rebellion from the Tidewater system is valid because in it he "asserts the principles of freedom and equality" (Porter 1981, 237), Sutpen's subsequent behavior reveals that he does not deserve whatever eminence he attains. His concern only for his own plight, his forgetting the condition to which his sister's and all his class's labor had been reduced, and his disregard for moral responsibilities lead him to disregard some of the values Faulkner implicitly has come to validate—an interdependence among all people, a determination of place in the social order based on merit, an obligation to the place one does hold, and a moral character.

Sutpen's demise seems supported by some cosmic justice, as if "the fates took revenge on him" (Gwynn and Blotner, 35); however, the novel also makes clear that the reasons for Sutpen's demise stem from his inability or refusal to adopt certain paternalist attitudes and his clinging to his own monadic isolation in the pursuit of wealth. In the story of Sutpen's rise, Faulkner questioned the aristocracy of heritage, the pseudo-aristoi; here, in the story of Sutpen's fall, Faulkner questions the aristocracy of wealth.[16]

Sutpen remains affiliated with the precepts of a liberal ideology, but this simple identification does not explain the whole story. As Andrew Jackson did for Thomas Jefferson, Sutpen, for Faulkner, represents the ramifications of a social system gone awry. Yet nothing in the social system itself seems to cause Sutpen's particular forms of depravity and indifference. There seems to be no reason, no logical explanation for why General Compson and Thomas Sutpen become different types of men. After a moment's consideration, though, that becomes the whole point: there is no logical explanation because the explanation is biological—they are *inherently* different types of men. Nothing in the social system explains Sutpen. His faults lie in his genes; his character is flawed at its root.

Thus, Faulkner's early explorations about the relationship between biology and character in *Light in August* find another application in his analysis of social history. Moreover, we can also begin to see more definitely the ways Faulkner works with the ideological formations characterizing the South and America. We move closer to a Faulknerian ideology, as it grapples with serious social questions at the heart of America.[17]

The very founding of the country had been based on the rejection of authority and rule based on an aristocracy of heritage. Various attacks on aristocratic rule by the founding fathers emphasized its corruption as well as its curtailment of freedom; these attacks carried into some assessments of the Southern plantocrats as corrupt, lazy, and autocratic in nature. Faulkner's own assessments of the Tidewater plantocrat parallel these criticisms. Yet, replacing an aristocracy of heritage with an aristocracy of wealth meant opening the doors of the ruling class to the shrewdest, most scheming and least moral, civic-minded individuals.

Debates in America during the nineteenth century focused on the discovery of some form of legitimate class subordination. Both Jefferson and John Adams came to think that a legitimate social order could and should be based on *natural* law. As Slotkin explains, "They asserted their belief that some men were better fitted than others for the exercise of political responsibility *because of their possession of a superior moral and intellectual endowment*" (1985, 73–74; my emphasis). This assertion of a naturally aristocratic character was seen as a resolution between an aristocracy of heritage and one of wealth.

In the careful creation of General Compson, Faulkner posits a figure who stands between polar opposites, the Tidewater plantocrat and Thomas Sutpen. Although he must have taken advantage of opportunities for social mobility and had increased his wealth and standing in society, General Compson also came to be guided by more than selfish motives. Faulkner's implicit assertion is that Compson's naturally aristocratic nature guided him. Through him, and figures like him, the dynamism of social mobility is reconciled with the preservation of order. Compson becomes an ideal figure who is simply biologically superior, while Sutpen embodies the dangers of unchecked social mobility.

In Thomas Sutpen's story, and through the depictions of Sutpen's interactions with General Compson and Wash Jones, Faulkner implicitly assesses the ideologies comprising the South's ideological milieu. In General Compson we see an alternative social vision to the ones offered by the competing ideologies of paternalism and liberalism. This aesthetic working of the general ideological formation reveals the way Faulkner fit himself into his world. Faulkner's authorial ideology—natural aristocracy—was his own subjective attempt to form a stance within the historical moment he found himself. Faulkner remains identified with paternalism and liberalism, to be sure, but his own struggle led him to assess, to criticize, and to take from each certain values that have become positive for him, values that would be positive for the social world as a whole if only it could be guided by them.

In this natural aristocrat we see Faulkner's imaginary relationship to the real conditions of history. Writing has enabled him to create a story in which alternative structures can be established. These alternate structures represent the way he worked not only within, but also on, the ideologies that shaped his life.

Of course, Jefferson's and Faulkner's ideal never became a reality. In the parallel story of Charles Bon, Faulkner's novel also indicates that his resolution to the real contradictions of history is indeed imaginary. Although Faulkner chose values from both paternalism and liberalism, his narrative remains sensitively aware that paternalism and liberalism are at odds. The tragic and noble nature of this ideology becomes revealed through Charles Bon, who both epitomizes the ideal and is canceled out by the irreconcilable contradiction. To understand his tragic story more fully we need to explore in detail the Southern ideology of race.

7 • *Absalom, Absalom!* and the Southern Ideology of Race

[B]attles lost . . . because of generals who should not have been generals who were generals not through training in contemporary methods or aptitude for learning them, but by the divine right to say "Go there" conferred upon them by an absolute caste system . . .

—Faulkner, *Absalom, Absalom!*

In *Light in August* and *Absalom, Absalom!*, one of Faulkner's major questions is, When does someone know whether he is black or white? Although he probes its absolute truth, the answer he offers is, When society tells him. In *Light in August* the rigid ideology of race characterizing Southern thinking is an *a priori* given, which characters do not question. Even abolitionist Joanna Burden thinks of Joe Christmas as a "Negro," as if that word had an essence to it. In *Absalom, Absalom!*, the Southern ideology of race operates as intensely, but it has not taken on a life of its own, and not all of the characters accept it without question. Here Faulkner explores in much greater detail and in a much more conscious manner the ways in which characters become "black," and he understands that this process is inextricably connected to the ways in which characters become "white." He implies that both "black" and "white" are inventions, constructed identities. Various characters attempt to assert their own racial identities. Some of these assertions are verified by society and others denied. Faulkner offers insight with which many people even today feel uncomfortable: racial identity and race relations are not at all *a priori* givens. Rather, they are social constructions formulated as conscious ruling-class policy for specific social purposes. In his explorations of these phenomena Faulkner reveals severe limitations to the South's form of racial paternalism.

From this perspective we can see in a new light Faulkner's descriptions of the white characters he labels "a different race." In *Light in August, Go Down, Moses,* and *Absalom Absalom!* Faulkner writes as if there are people whose skin color is white who are from different races. A quotation from *Go Down, Moses* summarizes this attitude: "that third race even more alien to the people whom they resembled in pigment and in whom even the same blood ran, than to the people whom they did not,—that race threefold in one and alien even among themselves save for a single fierce will for rapine and pillage" (277). Although this is seemingly an odd way to describe "white" people, it highlights a fact that is rarely discussed: the white race itself is socially constructed.[1] When we look at Sutpen's story from the perspective of an ideology of race rather than class, we see how Faulkner explores this insight. This perspective enables us to understand the implications of the character of Charles Bon for Faulkner's sense of natural aristocracy. In order to clarify, I need to discuss briefly ideas and theories about race that have affected scholars, including Faulkner critics.

As Theodore Allen explains in *The Invention of the White Race* (1994), there are two schools of historians concerning ideas about race relations and racial identity: the psychocultural and the socioeconomic. Represented by Carl Degler (1959 and 1971) and Winthrop Jordan (1969) the psychocultural historians believe that blacks will always be discriminated against whenever non-blacks have the power and incentive to do so because it is human nature to have prejudice against those who are different. The psychocultural historians claim that racial slavery and white supremacy were genetically or culturally foreordained even before the English settlers sailed into the James River.

The socioeconomic perspective differs sharply. Beginning with Mary and Oscar Handlin (1950) and carrying through such others as Eric Williams (1961), Lerone Bennett, Jr. (1967), Edmund Morgan (1975), and Theodore Allen himself, this approach claims that at one point in American history there was no discernible tension between the black and white inhabitants of the continent. People worked together, lived together, married, and argued without any intense influence from the color of skin, as Allen explains: "European-Americans in the continental plantation colonies showed little interest in 'white identity' before the institution of the system of 'race' privileges at the end of the seventeenth century" (1994, 14). This approach claims that white identity, and therefore black identity, was created through a concerted ruling-class policy to establish certain privileges for poor white people, especially men, in order to align them with ruling-class interests. This alignment was necessary for social control; it prevented poor whites from joining with free and enslaved blacks in resistance to the ruling class—as had occurred during Bacon's Rebellion and other outbreaks: "racial slavery and racism were a calculated form, designed to cope with problems of social control" (Allen 1994, 18). The socioeconomic school claims that only at this point did the notion of being white—and therefore black—come to have meaning. Eventually, as we all know, racism grew to have a life of its own. (See Allen 1994 and 1997.)

William Faulkner was born about two hundred years after the initiation of this ideology, in one of the places where it came to have a particularly virulent influence. As I have already discussed, he was not completely immune to it, but that he came to probe and question it at all is somewhat of a miracle. Even some of the most sensitive and concerned Faulkner critics have not been able to escape its effects completely. This situation reveals how much the Southern ideology of race has become the American ideology of race—no matter on which side of the imaginary color line one stands—and how much Faulkner criticism in general has ignored ideological theory as a productive way to analyze and understand Faulkner's work.[2] As is almost always the case, though, Faulkner's texts take Faulkner to places in his imagination where most citizens of his Mississippi and his America rarely go. Thomas Sutpen's story is one place where a Faulkner text pushes both author and reader to confront their own demons. Here, the demons happen to be powerful ones with a specifically American origin. Thomas Sutpen's life reveals, to use Theodore Allen's words, that the ordeal of Virginia clearly became the ordeal of America.

Historically, the ordeal of Virginia developed because of the significantly large number of poor whites living there. White bond-labor had been much cheaper than black for quite some time, and, unlike many other places in the New World, the plantation colonies, especially Virginia, had large numbers of poor whites. At the same time, plantation colonies were rigid societies, developed to produce profits for the plantation owners, and they offered little room for advancement or mobility for poor whites.

In 1676 Bacon's Rebellion revealed to the plantocrats of Virginia that frustrated poor whites could and would unite with blacks, free and slave, to change the social structure and the system of rewards. The solution these wealthy, powerful men decided upon was a systematic separation of poor white from black with the sole purpose of aligning the poor with the rich in a new category— "white" men. Certain privileges and rights were granted to poor white men and taken away from blacks, both slave and free. None of these affected the social structure one iota, but they did effect the means of social control the plantocrats sought. (See Allen 1997, chap. 13.) In effect, through a variety of means— clergy, court proceedings, electoral lectures, police—"the general public was regularly and systematically subjected to official white supremacist agitation" (Allen 1997, 251). These early developments in American history lead directly to "the social process of recruitment of Euro-Americans into the 'white race' social control formation . . . in the period between 1820 and 1860" (Allen 1994, 158)—the time, of course, of Thomas Sutpen's mature life.

As I discussed in the previous chapter, Sutpen begins to learn the difference between white and black on the way down the mountains as his family travels to the Tidewater. In his rebellion from the social structure in the Tidewater, he rejects the lessons about his assigned class position. He does not, however, reject the lessons he learns about racism and racial identity. One lesson he learns comes from what he sees while observing his sisters: "a certain flat level silent way his older sisters and the other white women of their kind had of looking at niggers, not with fear or dread but with a kind of speculative antagonism not because of any known fact or reason but inherited by both white and black" (186). Granted, in one sense Faulkner here implies a natural antipathy between white and black, something passed down through the blood of generations—perhaps an indication that Faulkner did not have all these ideas clearly formulated. However, other language about Sutpen learning the differences between white and black offers a different view—that indeed these differences are not genetic.[3] The claim that the antagonism between white and black is inherited more likely reveals the ways this racism had become part and parcel of many poor whites' existence at this point in the early 1800s. Racism was already a given and few poor whites questioned it.

This antagonism existed between the races despite the poverty and hardship of both groups' lives because of the ways in which the upper class divided rewards. Soon, Sutpen also sees that whites "lived in other cabins not quite as well built and not at all as well kept and preserved as the ones the nigger slaves lived in but still nimbused with freedom's bright aura, which the slave quarters were not for all their sound roof and white wash" (185). Here we can recognize the ways in which the plantocrats worked to create tension by offering their slaves better living conditions but offering poor whites freedom. Despite the probable sarcasm of Faulkner's comment, this line is historically accurate. Poor whites could do more than enslaved blacks. One of the acts they could commit without consequence, in fact, was beating up slaves. As Sutpen's father tells him with "fierce exultation": "'We whupped one of Pettibone's niggers tonight'" (187), and as Sutpen tells General Compson: "you knew that you could hit them . . . and they would not hit back or even resist" (186). The slaves' reluctance to defend themselves was due not to an inherent defect. Slave self-defense was forbidden by legal statute. (See Allen 1997, chap. 13.) Sutpen's recognition of his freedom cannot simply be brushed aside, especially since it is a lesson he learns quite well: one major aspect of this freedom, a right denied to slaves but open to poor whites, was the right to leave the Tidewater. The departure of angry poor whites acted as a safety valve; blacks, of course, would have been hunted down and returned, or perhaps killed to set an example.

Thus, although when Sutpen walks to the front door of the mansion he is "no more conscious of his appearance . . . than he was of his skin" (185), the same cannot be said when he makes his decision to leave. Sutpen's lessons have to do with what it means to be both poor and white. When he leaves the Tidewater it is with a distinct awareness that being white means something. When he decides to go to Haiti, it is clear that he has come to realize both that his whiteness means something and that it is all he has to offer. Sutpen finds no common ground between himself and the Tidewater planter whom he watches from the bushes; nonetheless, he eventually identifies with that man, rather than with the black slaves, because their shared whiteness is the only commodity he has in order to move forward and/or upward. This is exactly what the planters wanted. In Allen's words, "Though the squeezing out of . . . a poor planter to the 'frontier' negated the assumption of a common interest with the gentry, he was still 'made to fold to his bosom the adder that stings him,' the bondage of African-Americans" (1997, 257).

The effectiveness of the planters' actions as well as some of the long-term consequences is revealed in another aspect of the Sutpens' relations to the black slaves in the Tidewater. Faulkner clearly shows that the hatred of blacks by poor whites begins as hatred of upper-class whites. As Sutpen explains again: "you knew that you could hit them [slaves]. . . . But you did not want to, because they (the niggers) were not it, not what you wanted to hit" (186). Despite the fact they did not really want to hit the slaves, they did it because they were powerless to hit the rich white men. Their hatred could not be vented at the upper class directly, so it was directed at the black slaves.

Eventually, this anger toward the upper class was reified into an abstraction:

"that when you hit them you would just be hitting a child's toy balloon with a face painted on it" (186); Sutpen's father and his kind would not be hitting any "actual nigger, living creature, living flesh to feel pain and writhe and cry out" (187). Black slaves, then, become an abstraction to poor whites and in dealing with them white folks' reactions and behaviors had more to do with repressed anger toward the upper class and the reification of this repression than they did with anything black people said or did. As Faulkner was keenly aware, this intense ideology of race eventually took on a life of its own. In many other places in his fiction Faulkner explores the ways in which the Southern ideology of race affected the behavior of those who accepted it—in other words, the ways this process of abstraction worked: they lead directly to the blind race hatred of Percy Grimm in *Light in August*. Here, however, what Jameson (1981) would call Faulkner's political unconscious has led him to see how race relations in the United States originated in conscious ruling-class policy.

Another aspect of the novel supports the theory that Faulkner himself did not always accept the Southern ideology of race. For, though Sutpen learns the lesson about race relations and the value of his whiteness, he does not accept these lessons as moral absolutes. Sutpen always maintains the liberal belief that no man is inherently better than another. Quite subversively, he extends this thinking to the "black" people he meets, always holding to the belief that he has to prove himself to them as well. This type of thinking guides him in Haiti and with Eulalia. He does not "put aside" Eulalia due to natural antipathy; he does it purely because he has learned the social lesson of the Southern ideology of race so well: anyone with any African heritage is considered black.

In one sense, unlike his father, Sutpen does not reify his anger. He feels no anger against Eulalia, and later not even any against Charles Bon. He is clearly focused on the rich white man in the hammock, and he knows that in order to revenge himself on that man he must follow certain rules. Sutpen has rightly inferred that his very existence as a rich white man is founded on the idea of "black" people, who ensure against the possibility of social unrest by absorbing the frustration and anger of poor whites. He knows this implicitly, but seems to take no special race pride in it. His choices are social, not based on race hatred. In Sutpen, Faulkner implicitly criticizes the Southern ideology of race.

The novel also dramatizes the non-absolute nature of racial categories in the story of Mr. Compson's father's interactions with Charles Etienne Saint-Valery Bon. General Compson clearly indicates that he is aware that people are defined racially according to the social system in which they live. He knows that Charles

Etienne has "one-sixteenth black blood" and he tells Quentin: "'And your grandfather did not know either just which of them it was who told him [Charles Etienne] that he was, *must be,* a negro, who could neither have heard yet nor recognised the term 'nigger' . . . who had been born and grown up . . . where pigmentation had no more moral value than the silk walls'" (161, my emphasis).

These comments indicate the social construction of racial identity as well as a certain consciousness of the invented nature of racial identity within the upper class.[4] Later, General Compson offers Charles Etienne money to leave Mississippi, saying: "'Whatever you are, once you are among strangers, people who dont know you, you can be whatever you will'" (165). General Compson indicates a particularly distant perspective from the belief in the moral absolutes of pigmentation here, showing that the Southern ideology of race does not always determine his decisions. He does not make Charles Etienne a slave; he does not forbid him to leave Sutpen's Hundred as if the Sutpens own him. He tells Charles Etienne that he can will his own identity if he wishes, much the way Sutpen himself did and as Charles Bon tries to do.

Charles Etienne's reactions and decisions reveal he chooses both to accept and defy in suicidal fashion the Southern ideology of race, and his fate resembles that of Joe Christmas. Nonetheless, Faulkner's narrative reveals various perspectives on this ideology, characters who interact with it and are affected by it in different ways and by different degrees. One perspective clearly presents race as a social construction and the ruling class as conscious of this fact.

Sutpen's experiences in the Tidewater of Virginia have some direct connections to the historic ordeal of Virginia in the ways they reveal the tensions existing between poor and rich and between poor white and black. The social structure in the Tidewater was supported, both in the novel and in history, by a complete separation between poor white and black and by a forced allegiance between poor white and rich. Even those who felt the injustice, here Sutpen's father and Sutpen himself, had no possibility of changing this social structure, and they vented their anger and frustration toward those others as unfortunate as they. That the ordeal of Virginia became the ordeal of America is verified later in the novel and, one could argue, later in American history.

Thomas Sutpen's story, of course, only begins with his experiences in the Tidewater and Haiti. If his story emphasizes the creation of the Southern ideology of race, as I contend, one would suspect that his arrival in Jefferson and his eventual acceptance by the people there would also highlight various aspects of this process. Indeed they do. Much like Joe Christmas, Thomas Sutpen comes to Jefferson (in 1833) with no discernible or known past. Immediately it is suspected that he has some dark, specifically black past: "there were some among his fellow citizens who believed . . . that there was a nigger in the woodpile somewhere" (56). Sutpen, though, does not suffer the same fate as Joe Christmas because, unlike Christmas, he does not accept the ways society attempts to name or label him; he identifies and invents himself despite society. This process also has much to do with why and how the planters' social control attempts were constructed and developed.

Although the exact justification for Sutpen's acceptance by General Compson and Mr. Coldfield escapes Rosa as she tells her tale to Quentin Compson in 1910, she is clear that they did accept him. As Mr. Compson later explains to Quentin: "'if it hadn't been for your grandfather's friendship, Sutpen could never have got a foothold here'" (8); and Rosa muses that if not for her own father, Sutpen, "the ghost" could not have assumed "a quality almost of solidity, permanence" (8). This acceptance is mysterious to Rosa because she cannot understand how two respectable men with social position and moral standing could acknowledge and offer legitimacy to a man who lived with the black servants he brought with him from Haiti, who physically fought with these same men, and who flouted all the rules and mores of Jefferson society. As Rosa recognizes: "'Doubtless something more than this [what she explains] transpired at the time, though none of the vigilance committee ever told it that I know'" (34). Doubtless. Rosa observes correctly but misses the significance of her observations.

While the townspeople keep waiting for Sutpen to "show his true colors," so to speak, expecting that "the nigger" in the woodpile will appear any moment and inspire them to enact the so-called justice required by their customs, Sutpen is busy establishing his identity, his existence, his position. Essentially, he forces the town, and General Compson and Coldfield, to accept him and grant him the identity he has been so busy inventing. He accomplishes this task, it can be surmised, through the implicit threat he poses by rejecting the social mores in the first place and by revealing that he is a man capable of just about anything.

Living with his servants as he does, Sutpen proves to the town that he is different from many people who live there. He recognizes no distance between himself and his servants, and he acknowledges no innate difference between himself and them. Yet, "he led them" (27). Almost like a tribal chief, Sutpen leads the men on his land through will, strength, and daring. Certainly he poses a symbolic threat to the social mores of Jefferson, and the mob outside Coldfield's store is buttressed by its belief that moral law supports them. But, imagine the literal threat to Jefferson society—and specifically to the profit-making enterprises of Compson, his ilk, and Coldfield—that Sutpen and his "tribe" represented. They could burn fields, crops, stores, houses; they could steal goods, money; they could kill. And it would not be difficult to envision Sutpen engaging in these activities. In fact, Sutpen represents the ruling class's biggest nightmare. He is a shrewd and powerful man determined to make his own rules, leading a significant number of well-armed and loyal followers who have absolutely no stake in the social system and little to lose.

From this vantage point, Compson and Coldfield's acceptance of Sutpen makes perfect sense: they had much more to lose by not accepting him. As Rosa suspected, something more did transpire behind closed doors in Jefferson. By testifying for Sutpen, Compson and Coldfield establish the identity Sutpen has in effect demanded they establish: unlike what the townspeople think, Sutpen, they say, is "white." With this announcement, his heritage has been established; he is free.

The get-out-of-jail-free card that Compson and Coldfield give to Sutpen clearly establishes for the rest of Jefferson that Sutpen is indeed a white man. (When is someone white or black? When society tells him so.) Although the novel poses the decision in strictly moral terms, and though these men may have been thinking they were making a moral decision, the economic and social control factors cannot be ignored in the decision to grant Sutpen citizenship. Whatever these men's ideological conscience told them, we can see how Sutpen's story continues to have direct connections to the ordeal of Virginia. Thomas Sutpen is much more clever and shrewd than Joe Christmas is in *Light in August;* he has learned the social lessons well. On the other hand, Compson and Coldfield offer Sutpen legitimacy in order to maintain the social structure in its present form, for the peace and quiet and profit-making.

If we have any doubts that Sutpen's story unfolds, at least in part, with direct relationships to the socio-ideological development of the Southern ideology of race, we need simply note that Faulkner sends Sutpen to Haiti and remember the significance of the Haitian slave rebellion for Southern plantocrats. The overthrow of the ruling class in Haiti by a violent uprising of black slaves symbolized in vivid and gory detail Southern plantocrats' worst nightmare. That this occurrence was more than a foreign and distant concern was brought home quite intensely a number of times during the nineteenth century. In 1822

Denmark Vesey of Charleston, South Carolina, led a slave insurrection; in 1841, 135 slaves on a ship bound for New Orleans rebelled and took over the ship, sailing to the West Indies; in 1859 African Americans led by John Brown joined with about ten European Americans to raid the arsenal at Harper's Ferry; and, most significantly for my discussion, in 1831 Nat Turner led a slave rebellion in Southampton County, Virginia (Allen 1994, 165).

Turner's rebellion occurred just about the same time that Faulkner places Sutpen's arrival in Jefferson. There are, then, many historical precedents for the possibility of those like Sutpen leading a band of men, both white and black, against the citizens of Jefferson. The correlation between Nat Turner's rebellion and Sutpen's life certainly creates this context as a backdrop for the novel. The way Faulkner depicts the whole situation hints of the possibility, and it certainly must have crossed Compson's mind. Appeasing Sutpen, showing their "generosity," was a much less risky choice for Compson and Coldfield than resisting him.

That Compson and Coldfield allow Sutpen into the upper class of Jefferson society also starts Faulkner on a path of assessing Southern history in a way that considers the plight of Charles Bon from a racially neutral perspective. His assessments reveal that these men's decision indeed was not a moral one and that he sensed deep problems in the Southern ideology of race. Although Sutpen may have had the necessary money and power to be admitted into the upper class, Faulkner takes great pains throughout the book to show that he is not deserving of this status. Sutpen is described in many instances as a low-class kind of man who has various defects. First, "his face [is] exactly like the negro's save for the teeth" (16). Second, he gets involved in "fighting not like white men fight . . . but like negroes fight . . . as if their skins should not only have been the same color but should have been covered with fur too" (20). And perhaps the most damning description: "this creature . . . with eyes like (as you put it) pieces of coal pressed into soft dough" (51), a description that links Sutpen to a line of poor white characters in Faulkner who have moral and character defects: Popeye, Anse Bundren, Flem Snopes.

Faulkner's descriptions place Sutpen into that "third race" to which I referred earlier, implying that Sutpen should not have been accepted by Compson and Coldfield into the upper class—or even into the same race. Yet, the Southern ideology of race had created two and only two races. Sutpen was either black or white; neither Compson nor Coldfield could change the terms of the choice. That was the problem. Thus, added to his criticism of an aristocracy of heritage and one of wealth, discussed in the previous chapter, Faulkner adds an assessment of the Southern ideology of race: Compson and Coldfield's choice upholds an ideology of race that was flawed in the ways it adjudicated the terms of position and merit. To Faulkner's imagination, some new form of adjudication should have existed then and was needed now.

We return, then, to the notion of natural aristocracy with which Faulkner answers this crisis. This notion claimed that a deserving member of society could achieve aristocratic status, even to the extent that he could pass his traits and qualities to an heir. It seems crystal clear that Sutpen engages in precisely this task in order to prove his worth to that aristocrat in the hammock. On one hand, the novel engages in the process of revealing how Sutpen does not fulfill the natural aspect of the ideal of natural aristocracy because of defects in character and because he does not pass on the proper character to Henry: Henry kills the most noble character in the novel. On the other hand, Faulkner criticizes the type of aristocracy created in the South. Like Compson and Coldfield, Sutpen too must live within the strict ideology of race. He cannot recognize Charles Bon as a possible heir because he knows that this recognition has the potential to topple the very structure on which Sutpen's Hundred has been built. This ideology made people believe that the upper class could be debased through sexual or marital connections between upper-class people and blacks or lower-class whites and that this debasement would threaten their elite status. (See Clinton 1982, chap. 1.)

This ideology was also enforced, and it was very likely that anyone engaged in these types of marital arrangements would be made to flee, or worse. Thus, Sutpen can be seen to base his rejection of Charles Bon on the recognition that his place and position rest squarely on the foundation of racial privilege. His very status as a rich white planter rests on the complete separation of white from black, and he seeks to preserve that status at all costs. His desire to get revenge on the Tidewater planter and his awareness of the social system defining race and privilege explain his treatment of Bon throughout the book. That the Southern aristocracy was formed in this manner causes Thomas and Henry Sutpen to look at Charles Bon in a particularly limited manner. They cannot judge him as a man. The novel implies, however, that the South would have been very different, better in fact, if they could have.[5]

Very much like Thomas Sutpen and Joe Christmas, Charles Bon enters Mississippi with no discernible past. Unlike them, however, his behavior shields him and gives him an immediate place within the social structure: "a man with an ease of manner and a swaggering gallant air in comparison with which Sutpen's pompous arrogance was clumsy bluff and Henry actually a hobble-de-hoy" (58). His character and manner are further validated in many instances in Mr. Compson's story: Charles was like a "youthful Roman consul making the Grand Tour of his day among the barbarian hordes" (74), and compared to him "Henry and Sutpen were troglodytes" (74). In fact, for as many instances where Henry and Sutpen are compared to low-class people and are described as being under-bred, Bon is described in terms comparing him to the best men of the South. Mr. Compson tells Bon's story, of course, without knowledge of Bon's ancestry, but this fact assures that his story reveals to us how Bon should be judged as a man. In short, Charles Bon is the real thing, and the respect and admiration Ellen, Henry, and Judith come to have for him seem justified.[6] (Leaving Compson ignorant of that information also shows Faulkner's awareness in this book of the effect the ideology of race would have had on his narrators' interpretations of the facts.)

Moreover, the rest of his story reveals that Bon's manner and behavior are not illusions covering an amoral or immoral character. Unlike the Tidewater aristocrat who lies around in his hammock and rides around on his horse, Bon receives admiration and respect from his peers, in both New Orleans and the university, because of character and behavior. He becomes an officer in the army because of his ability, not because of his name and background, and Judith falls in love with him because of his character. Unlike Sutpen, nothing comes to him because of possessions; everything he receives from others he has earned through his own efforts and behavior. To validate his character, Faulkner has him tell Henry that "'if you haven't got honor and pride, then nothing matters'" (279), and has Bon write a letter to Judith near the end of the Civil War, which partly reads, "within this sheet of paper you now hold the best of the old South which is dead" (104). Later, knowing Henry will most likely kill him, Bon places the picture of his octoroon wife in his pocket on the way to Sutpen's Hundred so Judith will not grieve after he has been shot. He also refuses to be bought by the New Orleans lawyer. On all these accounts, Faulkner places Bon in a positive light. The comparison between Bon and Henry is similar to the comparison between General Compson and Thomas Sutpen, and Bon can be seen to be another example of the authorial ideology supporting the text because he has deservedly risen to certain positions due to innate characteristics and abilities and a worthy character.

Yet, Bon cannot survive in the social structure embodied within the novel; his murder reveals that he defies the real history governing the ideological matrix of the text's sociohistorical milieu. Faulkner had not written a fairy tale here. Every paternalist society needs criteria through which people become assigned a place within its stratified order. Not just anyone—no matter how qualified—can be a leader, and Bon did not have the necessary requirements to become part of the upper class within a South defined by a strict ideology of race. The Southern social order, one that claimed—as all stratified, paternalist orders do—that some men are indeed better than others, was based on notions of savagery and society, primitivism and civilization. Many lower-class whites were seen to be unqualified to become natural aristocrats because their inherent natures (supposedly) were aligned with savagery. This trait was seen to be embodied by native and black Americans. This stratification and the racism it led to in the South disallow Bon as a social agent: the ideological matrix demands his murder. Faulkner's novel accurately portrays the historical Southern world and implicitly criticizes and judges this world that came to accept the Sutpens rather than the Bons.

This point brings us to Faulkner's most intense criticism of the Southern ideology of race. Bon assertively denies his relegation to "'the nigger that's going to sleep with your [Henry's] sister'" (286). He refuses to be relegated to property, refuses to be seen as savage, and claims an inherent value in the actions and labor of his life. He defies Southern racial categories to struggle for his right to marry Judith. Very much unlike Joe Christmas, Charles Bon knows exactly the makeup of his biological heritage, but he places no moral value or meaning on it. Bon wants to be judged based on what his behaviors and actions reveal him to be. He implies that a different way to adjudicate merit and position in society needs to be found to replace one strictly defined by an ideology of race.

These actions reveal Bon to be very much like Sutpen in the way both men choose to will themselves into existence, choose to define and invent themselves on their own terms. Bon defies Southern racial categories while Sutpen accepts them, but Faulkner's text elevates Bon. Faulkner's own authorial ideology allows for the existence of Charles Bon; its vision transcends the limitations of racial paternalism in favor of one based on character and ability.

While acknowledging the specific historical criteria supporting Southern paternalism, *Absalom, Absalom!* indicates the distance Faulkner's imagination could travel from this history at particular moments. In bringing the full weight of his historical imagination to bear on an investigation into the roots of

Southern society, Faulkner exposes problems in the way in which Southerners decided their destiny. Their allegiance to a strict ideology of race was, here in *Absalom, Absalom!*, an intense limitation, one that effectively influenced the South to choose those like Sutpen over those like Charles Bon. Telling a more comprehensive tale than the one each of his narrators tells, Faulkner can answer Quentin's desperate curiosity about why the South lost the war: it had forsaken the ideal of natural aristocracy. Rather than choose the fate Quentin eventually chooses, though, Faulkner transcends the limitations of his world through his art—"those who can, do, those who cannot and suffer enough because they can't, write about it," he indirectly comments in *The Unvanquished* (1938, 262). In essence, Faulkner identifies with a line from *Absalom*—"there is that might-have-been which is the single rock we cling to above the maelstrom of unbearable reality" (120).

Faulkner's assertion is both noble and tragic: noble in that it had been imagined at all, tragic in that it was so only in fiction. Though Faulkner seemed aware of this tragedy, he would guide his own life and career by the values incorporated into this ideal. After the writing of *Absalom, Absalom!* and as his reputation became more firmly established, Faulkner would become a much more public figure than he had ever been previously, more public a figure than one could have ever imagined based on the first half of his life. He had, I would argue, proven his character and ability and remained true to the responsibility inherent in the position he had attained—sometimes even though it was clearly difficult for him. Thus, though the process had its beginning explorations in the early part of his life, it was in the writing of *Absalom, Absalom!* that Faulkner, in essence, wrote himself into history. He articulated an ideal to which he could be true in both his public and private life, and he continued to pursue this ideal from that point forward. He would also continue to explore in his fiction the effects on a society that had forsaken this ideal.

To a great extent *Go Down, Moses* confronts and works within the same set of questions and problems Faulkner poses in *Light in August* and *Absalom, Absalom!* Both Ike McCaslin and Gavin Stevens are white characters who do the best they can, but they act within and under the influence of the Southern ideology of race. Sam Fathers exists as the natural aristocrat figure, and though he tries to pass his legacy to Ike, he does not have a true heir who can carry forward his legacy. Here again, Faulkner's imagination is more noble than history, and his narrative reveals a deep historical problem with the natural aristocrat figure—he did not travel into the city. As Sam Fathers's destiny reveals, the city will not accept his kind. The strict ideology of race and the growth of liberalism were solidifying Jefferson society around the values and principles of those like Jason Compson, Percy Grimm, and eventually Flem Snopes. However, as Ike McCaslin reveals, the process also developed, for Faulkner, because gentlemen within the upper class abdicated and because they could not see through the ideology of race (as Ike cannot in "Delta Autumn").

The only upper-class white man in *Go Down, Moses* who agrees with Sam Fathers is General Compson. Unlike in *Absalom, Absalom!*, however, here General Compson has no social power; he and his kind have been usurped by the de Spains who have come to have social power in the capitalist society of the New South. Thus, at the end of *Go Down, Moses* Faulkner stands in the same place, confronting the same issue, as he did after *Absalom, Absalom!*: what happened to the upper class of the South? What has happened to that class of men who could lead society with wisdom and insight, combining social mobility with character and moral fiber? The Snopes trilogy takes this topic as its central concern.

Part Four • Faulkner's Social Vision

8 • The Snopes Trilogy as Social Vision

The later novels engage in an ideological work of recuperation . . . they urge the reader to consider the issues and become wiser. The know what wise is.
—Philip Weinstein, *Faulkner's Subject*

It's the generals they have nowadays . . . General Johnston or General Forrest wouldn't have took a Snopes in his army.
—Faulkner, *Flags in the Dust*

Absalom, Absalom! stands as a watershed moment in Faulkner's career. In this novel he created a vision to embody his values; this vision was both a response to the conflicts in history and to his need for identity. Faulkner's authorial ideology embodies his sense of himself, his subjectivity. Soon after this work, Faulkner's fiction took a decided turn toward the contemporary social world in which he lived. This movement can be seen to stem from his newly articulated subjectivity, which gave him a set of values and ideological parameters with which to confront his world. "Faulkner's new fictional emphasis . . . may well have stemmed from the fact that he was no longer driven by his private anxieties" (Wittenberg 1979, 191). It shows that Faulkner felt more qualified and able to instruct others, and that he was now ready to depict and judge the New South, which he did not consider the South at all. In the Snopes trilogy—*The Hamlet, The Town,* and *The Mansion*—Faulkner seeks to edify others about the dangers and consequences of his society's refusal or inability to follow the ideals of natural aristocracy.

In the years immediately after the publication of *Absalom, Absalom!,* Faulkner worked on both *Go Down, Moses* and *The Hamlet.* Two different books; two different worlds—or so it seems. The two aspects of the South's heritage that Faulkner explored so intensively in one book, *Absalom, Absalom!,* now become split, and Faulkner does not proceed to develop ideas and stories about the

Southern ideology of race the way he does about natural aristocracy. Seemingly, he backs away from the critique he uncovers in the story of Charles Bon; that part of his literary quest seems over.

Many have wondered why and have drawn various conclusions about Faulkner's fiction based on this choice. From my perspective, Faulkner's direction and choice makes much sense. By Faulkner's lifetime (and still in our own), the ordeal of Virginia had progressed to become the ordeal of America. The very status and position of the ruling class was based on the ideology of race. In the South especially, the worlds of black and white people had become intensely separated. Although Faulkner bravely pursued his historical imagination to uncover the reasons why this separation occurred—and could see clearly the injustice—he could not change the fact.

Perhaps another writer might have pursued these rather radical insights into American racial history and turned his attention to fictionalizing incidents where poor whites and blacks worked together, to encouraging the lower classes of poor white and black to resist and reject this ideology and join forces. But Faulkner, as I have argued throughout, was not *this* writer. There were always social and psychological forces working on him, influencing his choices and the course of his fiction. Despite where his imagination might have taken him, Faulkner's vision would be affected by the specific historical realities of his life, and Faulkner's concerns were always mainly focused on the ruling class. The Snopes Trilogy remains consistent with this focus. Thus, the direction of Faulkner's career after *Absalom* reveals another way in which Faulkner was, to some extent, shaped by his world. As always, Faulkner was produced, to some extent, by history.

Between the publications of *Absalom, Absalom!* and *The Hamlet,* Faulkner perceived his status as a natural aristocrat to be verified. He received a generous advance from Random House on *Absalom, Absalom!;* his publishers were truly impressed with the work. He quickly proceeded to complete *The Unvanquished,* a novel about Bayard Sartoris's growth from youth to manhood focusing on his development of an independent moral code, and then *If I Forget Thee, Jerusalem* [*The Wild Palms*], a novel about a passionate and doomed love affair.[1] Although not usually considered two of Faulkner's greatest novels, they contributed to his standing in the literary and intellectual circles of the day. Following the publication of *The Wild Palms* in 1939, the prestigious National Institute of Arts and Letters elected Faulkner to membership, and *Time* magazine put his picture on its cover. When sending the manuscript of *The Hamlet* to his publisher, Faulkner declared, "I am the best in America, by God" (Blotner 1977, 113). His status as an artistic aristocrat, and his desire to be one, seem clear.

In his personal life, he bought the farm of one Joe Parks, a man who had usurped this same farm from Faulkner's grandfather some twenty years earlier. The money had come from the sale of the movie rights to *The Unvanquished.* Faulkner's ability as a writer had permitted him to restore the land to one who appreciated its value. He installed his brother John as manager of the farm, taking four more dependents into his extended family, acting the true patriarch. Faulkner, unlike the ineffectual Horace Benbow, was able to restore one of his patrilineal homes.

All of these personal and professional events gave Faulkner confidence in the importance of his work as well as in himself as a social, public figure. For the first time he showed political and social commitment, giving a manuscript of *Absalom, Absalom!* to a group raising money for the Spanish-Loyalist cause and telling them they could sell it and keep the money. He also spoke publicly on behalf of this cause. Although Faulkner often complained about money during this period, he was only cash poor. He remained the owner of large tracts of land as well as a mansion in Oxford and was wealthy by comparison to others in the depression thirties.

During this period of his life, he proved his ability to succeed, and he revealed his moral character through his works and actions. His behavior at this point, and for the rest of his life, accorded well with the authorial ideology projected in *Absalom.* As Zender (1989) has commented in another context, the period before and after the publication of *The Hamlet* "reveals itself to be the outgrowth of a complex internal dialogue, one involving central questions about Faulkner's attitude toward patriarchal values and beliefs, toward a liberal, progressive vision of human experience, and toward his own development as an artist" (110).

During the forties and into the fifties Faulkner's sense of public responsibility would emerge more and more, and he would actively attempt to fill the social role he had projected in his novels. He articulates this role in a letter to his stepson, Malcolm, who was about to enter World War II. Faulkner writes that when the war is over, "the time of the older men will come, the ones like me who are articulate in the national voice . . . and have been vocal long enough to be listened to" (Blotner 1973, 166). During and after this war he sporadically works on *A Fable,* his self-declared *magnum opus,* a book that attempts to offer a vision of salvation to the modern world. In both instances, Faulkner implicitly identifies with the role of teacher in the public arena.

His sense of identity as a responsible, natural aristocrat becomes further manifested in his service as a university lecturer and as a State Department cultural representative during the fifties. These actions can be seen to stem from Faulkner's "heartfelt need to teach."[2] In the Snopes Trilogy Faulkner's specific edifications stem from his "deep-seated anxieties about the egalitarian forces at work in the South" (Grimwood 1987, 163), from his questions about "the kind of equality that equal access to money and commerce constitutes" (Snead 1986, 148), and his belief that if power in a society is not preempted by a benevolent paternal class of rulers, dispensing largesse according to the moral deserts of the individual, then society will always fall victim to Snopesism.[3]

With the understanding of the larger historical forces at work in the South and on Faulkner's fiction, I believe we can see that the crux of the trilogy does not lie in the "conflict between the non-aristocratic world of Frenchman's Bend and Snopes's world" (Warren 1941, 253; qtd. in Grimwood 1987, 143). These two elements of Mississippi society, like the Redeemers and the Progressives, are identified by an allegiance to the same set of values—in history and in the novels. The possibility of Flem's rise occurs, according to Faulkner, because those in the upper class associated with the values of an aristocracy of wealth have risen to dominance and their individualistic and materialistic ideology has come to replace any notions of paternalism except for a rhetorical commitment to it. Faulkner criticizes these elements as well as those who are not wealthy but identify with these values.

All have recognized how the world of the trilogy is indeed a fallen world for Faulkner, a world where the powers of greed have overcome the forces of love and community. Here, I will focus on the specific values and social interactions creating this world as well as the parallels to history and Faulkner's developing social commentary. Unlike his position in relation to *Absalom, Absalom!* Faulkner stands above and outside the trilogy, coolly paring his fingernails while he makes moral pronouncements.

The origins of the Snopes Trilogy go back to 1926, when Faulkner was working both on *Flags in the Dust* and a piece he then titled *Father Abraham.* Faulkner wrote only sixty pages of the latter novel, and his ideas were not as developed as they would come to be when he returned to the subject. As Phil Stone, Faulkner's early literary mentor, explains in the introduction to *Father*

Abraham: "The core of the Snopes legend . . . [was] that the real revolution in the South was not the race situation but the rise of the redneck, who did not have any of the scruples of the old aristocracy, to places of power and wealth" (Faulkner 1983, ii). Faulkner's opening lines of the fragment reveal his major target of criticism: "He [the man, Flem Snopes] is a living example of the astonishing byblows of man's utopian dreams actually functioning; in this case the dream is Democracy" (13). And later he reveals his agreement with Stone: "The Snopes sprang untarnished from a long line of shiftless tenant farmers—a race that is of the land and yet rootless . . . owing nothing to the soil, giving nothing to it and getting nothing of it in return" (19).

Faulkner's vision of the South here, though clear, is not as complicated and nuanced as it grows to be by 1940 when he writes *The Hamlet*. In this novel he identifies the conflicts as not simply between scrupulous aristocrats and selfish rednecks; in fact, he complicates this formula right from the beginning. He begins *The Hamlet* by describing its setting, Frenchman's Bend, "a section of rich river-bottom country lying twenty miles southeast of Jefferson" (3). Frenchman's Bend is the land of yeoman and tenant farmers, all supplied by the local furnishing agent, Will Varner, who owns much of the land. Essential to understanding Faulkner's depiction of this area is the knowledge that it is a fallen world right from the start, even before Flem Snopes appears on the scene. The area "had been the original grant and site of a tremendous pre–Civil War plantation . . . of once fertile fields" (3). The man who owned this plantation, "with his family and his slaves and his magnificence" (4) was gone now, "his dream, his broad acres . . . parcelled out now into small shiftless mortgaged farms" (4), and "the once-fertile fields had long since reverted to the cane-and-cypress jungle from which their master had hewed them" (3). This man's pride has become "but a legend about the land he had wrested from the jungle and tamed as a monument . . . his dream and his pride now dust . . . his legend [nothing now] *but the stubborn tale of money*" (4; my emphasis). Will Varner, who now owns the old mansion and the grounds of the once-fertile plantation, scans his property and ponders "what it must have felt like to be the fool that would need all this" (7); he considers the purchase of the mansion a mistake because it is the only thing he ever bought in his life he couldn't sell to anybody (7).

Although Faulkner does not give much description of the plantation owner's character, he depicts the old Frenchman as a man who had a dream and a vision he was attempting to actualize here at Frenchman's Bend. Because he had these qualities he possessed a magnificence that is now gone from this land. This contrast between past and present is heightened in an implicit way through the landscape descriptions. The old plantation owner had tamed the jungle but now it is allowed to revert to jungle-like condition by Varner. This imagery connotes the plantation owner's civilizing effects on the land, and this description reverberates outward to include his character, which inspired him to use the hand of husbandry to bring beauty and civilization to chaos.

These kinds of descriptions were used by Faulkner in both *Flags in the Dust* and *Sanctuary* in reference to Horace Benbow's patrilineal home, where the gardens had been allowed, in the new world of capitalist Jefferson, to revert to jungle conditions. In *The Hamlet*, the savage nature of the land, now under Varner's watch, points to Varner's own brand of savagery. The jungle imagery points to a world in which the strong feed on the weak, where the rule is survival of the fittest, interdependence, and reciprocal obligations be damned. Varner is thus immediately though indirectly linked to Thomas Sutpen; both men's savagery connects to their crass materialism.

The contrast between Will Varner and the old Frenchman indicates the changes occurring in the upper class of the South after the Civil War as well as Faulkner's attitudes to them. In Faulkner's canon the Varners and the de Spains serve as representatives of those involved in the Redeemers' business interests, who only adopted the pose of a paternalist ideology while incorporating the South into capitalist enterprises. In *Absalom, Absalom!* a group of men led by Major de Spain, the father of the de Spain of the trilogy, come to arrest Wash Jones for killing Sutpen. In their killing of Jones, they reveal their allegiance to Sutpen and wealth rather than to Jones and the paternalist morality that caused and justified his killing of Sutpen. (Importantly, this group does not include General Compson.) In *Go Down, Moses* Faulkner recounts how de Spain had purchased Sutpen's Hundred and then sold it to a lumber company and railroad interests. In the trilogy all these subplots become entwined with Varner. During this same postbellum period Varner had begun to purchase land, continuing his purchases throughout the 1870s and 1880s—the period when independent farmers all across the South were suffering and selling out cheaply. Later, in *The Town,* Faulkner recounts how de Spain and Varner go into the banking business with Bayard Sartoris. These developments mirror those occurring in Mississippi during the period in which the fiction is set and show how the upper class was changing in composition from men like the old Frenchman to those like Varner.

Among these men only Sartoris's behavior maintains a connection to paternalistic values: much like Faulkner's grandfather, Sartoris sends his bank clerk,

Byron Snopes, to school to learn bookkeeping. In the trilogy, he represents those aspects of the upper class identified with men like General Compson, whose influence wanes as that of Varner, de Spain, and Snopes rises. When Sartoris dies in *The Town*, Manfred de Spain, the son of Major de Spain, and Varner work out a deal that allows de Spain to become president and Flem to become vice-president of the bank. This union represents the Redeemers and Progressives' shared interests in Mississippi and indicates how this union led to the rise of the so-called redneck governors and senators, Vardaman, Bilbo and Russell. Faulkner finalizes this historical parallel by having Varner and de Spain support Clarence Snopes, a sardonic portrayal of Bilbo, for political office. Faulkner recognizes the coalitions in the upper class, the union of interests, and refuses to criticize only the rednecks.

The rise of the rednecks, then, and the decay of the aristocrats is not the central theme of the trilogy. For it is not the rise of the Snopeses that causes the decay of the Compsons' and Sartoris's class; it is the Varners's and de Spains's acceptance into that class and their eventual rise to dominance. Although in the trilogy paternalist values partly exist in the character of Gavin Stevens, when Sartoris dies they cease to have any social efficacy. Faulkner's criticism in the trilogy is not directed solely at the Snopeses and democracy, but against an aristocracy of wealth that engenders a repressive and exploitative system concerned with business and profit.

Faulkner's portrayal of Varner reveals the latter's control over Frenchman's Bend and the deficiency of his vision. Unlike the old Frenchman, Varner does not have a grand design; he just wants to get and to stay rich.[4] He is undoubtedly motivated solely by wealth and the concerns of profit, and he controls political and economic activity by displaying these values: "He was the largest landholder and beat supervisor in one county and Justice of the Peace in the next and election commissioner in both. . . . He owned much of the good land in the country and held mortgages on most of the rest. He owned the store and the cotton gin and the combined grist mill and blacksmith shop . . . and it was considered, to put it mildly, bad luck for a man of the neighborhood to do his trading or gin his cotton or grind his meal or shoe his stock anywhere else" (5–6). As Faulkner comments sarcastically in *The Town*, Varner had "the strictest of simple moral standards: that whatever Will Varner decided to do was right" (276). The rise of Varner and his values to dominance in *The Hamlet* has led men to establish "the foundations of their existence on the currency of coin" (220) and to think that the activities of other men's lives "aint none of our business" (79), even when those activities are seen as wrong or evil. This society founds itself, then, on the very aspects of a liberal ideology that Faulkner despised and regretted.

Both Varner's and de Spain's culpability for Flem's rise become further connected to their rejection of the values of a moralistic paternalism. Flem's father, Ab, has come to Jody Varner, Will's son, looking to rent some land to farm because he had been treated badly by de Spain and burnt de Spain's barn.[5] Ratliff implicitly warns Varner and hints at the need for kind treatment (27–29). Nonetheless, Jody Varner plans to exploit the Snopes family (27). Jody confronts Flem about Ab's past actions and asks Flem for assurances these actions will not occur again: he tries to protect his property while secretly planning to keep Ab around for the year to farm the land only to run him off right before harvest. Flem has come (rightfully) to distrust those like Jody, and he uses this chance to blackmail Jody into getting a job as clerk. Thus, the responsibility for Flem's drive to get into a business lies with Varner's and de Spain's actions. These men were exploiting farmers and demanding obedience, much as all paternalists would, but they did not feel any responsibility for the plight of the tenant in return. The entire notion of reciprocal obligations had been forsaken by them. Flem's reactions are understandable; the blame lies elsewhere.[6]

Indeed, Faulkner makes clear that the difference between Flem, a rising redneck Progressive, and Will Varner, an established Redeemer landowner, is a degree of audacity, not a fundamental difference in values. Varner comes to respect Flem for his shrewd ways. He recognizes that Flem "has passed Jody" (92), and allows Flem to become his assistant because Flem "never made mistakes in any matter pertaining to money" (62). Varner even permits Flem to ride with him around the country, watching the collection of debts and Varner's exertion of his pressure and power here and there. Flem learns these lessons so well that he becomes Varner's logical choice of a husband for his pregnant daughter. In the final analysis, Varner simply does not judge Flem morally; he judges him from within the values of an aristocracy of wealth, the very values that Flem has learned from de Spain and Varner and their ilk.[7]

Faulkner, though, judges both Varner and Flem through his value-system of natural aristocracy. In only a limited sense does Flem earn his new position. He proves himself more shrewd than Jody Varner, and in this way his talent and ability have won over Jody's right to his heritage. In a natural aristocracy, however, the heir to power should be he who deserves the position through talent and merit, as well as character: natural aristocrats would rise above crass materialism and resist the atomizing effects of the individual pursuit of profit. Flem does not possess these traits, and he does not deserve the place he attains here (or the place he eventually attains later in the trilogy). Varner makes an error in judgment, from Faulkner's perspective. He does not have the integrity to use his authority properly (and he will come to pay for it when Flem surpasses him too in *The Town*). Meanwhile, the rightful heir to Varner's power and domain gets bypassed due to Varner's lack of moral vision.

This rightful heir is none other than V. K. Ratliff, the itinerant sewing machine agent. Many critics have commented on the wisdom and moral nature of Ratliff, as well as on the fact that he knits the whole of Frenchman's Bend together in a sense because he retells its stories on his journeys to sell sewing machines. Some have noticed how much alike he is to Flem in that they are both traders and from the same class.[8] Faulkner also depicts very close affinities between Ratliff and Will Varner, and very strong differences between Ratliff and Jody. Early in the novel, Faulkner has Ratliff comment "'That there aint but two men I know can risk fooling with them folks [Snopeses]. And just one of them is named Varner and his front name aint Jody'" (30). He implies here that the other is himself and that only these two have the strength and intelligence to keep Flem at bay. Later, while Varner looks at Ratliff, he looks "at the man who was a good deal nearer his son in spirit and intellect and physical appearance too than any of his own get" (174). Later still, while Jody and Ratliff stand next to one another, the narrator comments: "they were the only two standing, and now, in juxtaposition, you could see the resemblance between them—a resemblance intangible, indefinite, not in figure, speech, dress, intelligence; *certainly not in morals*. Yet it was there" (352; my emphasis). The novel hints that Ratliff, rather than Flem, should have replaced Jody as Varner's rightful heir. Ratliff, who acts in this novel very much as General Compson does in *Absalom*, would have brought moral vision to the ruling class—for Faulkner, just what it needed.

This implication is supported further by the contrast between Ratliff and Flem. Unlike Flem, who is described in *The Mansion* as a man "belonging simply to Money" (419), Ratliff enjoys, as *The Hamlet* explains, "the pleasure of the shrewd dealing which far transcended mere gross profit" (75). Moreover, Ratliff exhibits behavior founded upon moral principles, something Flem knows nothing about, and these principles highlight his recognition of his interconnectedness with other humans. Unlike Flem, who refuses to return five dollars to poor, starving Mrs. Armstid, giving her a mere bag of candy for her children who have not had a decent meal for months, Ratliff exercises his power for the good of others. He offers Mrs. Littlejohn money to help her feed the retarded Ike, whom she has taken into her boarding house; he helps Mink Snopes's wife and children when they are left penniless after Mink's arrest. His actions here contrast him sharply with Will Varner, who helps Mrs. Snopes financially but not without recompense: he makes her sleep with him. Ratliff also stops the peeping toms from watching Ike's actions with the cow. Here, Faulkner makes clear, Ratliff refuses to accept that this situation is not any of his business. He refuses a society based upon the separation of one person from another into their individual and isolated lives and uses his strength to put right something that is wrong: "the reason I aint going to leave [Ike] have what he does have [the cow] is simply because I am strong enough to keep him from it. . . . Maybe all I want is just to have been righteouser, so I can tell myself I done the right thing and my conscience is clear now and at least I can go to sleep tonight" (219). Faulkner clearly implies that Ratliff has wisdom and character and that he is the more natural heir to Varner's power. Varner's lack of proper values, however, inhibits him from passing this power to Ratliff. Flem usurps this heirship as well and proceeds to master the accumulation of wealth based on people's alienation from and exploitation of one another.

The ultimate defeat of Ratliff at the hands of the union between Varner and Snopes comes in the salted gold-mine episode at the end of the book, and this resolution remains in keeping with developments in Southern history: the union of Redeemers and Progressives proved more powerful than the ideals of natural aristocracy. About this episode, during which Ratliff, Armstid and Bookwright buy the Frenchman's mansion from Flem, one of the men comments: "'Couldn't no other man have done it. Anybody might have fooled Henry Armstid. But couldn't nobody but Flem Snopes have fooled Ratliff'" (405). However, the novel makes clear that Flem does not beat Ratliff alone. Indeed, Ratliff had earlier gone head to head in some dealings with Flem and the two had bartered to a virtual standoff. Now, however, Varner has married his pregnant daughter, Eula, to Flem and has given him the old Frenchman's mansion and its surrounding property. For Ratliff, this gift bears some significance. When Bookwright asks him if he has allowed Armstid to talk him into buying this place, Ratliff responds: "'I don't think so. . . . I know I aint. . . . There's something there. . . . If there wasn't, [Varner] wouldn't never bought it. And he wouldn't a kept it, selling the balance of it off and still keeping that old house, paying taxes on it when he could a got something for it. . . . And I knowed it for sho when Flem Snopes took it'" (371–72).[9] Faulkner makes clear that Ratliff's respect for

Varner helps considerably in Ratliff's decision: the union between Varner and Flem, representatives of Redeemer and Progressive respectively, is too powerful for Ratliff to beat.

Although during the course of *The Hamlet* Ratliff has revealed wisdom and character and has used his power for moral purposes, he loses any chance for social power due to a lack of insight into Varner's character. Faulkner makes clear that meaning has been drained from Frenchman's Bend precisely because of Varner's false claims to authority and because others have supported these claims. Varner has reduced the story of the old South to the stubborn tale of money buried in the ground. This story has given Varner some authority in the eyes of others who value it. But this money does not exist; the story and the authority behind it are false. Faulkner condemns both those who give authority to the story and those who believe it—and Ratliff proves he is a believer. Ratliff had the potential to become a natural aristocrat; however, he makes the mistake of believing Varner, and this mistake allows Flem to enter Jefferson. (Ratliff paid his share of the purchase with his ownership of a restaurant there.) Ratliff comes close but gets defeated by his own, as well as Varner's, lack of vision, and Flem takes his values that rest upon the dead power of money into Jefferson.[10]

On one level, *The Hamlet* clearly parallels Mississippi history: the coalition between the Redeemers and the redneck Progressives defeated all challengers. Ratliff's defeat, however, seems to have little historical referent. His potential but ultimate failure seem more important for Faulkner's developing social vision. As I have explained, Ratliff's potential derives from his character, his moral fiber. His deficiency, on the other hand, would appear to stem from a lack of worldly wisdom about the possible duplicity of those in the ruling class, a lack of sophistication about people's motives—or, to put it more plainly, his primarily lower-class background. There is little rational explanation for this failure—in it exists a hint of Faulknerian class *ressentiment*—but there is a cultural history behind this depiction.

Proponents of natural aristocracy wanted, remember, to allow for the legitimate ambitions of the lower class for social mobility. Ratliff seems to have benefited from that possibility, and he reveals he has deserved that relatively improved social position. These proponents also felt that, in general, the biological origin of the naturally aristocratic character would mean that its exemplars would come from the existing wealthy and educated classes. Some from the lower classes might reveal this same character, but these would be biological freaks. Thus, though Ratliff shares the values of natural aristocracy, it would seem from the way Faulkner unravels his story that he is unqualified to fill that position.

After *The Hamlet* Ratliff never competes with Flem again. Although Ratliff continues to reveal wisdom and insight, Faulkner has him narrate only thirty pages of *The Town*, revealing his sense that Ratliff has had his chance to prove himself and has failed. In Jefferson, the battle against Snopesism—or rather, against the union between Redeemers and Progressives that it represents—will have to be fought by others. The major figure in the struggle in Jefferson becomes Gavin Stevens, lawyer and eventual district attorney, a man from the upper class. As Ratliff's struggle was not against Flem alone, but against Varner and Flem, Stevens struggles against Manfred de Spain and Flem. Thus, Faulkner's trilogy comes to operate within the tension between actual history of ideological conflict and the demands of Faulkner's own authorial ideology. On one hand, the trilogy symbolically depicts the ideological forces working on those in the upper class (ignoring other historical developments). On the other, it seeks resolutions to the real conflicts of history through the demands and parameters of natural aristocracy.

Faulkner begins *The Town* by making clear the union between Redeemers and redneck Progressives. Ever since de Spain, who is associated with the Redeemers through the dealings of his father, had come to Jefferson, a town ruled by "old Mr Adams the mayor with a long patriarchal white beard" (11), he had been looking for a way "to wrench Jefferson until the town fitted him" (10). When Bayard Sartoris and Mayor Adams pass a law forbidding cars on the streets of Jefferson, de Spain gets his chance. He runs for mayor against Adams; when he wins, "The new age had entered Jefferson" (12), and he becomes "the high priest in that new national religious cult of Cheesecake" (14). He was supported enthusiastically by "the ones who were not yet store- and gin-owners and already settled lawyers and doctors, but were only the clerks and bookkeepers in the stores and gins and offices, trying to save enough to get married on" (13). The middle-class elements in Jefferson rise to support de Spain against those of the old paternal class and they win the day. De Spain's rise in Jefferson parallels Varner's rise in Frenchman's Bend, and both ascents represent the replacement of the paternalistic elements of the upper class with those who value crass materialism. Stevens explains these men and their triumphs: "one generation more until that innocent and outrageous belief that courage and honor are practical has had time to fade and cool so that merely the habit of courage and honor remain; add to that then that generation's natural heritage of cold rapacity as instinctive as breathing, and tremble at that prospect: the habit of courage and honor compounded by rapacity" (35). In his own terms, Stevens explains how Redeemers wore the cloak of paternalism while operating by capitalist principles.[11]

Stevens, representative of all the gentlemanly values Faulkner feels are absent from this world, at first rises up against these men as the defender of Eula Varner Snopes. As Maggie Mallison, Stevens's sister, comments to him, " 'You're going to save her [Eula]'" (49). Stevens attempts to get Eula accepted into the community of Jefferson, to give her that social role through which she can offer the rebirth that her fecundity and power as Venus beckons—the exact role women are to play within a paternalist ideology. Gavin Stevens does not want to own or to use her sexually, as Flem and de Spain, respectively, do. He wants to give her back the communal and societal identity he feels a woman of her power and potential should have. He attempts in this way to undermine the power that de Spain and Snopes have as well as the system their values has instituted: though from the upper class, Stevens does not wish to share in the values characteristic of an aristocracy of wealth.

This crusade, as Gavin himself calls it, is represented in Gavin's conflict with de Spain. He even fights de Spain at the Cotillion Ball, and, when he loses proceeds to find some reason to sue de Spain in court. When the court comes to hear Gavin's complaint, they ask de Spain if he will resign as mayor in order to end the trouble: a perfect opportunity opens for Stevens to weaken de Spain's power. Gavin says, however, he does not want de Spain to resign. Later, at a court session over which Gavin's father presides, Gavin again refuses to press de Spain into resigning. Judge Stevens asks his son: " 'So you don't want him not to be mayor. . . . Then what is it you do want? For him not to be alive? Is that it?'" (99).

Here, Gavin gets caught between his allegiance to a moral code to which de Spain does not adhere and his allegiance to a class to which they both belong. His pitiful plea to his father reveals his absolute lack of the courage of his convictions and represents the absence of social power his ideals possess: " 'What must I do now, Papa? Papa, what can I do now?'" (99). His defeat, virtually at his own hands, symbolizes the growing impotence of gentlemanly values. Stemming from, now, the very residual ideological formation of paternalism, these gentlemanly values have become just another possible way to act in society. They have lost complete social efficacy because they do not unite those in the upper class in a shared ideology.

Significantly, Gavin's inability here stems from his refusal to judge de Spain on the quality of his character, a necessary element for a natural aristocrat, and his dependence on his father for advice reveals that he himself has not achieved a personal authority with which to guide his own actions. For Faulkner, Stevens simply does not earn or deserve a powerful social position because he fails in a manner similar to Ratliff. From the outside, in their political and social positions and achievements, both de Spain and Stevens are similar. Finally, these are the only criteria by which Stevens judges. In a conversation between Eula and Gavin, the former notices the difference between Gavin and de Spain, claiming: "'you're a gentleman and I never knew one before'" (94). However, Gavin himself does not recognize any difference, responding "'so is Manfred [de Spain]'" (94). The tension Faulkner creates here is a perceived difference between members of the same class—much the same as that between General Compson and Thomas Sutpen. Faulkner places a wedge between these two characters, but Gavin Stevens does not notice or utilize it. By siding with de Spain's class position rather than upholding his own moral values, Stevens reveals he will not become a natural aristocrat, unlike General Compson before him, and he thereby becomes complicit in the declining social power of gentlemanly virtues. These values become now simply personal property, not social mores. Gavin's fight with de Spain could have erupted into a social, intra-class conflict; but Gavin's defeat symbolizes the ascendant status of the liberal, bourgeois ideology dominating Jefferson.

Stevens's actions parallel the historical development involving the movement of humanist values into the personal arena, into a purely private as opposed to the public, economic realm. To his pitiful plea Gavin's father answers that he should leave the country, and Gavin goes to Germany to study. The historical recognition here, though an unconscious one, is that once the bourgeoisie rises to dominance, its ideological formations split. On one hand, individuals pursue wealth in free competition with other isolated, monadic individuals; on the other, individuals pursue the development of inner resources with which they can resist the alienation and anomie characteristic of these societal developments. Culture, in this sense, becomes an inner state all can supposedly develop, and it becomes increasingly divorced from people's daily interactions that are now guided completely by respectability and conformity. Stevens's acceptance of (or interpellation by) these humanist, yet liberal, bourgeois values becomes clear when he returns from Germany. He no longer fights Snopesism, concerning himself with the development of Linda Snopes's inner culture.[12]

The allegiance between Stevens and the liberal, bourgeois forces now represented by Flem Snopes becomes clear in their mutual struggle against Montgomery Ward Snopes, who has established a boutique whose back room offers men the opportunity to gaze at dirty pictures. When Stevens catches Montgomery, he realizes that there is no law on the books forbidding these actions. Momentarily, he uses the old law against the use of cars in Jefferson passed by Sartoris and ex-Mayor Adams to arrest Montgomery and gain some time to decide how to stop the activities for good. Faulkner reveals the inability of bourgeois legality to cope with situations requiring moral judgment: though Stevens feels Montgomery is wrong, he can only rely on a law passed, significantly, by old paternalists for some other reason. Stevens does not know what to do; Flem, however, does. He sneaks into Montgomery's boutique and plants whiskey, thus giving Stevens a pretext for which to press charges and send Montgomery to prison. When Flem returns to Stevens's office, Gavin comments to him: "'You're like me. . . . You dont give a damn about truth either. What you are interested in is justice'" (176).

Although Flem's external behavior may seem to Gavin to be motivated by justice, Faulkner makes clear that Flem is motivated by his own drive for respectability, behind which he can continue to pursue wealth unmolested: "'When you jest want money, all you need to do to satisfy yourself is count it and put it where cant nobody get it . . . But this-here new thing he has done found out it's nice to have, is different. It's like keeping warm in winter and cool in summer, or peace or being free or contentment. . . . It's got to be out in the open, where folks can see it, or there aint no such thing. . . . Call it civic virtue'" (175). Gavin's approval of Flem's actions gives Flem that respectability, but his approval is based only on the external behavior, not on Flem's motives or on the lack of character responsible for those motives. As Brooks (1963, chap. 10) has noted, bourgeois respectability is maintained by both Gavin and Flem. Most importantly, this allegiance to respectability—a commodity that increases one's social position—has replaced any real sense of morality.

The action of *The Town* develops along parallel tracks—Flem rising to the position of bank president and Baptist deacon, safely ensconcing himself within the realms of respectability and wealth, and Gavin Stevens attempting to educate Linda Snopes, "forming her mind" (179) and getting her out of Jefferson.

As Wilson (1980) has convincingly argued, Flem's actions on his way up the ladder are modeled exclusively on those of people who preceded him: the source of acquisitiveness and "evil" is not Flem but the systems established by Varner and de Spain. Gavin's actions are caused by his acknowledged lack of social power and his implicit acceptance of bourgeois ideology. The novel's denouement, however, occurs when these tracks converge, somewhat violently, for both Flem's presidency and Linda's departure occur after Eula Varner's suicide.

This act comes about through Eula's and Linda's common entrapment within a vicious web of connections concerning sex, money, and power, complicated interconnections among Eula's father, her lover, her husband, her daughter, and her daughter's mentor, Stevens. Flem has come to see how presidents of banks can embezzle money without getting caught, and this new knowledge causes him to want now to displace de Spain as bank president. In order to do this, he must get the backing of Varner's stock, something Varner is loathe to give: he has resented Flem ever since Flem beat him in the old Frenchman's mansion deal and surpassed him to get out of Frenchman's Bend. Flem holds half a trump card in Eula's affair with de Spain, about which Varner knows nothing. What he needs is Linda's assurance she will give him part of her inheritance from her grandfather. Flem knows that Varner will do anything to keep his money from him, even if it means letting Flem become bank president. In the meantime, Stevens has convinced Linda that she must leave Jefferson.

At first, Flem refuses to allow Linda to leave, for, if Linda gets beyond the confines of Jefferson, she will be more likely to discover that Flem is not her real father; then she will never offer her inheritance. After forbidding her for some time to leave, Flem suddenly gives her permission, mentioning something about the money in passing. In her gratitude, Linda signs a legal document relinquishing half her money to her father. Flem then goes to Varner with the document and exposes Eula's affair to him, and Varner rushes into town to set matters straight. At this point, Eula knows that de Spain's masculine pride and ego will not allow him to lose both his mistress and his job without a fight. Linda then will become aware of the affair, and society will try to make her ashamed of her own mother. De Spain will accept a trade, the presidency for Eula, but his identity as "a man" (331) will not allow anything else. Eula's departure from Jefferson with de Spain, however, will expose Linda to scandal as well. Realizing that none of the men will do what is best for her, Eula settles the matter in the only way she can: she sacrifices herself on the altar of respectability, masculine power, and economic lust.

Faulkner does not approve of this sacrifice. Eula has consistently been seen to offer some possibility for renewal in the barren worlds of Frenchman's Bend and Jefferson: as described in *The Hamlet* she "suggested some symbology out of the old Dionysiac times" (105); she was "the queen, the matrix" (128). For Faulkner, this crisis demands a figure of authority who can settle matters according to some moral principles. It implicitly demands one who can be guided by ideals and moral values while acting in the social world. But there is only Will Varner. The absence of any character possessing these values of natural aristocracy thus leads to Eula's death. This world continues to be guided by the power of money and by men who have no principles or who have forsaken their social power in order to keep some limited, purely personal ideals. At the close of the novel, when Flem begins to redecorate his new mansion in the antebellum style, *The Town* sardonically reveals what happens in a world in which the values of natural aristocracy have been abandoned.

This conclusion emphasizes the emptiness of the social vision ruled by the man in this mock-antebellum mansion. *The Mansion*, however, seeks to demonstrate that there is "a simple fundamental justice and equity in human affairs" (6) that can and will overcome those "belonging simply to Money" (419). This justice is enacted by Linda Snopes, Eula's daughter, a Communist, and Mink Snopes, Flem's farmer cousin. Although this coalition between Linda and Mink has a potential to undermine the very structures and inherent hierarchies of Faulkner's natural aristocracy, Faulkner takes pains to reveal that these two people recognize their place *within* these hierarchies. Only through this recognition do they become qualified to enact justice. Here, Faulkner's authorial ideology and his social vision combine to solve, imaginatively, the contradictions of history.

As Brooks (1963) has noted, "even in the foreshortened account of Mink given in *The Hamlet*, Mink has, with all his bitterness and viciousness, a sense of honor" (183). This honor, a vestige from an aristocratic paternalism similar to the one Wash Jones maintained in *Absalom*, and Mink's status as a farmer who recognizes his place in the social order, privilege him within Faulkner's trilogy.[13] Beginning in *The Hamlet* Mink describes himself as "'one cousin that's still scratching dirt to stay alive'" (85). In *The Hamlet* Faulkner offers poignant descriptions of Mink's home and fields to reveal the pitiful conditions of his life: "He emerged from the bottom and looked up the slope of his meagre and sorry corn and saw it—the paintless two-room cabin . . . which was not his, on which he paid rent but not taxes, paying almost as much rent in one year as the house had cost to build . . . his corn, yellow and stunted because he had had no money to buy fertilizer to put beneath it and owned neither the stock nor the tools to work it properly" (243–44). In *The Mansion* these conditions are described as having "continually harassed and harried him into the constant and unflagging necessity of defending his own simple rights" (7), for, in the land of Varner, no one else will: all is decided by the cash-nexus on the basis of man's separation from and competition with other men. The tragic violence of this cash-nexus system becomes revealed in the treatment Mink receives from Jack Houston and Will Varner.

Mink, who asked "no favors of any man, paying his own way" (8), had allowed his cow to stray onto the land of Jack Houston, "a man not only rich enough to be able to breed and raise beef cattle, but rich enough to keep a Negro to do nothing else save feed and tend them—a Negro to whom Houston furnished a better house to live in than the one that he, Mink . . . lived in" (9–10). Despite his better living conditions, Houston refuses to feed Mink's cow for free; indeed, he demands the full price of the cow in its present condition—an amount of money Mink has never seen. When Varner comes to adjudicate the situation, he basically agrees with Houston: offering to pay half but judging that Mink will have to work for the rest of the price. In another time, another man motivated by benevolent paternalism, by reciprocal obligations, might have paid Houston's price or might have judged against Houston—but not now.

After working out his time, Mink returns home for the evening, planning to get his cow the next day. Arriving at Houston's, Mink is told that he owes another dollar because he did not take his cow on the day he finished: the law says the owner of a cow will pay a one dollar pound fee to another man who houses his animal overnight. Mink is outraged; he goes to Varner to check the law and Varner verifies it. Here, Varner offers Mink the dollar, but Mink refuses. Varner's offer of money remains consistent with his values. Significantly, he does not go to Houston and tell him to forget about the dollar—that would have been the moral thing to do. Mink's refusal of Varner's offer reveals that he is not motivated by money. Indeed, for him this affair has nothing to do with money, and he decides to kill Houston, claiming: "'I aint shooting you because of them thirty-seven and a half four bit days. That's all right. . . . Likely Will Varner couldn't do nothing else, being a rich man too and all you rich folks has got to stick together or else maybe some day the ones that aint rich might take a notion to raise up and take hit away from you. That aint why I shot you. I killed you because of that-ere extry one-dollar pound fee'" (39). Faulkner's implications are twofold: Mink's rebellion has arisen from the denial of "simple justice and inalienable rights" (12), and those in power should be more morally minded or they will rightfully lose their positions.

In keeping with the legacy of natural aristocracy, Faulkner's criticism of these men in the upper class is rather severe. Natural aristocracy argued against intense autocratic power wielded in extreme exploitative means. It recognized the republican rights to life, liberty, and the pursuit of happiness, and often held out the yeoman farmer as the ideal of one who worked independently and who recognized his place within a natural order. As long as people in society did not break its natural relations in a frenetic quest for social mobility, and worked diligently, they should be respected and rewarded accordingly. Varner and Houston are here depicted as controllers of a rather harsh lien system of tenant farming where farmers were reduced to mere pawns in the hands of wealthy men who had no interest in the farmer or the land. Varner carries in his pockets as loose change an amount of money Mink will have to work thirty-seven half-days to earn. Meanwhile, Mink is shown to be cooperative to a point, not rebelling from the system, or demanding more. He seems willing to work his land, take the ups and downs of farming, asking for help only when he needs it. As in the town, here in the country values of natural aristocracy are not winning the day. Faulkner condemns Varner and Houston, sympathizing with Mink's plight.

This sympathy continues in Mink's experiences with Flem. After being sent to jail for Houston's murder, Mink thinks that Flem will help him, that Flem will have to help him "because of the ancient immutable laws of simple blood kinship" (5). And as Bookwright comments during the trial in *The Hamlet*, "'Even Flem Snopes aint going to let his own blood cousin be hung just to save money'" (294). Yet, though Mink is not hanged, Flem does not help him in any way, thereby abrogating the connections of kinship and validating only the bonds of money. Sitting in jail, waiting for thirty-eight years, Mink never forgets Flem's betrayal of the bonds between them. Neither does Faulkner.

Mink's value as a character stems from his recognition of other values besides those of money as well as his recognition of the natural ties and responsibilities between people. He comes to represent also the necessity for change in this social structure. Before Mink enacts vengeance on the upper class, though, he will reveal his acceptance of the proper social structure. This acceptance involves Mink's realization of his place within the overall scheme of society.

Indeed, only after Mink's acceptance does Faulkner release him from jail to kill Flem. In thinking of Flem, Mink had at one point felt that Flem "had either been born with or had learned, taught himself, the knack or the luck to cope with, hold his own, handle the They and Them which he, Mink, apparently did not have the knack or the luck to do" (35). Now, in prison, Mink realizes "that there was no such thing as bad luck or good luck: you were either born a champion or not a champion and if he had been born a champion Houston not only couldn't, he wouldn't have dared, misuse him . . . that some folks were born to be failures and get caught always, some folks were born to be lied to and believe it, and he was one of them" (89–90). This knowledge does not depress Mink or make him suicidal, however; rather it gives him peace. In a conversation with the Warden, he says: "'You dont need to write God a letter. He has done already seen inside you long before He would even need to bother to read it. Because a man will learn a little sense in time even outside. But he learns it quick in here . . . all you got to do is jest take back and accept [Judgment]'" (100). As Faulkner orchestrates it, judgment helps Mink acquire the salvation he seeks, getting him to Memphis, then to Jefferson, past the bodyguard and into the mansion where he kills Flem. The recognition of his supposedly God-given place in life is precisely what permits him, from Faulkner's perspective, to achieve what he desires. In short, Mink sees that there is, supposedly, a natural order in society, recognizes a system governed by the rules of natural aristocrats, and admits he is not a natural aristocrat. This realization gives him a place within the "celestial and *hierarchate*" universe (433; my emphasis) and among his fellow human beings.

The depictions of Mink's realization process in *The Mansion* reveal more clearly what had been implied in earlier novels: the inherent hierarchy of Faulkner's social vision and the degree of class *ressentiment* on which it was based. Certainly, Mink is seen through a dual lens. On one hand, he is sympathetic and comes to be the instrument of justice; on the other, he is sympathetic only because he accepts a low place in the social order and he is not seen to be the sole agent for the justice he enacts. (The question about whether he has any agency at all remains open.) As Grimwood comments: "As long as the poor stayed in their place . . . they earned [Faulkner's] deep respect" (1987, 164). Mink certainly fits these requirements. Moreover, his desire for revenge is greatly abetted by a more aristocratic nature—Linda Snopes Kohl.

The roots of Linda's qualifications to play an assertive role in the enactment of justice on Flem stem from her connection to her biological parents, her recognition of responsibility to family and the desire to be responsible to the human family at first represented by her drive to go to Spain.[14] Before she had gone overseas, Gavin had arranged for her to meet her real father, Hoake McCarron. McCarron is "the only child of a well-to-do widowed maw and only educated . . . in that select school that even in that short time some of them high standards of honor and chivalry rubbed off on him by jest exposure" (125). After this experience Linda comes to understand Flem's cruel role in her mother's death and "that someday her maw would be saying to her, "'Why didn't you revenge me . . . instead of jest standing back and blind hoping for happen-so?'" (431). Linda now seems to be heavily influenced by the values represented by her biological father, with all their roots in the Old South, and by her mother, the queen, the matrix. She comes to compare their values to those of Flem. She realizes that she can (and must) fight evil right in her own hometown in order to defend the values both her gentleman father and courageous mother represent. As Ratliff says, after the war "'she'll come back here [to Jefferson]'" (178). The implication is that she will come to set matters straight. When she signs a petition to free Mink from jail, we understand how she plans to do this.

As Ratliff comments: "'She could a waited two more years and God His-self couldn't a kept Mink in Parchman . . . and saved herself not jest the bother and worry but the moral responsibility too, even if you [Gavin] do say they aint no morals. Only she didn't'" (431). Gavin has, in a sense, been right—there have not been any morals. This condition has been caused by the rise to dominance of the Varners and de Spains and the Flem Snopeses and by their acceptance by people like Gavin. Linda refuses to accept this dominance and works to fight the aristocracies of wealth, whether they be in Spain or in Jefferson. She recognizes her moral responsibility and chooses to act upon it—as her attempts to help the black tenant farmers reveal. Linda has been touched: "'The Lord touched her, like He touches a heap of folks better than you [Mink], better than me [black tenant farmer]'" (401). Unlike Mink and the black farmer, Linda stands near the top of the celestial hierarchy. Without her assistance, Mink might never have gotten to serve as the instrument of justice.

Linda's moral responsibility, her recognition that she has obligations to other human beings in the world, and her willingness and ability to act upon these are precisely the requirements of a natural aristocrat. They serve to contrast her sharply with Gavin Stevens, who calls himself "'a humanitarian'" and then realizes "'that word is customarily used as a euphemism for [coward]'" (379). Despite these character traits, Linda does not get to renew the social vision operating in Jefferson. She acquires no social power. In fact, after it becomes clear that she and Gavin will never marry, she leaves Jefferson. Faulkner, that is, sends her away.

As Polk has commented about this ending: "The ending of the trilogy seems to me . . . very bleak. If violence, if murder, is the only way we can deal effectively with Snopesism, if the world has to depend on the like of Mink Snopes to save it, then we are in sorry shape indeed" (1983, 125). Polk's point is precisely Faulkner's point: the worlds of Frenchman's Bend and Jefferson are in sorry shape. For Faulkner, they have been led astray, on one hand, by the values of an aristocracy of wealth that imprisons people in an exploitative system that disregards the value of day-to-day human interconnections and the obligations that should bond people together in some ordered hierarchy and, on the other, by the inefficacies of a cowardly humanism that rationalizes the personal pursuit of inner culture as an ideal pastime while ignoring the quality of the social and cultural life of a community. The corrective for Faulkner is a class or group of gentlemen who will control egalitarian impulses to pursue individual self-interest and whose wisdom is worldly, moral, and civic-minded. As Slotkin explains: "the ideological mission of the doctrine . . . of 'natural aristocracy' is to provide solutions to the social conflicts of the Metropolis" (1985, 78); in it, "the dynamism of social mobility could be reconciled with the preservation of order" (307). In a sense, because he has set matters straight in the world of Jefferson, Faulkner projects himself as the natural aristocrat who has the wisdom and ability to be a leader of society.

In the resolutions to this novel we also can see the limitations affecting Faulkner's social vision. Since Linda is not literally the one who acts against Flem—that is, she does not pull the trigger—Faulkner perpetuates the notion that action in the world is a masculine trait. By sending Linda out of Jefferson once it is clear Stevens will not marry her, Faulkner implies that her proper roles are those of mother and wife. The social and political changes her agency might have brought to Jefferson seem not to be Faulkner's concern. Moreover, Mink becomes "equal to any, good as any, brave as any, being inextricable from, anonymous with all of them: the beautiful, the splendid, the proud, and the brave" (435), but he does so only in heaven, not here on earth. On earth, Mink finds his way, not surprisingly, to the old Frenchman's mansion. The trilogy comes full-circle as Faulkner returns to the symbol of the old South, and, in definite ways, to a romantic vision of that world as well. Linda and Mink have cleaned the slate, have opened a gap in the power of the aristocracy of wealth, but neither can fill that gap for Faulkner. This conclusion parallels developments in other Faulkner novels. If Faulkner had been more aware of or concerned with the range of possible subjectivities for his women and working class characters, the directions and resolutions of his novels may have been quite different. He was, though, more concerned with the subjectivity of upper-class men. Linda and Mink act according to the values of Faulkner's implied ideological position, but neither can become the leader of a society based on these values. Both of these components define the parameters of Faulkner's natural aristocracy.

By the end of *The Mansion*, the noble and tragic vision underlying *Absalom, Absalom!* has come to be one of idealism and irony. Though much more conservative here than in *Absalom*, this vision maintains a level of idealism in confronting the ravages of capitalism. Like Charles Bon, Faulkner wants people to be judged by their actions and their behaviors, not by the money they have or whom their family happens to be. However, as is always the case, someone needs to be the judge, and the irony of the Snopes Trilogy is its implication that upper-class men need to be those judges. Like Faulkner, one could wish for better men; however, one could also wish for the inclusion of Mink and Linda in the social order (and by implication, Charles Bon). Faulkner could see exploitation and feel for the plight of those suffering from it; he could desire for these people a viable social role deserving respect; however, he did not give them any form of social power. Ultimately, Faulkner's social vision becomes deeply romantic. Rather than exploring the subversive possibilities of some of his most accurate and far-reaching insights—recognizing the social roles women, poor whites and blacks have played and continue to play in our society—Faulkner returns to the fathers and husbands, these good men. Although during the decade of the 1950s Faulkner was fulfilling, on a personal level, the image he had of himself—he wrote himself into history as a natural aristocrat—the process of history itself becomes the nightmare from which he and his fiction had to escape. To finish detailing his social vision, to create the natural aristocrat in fiction, Faulkner would cease his creation of symbolic histories and turn instead to "a reminiscence." Faulkner thus follows his political imagination, overdetermined at it was by its immersion in paternalism and liberalism, to its logical conclusion: he creates a natural aristocrat who leads society in *The Reivers*.

9 • *The Reivers*

Imaginary Resolutions and Utopian Yearnings

> I mean, I didn't want to be *is* anywhere. If I had to be something, I wanted
> to be *was.*
>
> —Faulkner, *The Reivers*

> If you ask, Which is the worst? I answer: This which we now have, that
> Chaos should sit umpire in it; this is the worst.
>
> —Thomas Carlyle, *On Heroes*

In an essay about *Sartoris,* Faulkner confirms the force of my own argument about his Yoknapatawpha project: "I contemplated those shady but ingenious shapes by reason of whose labor I might reaffirm the impulses of my own ego in this actual world without stability, with a lot of humbleness, and I speculated on time and death and *wondered if I had invented the [teeming] world to which I should give life or if it had invented me*" (Blotner 1973, 124). My contention throughout has been that Faulkner's Mississippi did, to some extent, invent him. Although he would move some distance away from the noncritical version of the South offered in *Flags,* late in his life Faulkner was returning to this version more and more, and in *The Reivers* he returns very much to the South he pictured in *Flags* and to the noncritical depiction of it. Along with his conclusion to *The Mansion,* this move reveals just how deeply Faulkner was affected and influenced by that South, how difficult it was for him to separate himself from it, even though he could criticize it in detail in some of his books. With the character of Lucius Priest, Faulkner offers a clear picture of his ideological position—the representation of his imaginary relationship to his real conditions of history.

Toward the end of his life Faulkner was, it seems clear, enjoying the image he had attained for himself as a natural, artistic aristocrat. His settling in Char-lottesville, Virginia, enjoying the "snobs," as he called them, seems indicative of the subjectivity with which he identified and implicitly of the social vision he sponsored. Although there are contradictions in his ideological position in fiction and history, there is indeed a degree of glory in it for Faulkner's life. For, truth be told, Faulkner not only wrote his way into history, he did so according to the values he cherished and articulated. In his own life, in the distinct arena of literary production, Faulkner did indeed resolve the contradictions between liberal and paternalist ideologies. Faulkner proved he was a man of action when it came to writing; he demonstrated his talent, skill, and vision over a long pe-riod of time. Moreover, what he considered his inner, inherent talent and worth became verified by larger communities, and he assumed what he considered his rightful place, eventually, in both literary and social circles.

In fact, I sense that part of what makes Faulkner so attractive to literary critics is that he proved, in definite ways, that ideals of a meritocracy and high standards of artistic production can and do go hand in hand. University culture in America remains a world in which Faulkner's ideal of natural aristocracy still has effect and impact. Students and professors alike, the theory goes, who work hard and produce well *will* succeed to the upper echelons of status. There is also a tendency to believe that some students, some people are indeed naturally bet-ter, smarter than others. Meanwhile, money and the commercial spirit have little to do with the day-to-day life on campus. Literary critics tend to operate in a world filled with values from liberal and paternalist ideologies; we tend to function within a world filled with contradictory forces; and we strive for suc-cess, recognition on our own terms. How could we not admire a man who bal-anced these forces as well and as successfully as Faulkner did? Whatever the parameters and limitations of his political imagination, Faulkner achieved suc-cess through talent and industriousness. He proved the system works as we all hope it does or can or will.

Admiring Faulkner does not mean we have, on the other hand, to glorify his social vision. In the final analysis, and in its final manifestation, this vision be-comes a deeply romantic, nostalgic vision of people's places and possibilities in society. *The Reivers: A Reminiscence,* Faulkner's last novel, clearly substantiates these claims. Here, in a *bildungsroman* somewhat reminiscent of *Intruder in the Dust,* the old Lucius Priest recounts to his grandson his own maturation and his initiation into the "gentlemanly code." The overt theme of this novel is stated by Lucius's own grandfather near the end of the story: "'A gentleman can live through anything. . . . A gentleman accepts the responsibility of his actions and bears the burden of their consequences'" (302). The heretofore absent natural aristocrat now appears on the scene recounting lessons and values to perpetuate his societal and ideological position. This position is defined more directly than anywhere else in the Faulkner canon, and this scenario—old men telling tales that incorporate their version of proper values—seems oddly appropriate: the contents of these lessons became, in a sense, Faulkner's final message. (Faulkner died soon after the completion of this novel.) Delving into Lucius Priest's tale of initiation reveals how his story continues and develops from various Faulkner concerns. Through this process we come to see even more clearly what Faulkner's authorial ideology values and represents and how deeply it remained affected by history.

During his trip to Memphis with Boon Hogganbeck, a poor, white handyman in his mid-twenties, Lucius, at the age of eleven, realizes: "I was smarter than Boon. I realised, felt suddenly the same exultant fever-flash which Faustus himself must have experienced: that of we two doomed and irrevocable, I was the leader, *I was the boss, the master*" (53; my emphasis). This realization comes to Lucius as a God-given or natural truth. It is irrevocable; he cannot do anything about it. He is simply a better man (if an eleven-year-old can be a man) than Boon. An inherent hierarchy of men has placed Lucius in the upper class and Boon in the lower, and the social order is here clearly based on predetermined natural conditions. Lucius's realization is the converse of those of Mink Snopes and Wash Jones: Mink and Wash realize and accept their low position in the natural/social order; Lucius, his exalted one. Here, the various explorations Faulkner undertook in *Light in August* and *Absalom* become instituted into his ideological position: certain men are better than others, by nature; people do have a natural identity; and the social order must be in alignment with the natural order. Like others before him, Faulkner asserts that some men were better fitted than others for the exercise of political responsibility because of their superior intellectual endowment and an unselfish devotion to the public good. Moreover, he believes that these men will typically be found among members of the existing wealthy and educated classes.[1]

Much of the novel proceeds from this realization to focus on the ways Lucius reveals his pedigree (so to speak). Like Quentin Compson and Horace Benbow before him, Lucius adopts a protective role in relation to women. Women, for him, are ladies. He manifests this feeling when he fights the fifteen-year-old

Otis, who has a knife, for being a peeping Tom and defiling Everbe's femininity. Lucius's actions then come to have inspirational effects: based on them Everbe stops whoring and becomes a respectable woman. Later, Boon decides she is worthy enough to marry, claiming, "'if you [Lucius] can go bare-handed against a knife defending her, why the hell cant I marry her?'" (299). Both Everbe and Boon see "refinement" (203) in Lucius, and, so Faulkner would have us believe, they have become inspired by his character. Hoping that these characteristics might be transferable, they name their son, Lucius Priest Hogganbeck.

On one hand, the effects Lucius has on others points to the beliefs that the characteristics of the natural aristocrat could be distributed through a democratic society—that they would become infused to some extent through the populace. As noted in chapter 6, this process is the one that explains the possession of these traits by General Compson in *Absalom*. On the other hand, the Hogganbecks reveal the same hope that Thomas Sutpen had—that traits might be transferable to one's heir or, here, to one's namesake. In both ways, Faulkner's text reveals a continued involvement with the ideas and values of natural aristocracy—an ideal that attempts to give order to an otherwise chaotic capitalist, democratic society.

The other aspect of Faulkner's implied social vision that becomes manifest in *The Reivers* is the relationship between black people in the South and upperclass whites—and the corresponding attitude toward poor white people. It is not surprising that the difficulty Lucius, Everbe, and Boon have with the sheriff is resolved with the help of Ned and Uncle Parsham. As is often the case, Faulkner posits a kind of savagery in certain elements of the lower-class white population—that third race notorious for rapine and pillage. Meanwhile his black characters play the noble and humble chorus to the wealthy white leaders. As is often the case, black characters have a nobility that poor whites lack, and again, only certain people in the upper class—here represented by Grandfather Priest, Colonel Linscomb and Mr. van Tosch—can recognize this. Thus, Faulkner's attachment to the supposed ideals of the Old South remains a constant influence on his version of natural aristocracy.

As is clear from these brief descriptions, this particular ideological position can easily be seen to mask a repressive and limited social vision. To deny, seemingly, effective social agency and independence to poor whites, who are seen often as savages, blacks, who are seen as noble but always dependent, and women, who are supposed to be wives and mothers, has been a paternalist legacy for some time, and a strong case indeed could be made that Faulkner's social vision—in the final analysis—is conservative, even reactionary. I will leave that case for others to make, however, and attempt to explain and understand Faulkner through the lens of ideology, reiterating some of my earlier points. Individuals, including Faulkner, rarely admit or see that they are indeed determined or produced by their place within a subtle network of interlocking forces. Instead, they develop an imaginary representation of themselves that satisfies an unconscious need for coherence and unity. An authorial ideology of natural aristocracy offered Faulkner a compelling sense of reality—seen from where he stood—in which contradictions between himself and his social order appeared resolved. Thus, Faulkner can be seen to have been aware of the deep problems and conflicts of his South, aware that solutions were intensely difficult and perhaps impossible in his lifetime, and interested in projecting some imaginary means of resolution. Labeling *The Reivers* "a reminiscence," which has the ring of fairy-tale to it, Faulkner seems aware that he is playing with reality, that he is projecting only an imaginary world. But, when dealing with and confronting contradictory and irreconcilable ideologies, an imaginary projection seems almost the logical, necessary, shall we say, natural next step.

As another aspect of *The Reivers* makes clear, Faulkner was struggling, to some extent, against a liberal society that had achieved hegemonic status. As Priest comments: "we had democracy too: the judges were the night telegraph operator . . . and Mr McDiarmid, who ran the depot eating room, who, the legend went, could slice a ham so thin that his entire family had made a summer trip to Chicago on the profits of one of them; our steward and marshall was a dog trainer who . . . was now out on bond for his part in . . . a homicide . . . did I not tell you this was free and elective will and choice and private enterprise at its purest?" (235). Faulkner also had the historical perspective to see that various responses to liberalism and capitalism had not been very successful. Why not an imaginary resolution that tied into his utopian yearnings for a better world?

In *The Reivers* Faulkner returns to the early-twentieth-century world of intense struggle, conflict, and repression that he knew well, yet he paints an idyllic picture. With the creation of the recognizably paternalistic Lucius Priest and friends, and through Uncle Parsham, the black paternalist who sees things the same way as the white men, Faulkner implies that all would have been well with Southern society if only these kinds of men existed to set matters straight, so to speak. Faulkner's yearning for a social haven established under the benevolent rule of natural aristocrats can be seen to stem from the loss he felt living in an emergent capitalist social formation that encouraged monadic isolation and produced alienation and reification. Faulkner yearns to return to a time, an imaginary time that existed only in fairy tales, when the content of one's character was judged according to one's manners and morals. In the final scenes of the novel Faulkner even implies that everyone in this world, once it is reorganized by Grandfather Priest and Colonel Linscomb, lives happily ever after.

Faulkner did indeed only imagine this version of Yoknapatawpha. This reminiscence purposely has little to do with history; it connects more to Faulkner's imaginary resolutions to the real conditions and contradictions he witnessed. This novel tells us much more about Faulkner than about history.

Various Faulkner critics have discussed how Faulkner was hurt into greatness, and how writing for Faulkner was an attempt to fill a loss he deeply felt.[2] From my perspective, Faulkner was hurt by history, that irrevocable and ineluctable process that refuses to be guided by one's individual desire. History placed limits on him. Viewing Faulkner through a historical lens and placing his work in relation to its sociohistorical environment allow us to see his literary project as a quest to define an ideal social world and to delineate his position within this world—to write his way into history on his own terms. Like many literary projects before his—those of William Wordsworth, Samuel Coleridge, Thomas Carlyle, Matthew Arnold, Charles Dickens, R. W. Emerson, T. S. Eliot—Faulkner's solves the social problems of capitalist social formations with a nostalgic glance backward to an imaginary time and/or to imaginary authoritarian figures possessing putatively ideal qualities. Certainly, Faulkner knew this response to capitalism was not the only one. Living through the American 1920s and 1930s, contributing to the Spanish Civil War, responding to communism, Faulkner was well aware of other responses to the ravages of capitalism he despised so vehemently. To wonder—*why this response?*—leads to the argument I have presented here: Faulkner's responses to the social crises he witnessed were overdetermined by his identification with certain aspects of the ideologies most influential on him. On one hand, Faulkner objected to the impulse of capitalism that leads to the constant destruction of social relationships, the uprooting of communities and the atomization of social life; on the other hand, he was interpellated, as Althusser defines that term, by paternalism and liberalism in such a way as to define his social vision through the position of natural aristocracy.

To find other historical potentialities in Faulkner's canon, readers must focus their vision more on what I have called the latent content of Faulkner's authorial ideology. In contrast to the manifest content of this ideological position with which I have been concerned, this latent content reveals Faulkner's political unconscious and the utopian impulse behind his rewriting, his re-vision of history. Focusing on the utopian function would highlight characters such as Caddy Compson, Addie and Darl Bundren, Charles Bon, even the coalition between Mink Snopes and Linda Snopes Kohl. These characters stand in opposition to Faulkner's authorial ideology of natural aristocracy and threaten to subvert it in attempts to re-vision history differently, to initiate a different narrative. That they appear in the texts in this way reveals that Faulkner may have unconsciously desired them to subvert the overt ideological system guiding his Yoknapatawpha. Faulkner's political unconscious becomes manifest in the utopian impulse to wish for human freedom and the fulfillment of the human community's potential that his own narrative curtails. Though I do not focus on these characters, their existence and their relationships to the texts' dominant structures only reinforces my point about the existence of an ideology guiding Faulkner's fiction from near its beginnings. Seeking reasons for *why* certain characters are repressed from the narrative, from telling their own stories, or from playing different roles in the worlds in which they inhabit leads us, again, to the argument I have presented: Yoknapatawpha functions as a world guided by an ideology that both legitimizes and represses.

Faulkner's novels intersect in some ways intensely with the central concerns of American literature, with issues of American culture, and with America's visions of itself as a nation. His fears of democracy are not unique—they go back as far as Hamilton and Jefferson, who often debated about the directions American society should take and who sought answers to the perplexing problems created by a liberal ideology's overthrow of an aristocratic paternalism. They also connect to the concerns of British writers of the nineteenth century, who witnessed the rise of democracy and the consolidation of capitalist society. Faulkner's American response, in fact, shares much with Thomas Carlyle, John Ruskin, and Matthew Arnold, all of whom sought, in effect, the creation of a class of leaders who would be civic-minded and cultured, safe from the corrupting effects of commercial society and the debilitating effects of poverty. To address this need, these men placed emphasis on the development of inner, personal culture. In this emphasis on inner culture, which would prohibit the development of outer, social anarchy, these men ignored the way in which culture could or should be conceived as the entire network of social relationships—how people within a given society, and across classes, perceive and interact with one another, how indeed we are instructed to perceive and interact with each other.[3]

Faulkner's struggle remains, in many ways, our own. Faulkner's solution highlights an idealistic response to a conflict at the heart of American society. It is an ideal that many hold, both inside and outside educational institutions, and its ultimately romantic nature highlights the full implications of this ideal for us. We can see ourselves in Faulkner and learn to what end our own seemingly idealistic gestures will lead. Certainly we can come to question capitalist social formations with a similar intensity, but we must also see how his vision failed to push democracy to its egalitarian potentials. Faulkner's literary project remains perhaps the most far-reaching in all of American literature; however, I believe that we need to become more aware of the underlying ideological features of this project, as well as the possible reasons why we have come to value his writings so highly. An ideological analysis allows us to see the limits of Faulkner's social vision. We can also hope that it can help articulate the world that Faulkner's political unconscious projected. Faulkner's work clearly reveals the seeming permanence of the past; perhaps new imaginative energy can change our memories of ourselves and our relation to one another so that we too can endure and prevail.

Notes

PREFACE

1. The breadth of Faulkner scholarship certainly cannot be summarized in one sentence. There are others, besides the critics mentioned earlier, who investigate Faulkner's immersion in and relation to history, most notably perhaps Pamela Rhodes (Pamela Knights), Richard Godden, Cheryl Lester, and Charles Hannon. (See Knights 1989; Rhodes and Godden 1985; Godden 1989, 1993, 1994; Lester 1987, 1988, 1994, 1997; Hannon 1991–92, 1997.) Nonetheless, the troubled relationship between ideological analyses and Faulkner studies can be seen in certain places. See, for example, Kartiganer and Abadie (1995). There, certain essays argue against the validity of the very topic of the collection—Faulkner and ideology.

CHAPTER 1. FAULKNER'S MISSISSIPPI:
IDEOLOGY AND SOUTHERN HISTORY

1. Granted, the possibilities discussed in this paragraph are speculative; nonetheless, Faulkner's figures for the population of Yoknapatawpha basically coincide with these estimates. There were 9,313 blacks in Yoknapatawpha and 6,298 whites. For map of and figures about Yoknapatawpha see *Absalom, Absalom!* My figures about populations in Mississippi counties come from Kirwan (1951, 40 and maps after 162).

One book I discuss, *Absalom, Absalom!*, confronts a historical period other than the one described in detail here. I will deal with its historical origins in chapter 6; however, like all books within Faulkner's canon, *Absalom* is deeply affected by Faulkner's authorial ideology, which stems from the period I describe.

2. The extent to which the Old South was indeed a paternalist society as well as how long any paternalist influence lingered after the Civil War are both ongoing discussions within historical scholarship. My interpretation agrees with the Marxist historians Eugene D. Genovese, Jay R. Mandle, Jonathan M. Wiener, and Dwight B. Billings to the extent that I find strong evidence for paternalism—as Oakes defines it—as an active ideological force in Mississippi before and after the Civil War. Nonetheless, the evidence seems also convincing that the ruling class was not—perhaps was never—unified in its allegiance to this ideology. And, as the South and Mississippi developed after Reconstruction, the ideology of liberalism came to have more and more of a hold on the entire society, including the ruling class. For a brief synopsis of the historical scholarship, see Wayne (1983).

3. In *Black Reconstruction in America* (1969) W. E. B. DuBois discusses the missed chance epitomized by the decision against land confiscation. A real democracy founded on the economic freedom of its citizens could have been established in the South, he argues, but Northern leaders felt the move was too extreme, too much like socialism. In valuing private property, Northern Republicans were true to their colors—white and capitalist. The freed black population would have to make it on its own abilities as free men; tragically, the Radicals did not realize the wholly abstract quality of this freedom.

DuBois recognized that the potential in this kind of decision, if it had been made, was enormous for blacks. This potential was shown during the years from 1863 to 1866, when Davis Bend, the plantation of Jefferson Davis himself, was divided among freed slaves. Five thousand acres were divided among approximately 1,800 blacks. They established 181 companies, opened stores and schools, and established a system of self-government. At first supported by federal government loans, they cleared a profit of $160,000 and paid back the money. When Johnson decided against land confiscation, Davis Bend was returned to the Davis family; the blacks were left to fend for themselves. (See Loewen and Sallis 1974, 135–37.)

During the past twenty years or so, historians have diligently pursued DuBois's early lead. Ideas about the roles played by black Americans, their assertions of autonomy and independence, in slavery and Reconstruction, have been changing dramatically. This branch of historical inquiry has reinterpreted these time periods to understand the full potential and efforts of black Americans much more clearly. (See Genovese 1972; Litwack 1979; Gutman 1976; Foner 1988.)

4. James Alcorn, Mississippi's first Reconstruction governor, a scalawag, had been a Whig. After the war he was immediately attracted to the Republican party because it represented business interests. Alcorn wanted decisions to be based primarily on business concerns, allowing issues of reform and education to be stalled. He was replaced by Aldebert Ames, a carpetbagger, because he was doing little for the newly freed blacks. One major issue of this race concerned proposals to curtail the operation of the newly formed Ku Klux Klan. The Klan essentially served as a police force for large planters, keeping blacks on plantations through its threats of violence and death. Alcorn did not want Klan laws passed, while Ames did. For the moment, Ames won. (See Clark and Kirwan 1967, chap. 2.)

Under Ames's administration, the large landowners were taxed more heavily to help pay for the state's rebuilding and reform efforts. This heavy taxation helped swing key wealthy landowners to support the Democratic ticket in the elections of 1875, when Republicans lost their hold in Mississippi.

Men like Alcorn were in better position to begin again after the Civil War as well, primarily because they did not have to fight during the war. For every twenty slaves owned, one white man was entitled to remain in order to supervise the slaves and to protect the women. Also, men could pay others to go fight for them. These were legal practices during the war. Thus, many wealthy men—especially those like Alcorn who did not totally support secession—did not fight. They could keep their affairs in better condition and be prepared to begin again when the opportunity arose, as it did after Appomattox.

5. For a discussion of these points, see Cobb (1992) and Wayne (1983). My focus in this history is on the developments affecting and influencing the upper class in Mis-

sissippi, primarily because this is the class to which Faulkner himself belonged. As I have already mentioned, accounts of Reconstruction itself have changed dramatically, and more recent accounts emphasize the contributions of freed black Americans and how much they influenced the direction of Southern history. I only point to these events here, but my account does not at all mean to deny or downplay these occurrences.

6. For discussion of these points, see Genovese (1969, 63), Ransom and Sutch (1977, chap. 5), and Brandfon (1967, chap. 6).

One must mention here that this system of paternalism included the penitentiary and the convict-lease system of forced labor. Paternalists' benevolence was self-serving and supported by a system of institutional violence; however, the treatment of blacks in the convict-lease system and on the plantations shows that although the system was created and maintained by white men, it nevertheless required both blacks and whites more or less to follow a set of rules and codes that implied certain reciprocal obligations. But when a black man broke these rules and was sent to the penitentiary, white men no longer followed the rules, and their behaviors here demonstrate the underlying violence that supported the whole system. (For a discussion of the penitentiary at Parchman, Miss., see Oshinsky 1996.)

To some extent, also, these developments explain how Southerners, even those identifying with liberalism in general, had some stake in the social structure developed by paternalism. Many poor whites felt much more threatened, economically and personally, by the freedom of black Americans than did wealthy landowners whose ideological heritage enabled them to feel superior to both blacks and poor whites. By keeping freed blacks on plantations and in the country, wealthy whites secured the support of poor whites, allowing them to continue in their positions of power for a time. Although these poor, liberal-minded whites did not adhere to the same values as the paternalist plantocrats, they did not rebel until their interests were more obviously threatened.

7. The legacy of racism in this country has its origins in these very specific social arrangements and historical developments. A type of paternalism based solely on race was instituted in Mississippi and in much of the South. Nowhere else in the world did this type of particularly virulent racism continue after the end of slavery and the establishment of rights. Paternalism itself does not simply explain the racism of the South, for paternalist attitudes would extend to any and all in the lower classes. The main voice of this kind of thinking in the South was George Fitzhugh; however, it never developed. (See Fitzhugh 1960.) The complex web of forces keeping both paternalism and liberalism tied in a tense but effective relationship was the creation and legacy of the Redeemers, not those associated with paternalism. (For a discussion of how white supremacy can explain the uniqueness of American development, see Goldfield 1991.)

8. Devised to ensure white supremacy on the political level, the Mississippi Plan was developed initially to control the outcome of the 1875 elections. This plan consisted of terrorist tactics against both whites and blacks. Whites who had voted Republican were publicly ridiculed as lovers of blacks and traitors to their race, their shops and stores were boycotted and often their lives were threatened, and their children and wives were ostracized from society and ridiculed. The livelihoods and lives of blacks who had voted were also threatened; they were no longer allowed to buy goods or supplies for their farms and families.

The Mississippi Plan ended the two-party system in the state. Planter and Delta

Republicans had no choice but to vote Democratic; they were in effect forced to join the Democrats, and all political battles in the South were thereafter to be fought within the confines of the Democratic party.

9. The myth of the lost cause was popularized by Edward A. Pollard in his 1866 book *The Lost Cause: A New Southern History of the War of the Confederates.* There and in *The Lost Cause Regained* (1868), he glorified the world of the Old South and its heroes, especially Jeb Stuart. (See Osterweiss 1973, esp. chap. 1.)

10. For a discussion of the Mississippi Plan see Woodward (1951, chap. 12). For a discussion of Whig ideologies, deference and paternalism, see Slotkin (1985, chap. 4).

These men were safely ensconced in power partially because of the representative selection system and the convention system of electing public officials. There were no direct primaries in Mississippi for state and federal officials; only county representatives were elected, and they were not the only people from the county to go to state conventions: others were appointed. County electors—those who counted votes—were also appointed officials, and many elections in Mississippi were notoriously corrupt. Changes against the establishment were thus very hard to effect. Farmer and agrarian interests would constantly be frustrated by this system, and it was changed only in 1903, when James K. Vardaman ran for governor.

11. Although this form of rebellion was difficult, it indeed existed. Theodore Allen (1994, 150–51) lists several cases in which blacks and whites united to resist the efforts of wealthy planters. They are significant because they refute the argument of the time that it was natural for whites and blacks to feel antagonistic toward each other.

CHAPTER 2. FAULKNER'S IDEOLOGY: IDEOLOGY AND SUBJECTIVITY

1. For a discussion of these ideas, especially the concept of internally persuasive discourse, see Bakhtin (1981). Weinstein (1992) discusses how Bakhtin's theories relate to Faulkner's characters, but he does not address whether or how they apply to Faulkner.

The term *authorial ideology,* which I use extensively, is defined by Terry Eagleton as "the effect of the author's specific mode of biographical insertion into GI [General Ideology], a mode of insertion over-determined by a series of distinct factors: social class, sex, nationality, religion, geographical region and so on" (1978, 58).

2. Jehlen (1986, 11). In her introduction to *Ideology and Classic American Literature,* Jehlen's own sense of ideology has developed significantly from her discussion of Faulkner's work in *Class and Character in Faulkner's South* (1976). There, she had a much less formulated idea of ideology and its significance, and this affected the argument of the whole book. Nonetheless, Jehlen needs to be credited for beginning a still relatively unexplored avenue of investigation in Faulkner studies. Her work was certainly inspirational for me.

3. My explanation here is indebted to James Kavanaugh (1985). Although his article "Shakespeare in Ideology" naturally focuses on Shakespeare, there is an initial discussion of Marxist ideas as they relate to literary criticism.

4. Faulkner was amazingly sensitive both to the manifest and latent contents of his ideological milieu, almost as if he knew his sense of himself was tenuous and based only on the repression of various, other aspects of his surrounding world. This sensitivity and the ability to "let the voices speak for themselves" are partly responsible for his achievements and also for the constant tension in his work. Finally, we should remember that

the manifest and latent content, the dominant and repressed ideological content, are, of course, inextricably linked and mutually interdependent.

5. The information about Faulkner's relatives in this chapter comes mainly from Blotner (1974), books 1 and 2. For other takes on Faulkner's life, see Minter (1980), Oates (1987), and Karl (1989). Although these are rather different interpretations of Faulkner's life and art, they do not offer more information about Faulkner's relatives. In *William Faulkner and Southern History* (1993), Williamson offers many insights into the Falkners' lives and provides a good deal of new information; however, he too follows Blotner's lead in his understanding of Faulkner's relationship to his great-grandfather and his grandfather. The interpretive slant on Faulkner's relatives in this book is completely my own.

It should be noted that Karl's attempt to define Faulkner as an *American* writer has some connection to my overall project of seeing Faulkner as struggling with a heritage that is uniquely American. The ways we approach this question, however, and our outlooks on it, are different.

6. For those familiar with the discussion in Carolyn Porter (1981), this description of Faulkner's great-grandfather will not sound at all strange. I certainly agree with Porter's assessment of W. C. Falkner's character and place in society. I do not agree, however, with Porter's assessment of paternalism as simply a ruse or a front for capitalistic goals and enterprises. As I have explained, although some may use the images and language of paternalism to shield capitalistic pursuits, this does not mean paternalism itself is an illusion. Porter also does not discuss how W. C. Falkner's life and Sutpen's life story were affected by their identity as whites. The differences between Porter and myself will be explored in chapter 6.

7. For a discussion of Faulkner's desire for heroic action, see Bleikasten (1983); to understand Faulkner's feelings about the New South, see Meriwether (1973).

8. Interestingly, Mrs. Oldham would not allow Estelle to attend parties given by Sallie Murry, Faulkner's aunt, because of what she considered to be the democratic selection of guests. Faulkner was attracted to Estelle either despite or partly because of attitudes such as these. My reading is that he identified with that class and with those values and wanted to be part of it. For a discussion of the Oldhams, see Williamson (1993, chap. 5).

9. Although I approach this question from a different angle than Sensibar (1984) and Lind (1986), I do think there are many similarities between the insights Sensibar and I make about Faulkner's life and mind, especially as articulated in my chapter about *Sanctuary.*

10. My claim is that Faulkner did not just want to make a living as a writer, he wanted to gain widespread recognition. A comment he made in 1922 supports the contention that, to use other words, other people's opinions did indeed matter: "'I'll write a book they'll read. If they want a book to remember, by God, I'll write it'" (quoted in Williamson 1993, 193). Faulkner made comments such as these throughout his life. About *Flags in the Dust*, he wrote, "I have written THE book" (Williamson 1993, 210.) And, in a 1939 letter he wrote, "I am the best in America, by god" (Blotner 1977, 113). Recognition was indeed important to him.

11. In *The Politics* Aristotle was probably the first to discuss the concept of what we know today as natural aristocracy. This idea—that some men were born to rule and others to obey—was refined by Jefferson to mean that those who had so-called natural abil-

ity would reveal it when given the opportunity to compete with others in a democratic society.

My definition of this ideology is meant to be purely descriptive, not evaluative. Though I focus here on the ideology of natural aristocracy from the inside, so to speak, in the way Faulkner himself pictured it, we must always keep in mind that it can also be seen as a repressive and discriminatory system as well, especially for women and minorities, whose role in any system partially shaped by paternalism has always been subordinate to white men's no matter how important some of their functions might be.

12. In his preface to *Faulkner: The House Divided* (1983), Eric Sundquist claims that this public role was thrust upon Faulkner. I would argue that Faulkner accepted this role because it meshed with some deep-seated vision he had of himself, and that he took the role of responsible teacher seriously.

CHAPTER 3. *THE SOUND AND THE FURY:*
FAULKNER'S BIRTH INTO HISTORY

1. This quotation is from the 1972 edited version of Faulkner's introduction to *The Sound and the Fury* (Meriwether 1972, 708).

2. I utilize the term *Cavalier paternalism* in this chapter as a synonym for the paternalism I describe in chapter 1. After the Civil War, the ideology of the Old South was associated with the term *Cavalier* in discussions of the myth of the lost cause. Faulkner uses this term in the novel to point to that Old South system of values.

Discussions of Quentin have vacillated between seeing him as representative of a decaying aristocratic tradition, a remnant of the Old South gone sour due to some biological or metaphysical taint, and seeing him as "a more modern character trying merely to make moral sense out of the doom which has overtaken his family" (Jehlen 1976, 41), a Hamlet-figure trying to make sense of a senseless world. In *Figures of Division* James Snead moves away from these types of analyses, connecting Quentin's plight to the social situation by claiming that "the terms of his identity are collapsing all around him" (1986, 26). More in keeping with Snead, I will argue that Quentin Compson embodies an ideological orientation within Faulkner's sociohistorical milieu, one losing the social power it once possessed.

3. For historical dimensions to an ideology of race see chapter 1, and for a specific discussion of it and how it works in *Absalom, Absalom!* see chapter 7.

4. For a discussion of male role expectations within Cavalier ideology, and especially their implications for women, see Clinton (1982, esp. chaps. 3, 5, and 6) and Taylor (1979, esp. chaps. 5 and 6).

5. Horace Benbow, also associated with this class, has similar visions of grandeur in *Sanctuary,* a book where Faulkner explores these attitudes in detail and with a more critical eye.

6. The attitudes and behaviors of Bland, Head, and Ames toward women are very similar to those of the townsmen who discuss Temple Drake outside the courtroom in *Sanctuary.* There, one man states: "'I wouldn't have used no cob'" (1985c, 309).

7. Jones (1981) here quotes John Dollard (1957).

8. I think there are various connections between Quentin's psyche and the world Faulkner explores in *Sanctuary,* and the full social-psychological ramifications of Quentin's ideological affiliation will be explored in the next chapter. In linking Quentin's

section with *Sanctuary* I am in agreement with Noel Polk: "Add to this possibility the fact that during the winter and spring of 1929 Faulkner revised heavily the Quentin section of *The Sound and the Fury,* and it is possible to demonstrate a close compositional relationship among *Flags, Sanctuary,* and *The Sound and the Fury* that may well symbolize the degree to which all three spring from the same matrix" (1985, 18).

9. The figures most obviously connected to the old values of the past are Horace Benbow, Ike McCaslin, and Gavin Stevens, all of whom have little social power, who indeed renege on their chances for social power. Like he does with Quentin, Faulkner draws somewhat affectionate portrayals of these characters, but he also reveals their weaknesses and limitations, their almost churlish attachment to the past.

Faulkner himself, however, knew this feeling of estrangement from the world. In a 1925 review of a book of poems written by William A. Percy, Faulkner wrote: "Mr. Percy—like Alas! how many of us—suffered the misfortune of having been born out of his time" (Collins 1962, 71).

10. Though other characters in earlier works certainly could be said to be contemporary figures, none of them—not Bayard Sartoris, Horace Benbow, Donald Mahon, or any of the characters from *Mosquitoes*—are really important as social figures. They are more important as psychological types or for their place within an artistic plan and design.

11. Again, we need to remember the fine line one treads when talking about the conflict between paternalism and liberalism, and the sentiment expressed here does not mean to idealize paternalism or its social order. To quote Michael Wayne: "There is no need to exaggerate the benevolence of the former slaveowners. Their humane actions . . . derived from a perceived self-interest and an ideology deeply rooted on the old regime. If this ideology told them to care for the aged [of those families working on their fields], it also told them that they were entitled to unquestioning obedience from all blacks" (1983, 115). In some ways, the paternalist system had advantages; in other ways the one led by Redeemers had advantages. Neither allowed for freedom within the lower ranks of society.

In discussing Jason Compson, one could also easily make the case that indeed "all the Compson gave out before it got to [Jason]" as *The Sound and the Fury* claims (Faulkner 1984, 197), that within Faulkner's canon the Compson men embody the values, behaviors, and attitudes of paternalism until we get to Jason IV. Even in *Absalom, Absalom!* General Compson clearly functions from within this ideology and the contrast between him and Thomas Sutpen is made all the sharper because of it.

Assessments of Jason range from Bleikasten's comments that "[Jason's] ideas are all second-hand . . . they all come from the threadbare ideology of his cultural environment. The very texture of his speech testifies to his mental barrenness" (1976, 164) to Wittenberg's more positive remark that "running the household mark[s] him [Jason] as the one real 'adult' in the Compson family by 1928 [and] it is difficult not to be a little sympathetic with him" (1979, 85). My own interpretation of Jason's social and ideological position leans in the direction of Bleikasten; however, his argument about Jason's "mental barrenness" dismisses Jason's position as a viable, and indeed powerful, social force within Southern (one could argue American) history. Though Faulkner's account does imply the threadbare nature of Jason's ideology, this ideology also connects to powerful social developments—which originate in reassessments of the Southern past and continue with redefinitions of Southern futures.

12. Thadious Davis (1983) argues that Faulkner portrays the black community in *The Sound and the Fury* as a homogenous folk culture of simplicity and basic Christian faith. She sees these characterizations as positive and, to some extent, realistic. I agree with her insights into Faulkner's characterizations, but I contend that we must see all attempts to essentialize a black community, or the black race in general, as limited. And I would argue further that we need to do so especially when a black presence is romanticized to serve an underlying conservative social vision. Black culture in *The Sound and the Fury* is part of the Old South paternalist vision of a structured society where everyone has a place, but it can be positive only in a romanticized account. Finally, we must also remember that black religious experience in this country developed in part as a direct response to the specific historical conditions blacks faced, not as a natural outgrowth of so-called black culture.

Dilsey is far more important, I would argue, for what she reveals about Faulkner and Faulkner's view of the world than she is as a representation of what might be labeled real black experience in Mississippi. As Jehlen (1976) and Snead (1986) both point out, Dilsey's salvation has absolutely no social significance; it offers no social salvation and enables Dilsey to find meaning in her life only if she accepts her oppressed social role. As one black preacher expressed it in 1941: "'We are the policemen of the Negroes. . . . If we did not keep down their ambitions and divert them into religion, there would be upheaval in the South'" (qtd. in Tindall 1967, 566).

CHAPTER 4. *SANCTUARY:* THE SOCIAL PSYCHOLOGY OF PATERNALISM

1. Until recently, when feminist readings of *Sanctuary* began to surface, Freudian analyses had been the most convincing and stimulating discussions of this novel. Perhaps the best is John T. Matthews, "The Elliptical Nature of *Sanctuary*" (1984). Another very good psychoanalytical reading of this novel is John T. Irwin, "Horace Benbow and the Myth of Narcissa" (1992). For a feminist reading see Diane Roberts, "Ravished Belles: Stories of Rape and Resistance in *Flags in the Dust* and *Sanctuary*" (1988–89), and her 1994 book *Faulkner and Southern Womanhood*.

2. Matthews (1984) first claimed that the dynamics of Horace Benbow's world set the conditions for Temple Drake's story.

3. These quotations appear in the revised version of the novel (Faulkner 1985c, 295 and 280, respectively). Throughout this chapter I quote extensively from both the revised and the original versions of the novel, seeing them as two parts of an extended text, as suggested in Polk (1985). The references will be cited as Faulkner (1981) for the edition of the original text and Faulkner (1985c) for the edition of the corrected text. See bibliography.

4. Many critics have labeled Horace Benbow and his world bourgeois. This label is often used to refer not to a historically specific class or a specific society, but to a set behaviors or qualities the critics have disliked. Being bourgeois can be associated with relying on appearance over reality, as in Petesch (1979), or with effeminate, superficial qualities, as in Polk (1984).

To clarify the connection between Horace and Judge Drake and to indicate that Horace's status as a gentleman is not purely a description of personal behavior but a social-class designation, Faulkner also makes definite connections between Horace and the title "judge." In a few places in both texts, Faulkner has Clarence Snopes call Horace

"Judge Benbow" (1985c, 182). More than a simple mistake, Snopes persists in using this designation even after Horace corrects him, indirectly connecting Horace to his own father—Judge Will Benbow—and the social position his father held in a different type of society. Considering also the prominence of Temple's refrain, "My father's a judge," Faulkner also indirectly links Horace to Judge Drake. A real connection exists, then, between the personal, descriptive label of gentleman and the social, class designation of judge.

5. The description of the Old Frenchman's Place reads as follows: "The house was a gutted ruin rising gaunt and stark out of a grove of unpruned cedar trees. . . . gardens and lawns long since gone back to jungle" (1985c, 8). The description of the Benbow home reads: "The house was of red brick . . . in the uncut grass that year after year had gone rankly and lustily back to seed. . . . The cedars needed pruning too, their dark tips . . . breaking on against the house itself in a fixed whelming surge" (1985c, 61).

Though my focus in this discussion will be on Horace Benbow, the association of Horace and other male characters such as Quentin Compson and Gail Hightower purposely implies that what will be said about Horace applies equally to these others. Horace becomes representative of a certain type, if you will, that appears frequently in this early part of Faulkner's life in various guises. Its appearance indicates how significant this ideological perspective was for Faulkner. In addition, if we doubt the relation between Theweleit and Faulkner, we should keep in mind Faulkner's character Percy Grimm in *Light in August;* about Grimm, Faulkner commented that he had "created a Nazi" before Hitler did (Cowley 1966, 32). Grimm, like Horace Benbow, was interested in order and civilization, and though he was more active than Horace, my discussion will reveal ways in which the two are very similar.

6. From this discussion we can see how *Sanctuary* is the Faulkner novel most specifically focused on what some would call an ideology of gender. Although I understand the term, I find it a bit misleading, for ideologies of gender do not exist separately and distinctly from ideologies of class, for the most part.

7. Roberts (1988–89, 22). Roberts discusses, here and in her book *Faulkner and Southern Womanhood,* how in Faulkner's canon evil is a code word for female sexuality. I agree. There are many similarities between the way Roberts and I read both the South's sexual politics and *Sanctuary,* although our insights come from different avenues of investigation.

It is also easy to make connections between these images and those related to Caddy Compson, her "dirty drawers," and Joanna Burden, who relishes Joe Christmas being "Negro."

8. Other critics have assumed that Horace's identification in this scene is with Temple, that he "becomes" Temple, primarily because of the reference to the shucks. I believe, however, that the movement of Horace's thoughts is away from Temple to envisioning Little Belle in a scene like the one Temple experiences. Earlier in the book, Horace remembers his trip on a train with Little Belle, and this horrific scene seems to place her back on a train without Horace—that is, unescorted, as was Temple. Her deflowering seems to be enacted in Horace's nightmare.

9. In relation to this point, we can recall Quentin Compson's remarks to his sister Caddy in *The Sound and the Fury,* when she discovers him fooling around with Natalie in the barn. He calls Natalie "a dirty girl" (1984, 134).

10. That Horace is undergoing this implicit conflict is indicated in a couple of places

in the novel. After he tells Ruby that God might be foolish but at least He's a gentleman, she tells him that she always thought He was a man (1985c, 295). Later, in conversation with Horace, Lee comments, "'What sort of men have you lived with all your life?'" (1985c, 295)—implying that Horace is no kind of man at all. In this new world, this new social structure, all that had maintained Horace's definition of masculinity is in the process of fading.

Gowan's situation also indicates a struggle between definitions of gentleman and man. Gowan overtly attempts to decipher whether Temple is either a lady or a whore so that he will know how to treat her. However, as his embarrassment about getting drunk and vomiting and his interactions with both Narcissa and Temple reveal, he more covertly struggles with whether he is a gentleman or a man. In his treatment of Narcissa, Gowan seems to want to adopt all the trappings of the Southern gentleman courting the lady. In his treatment of Temple, he seems to want to prove he is a man by "having his way with her." He never seems to resolve any of these conflicts; thus, he can also be said to show that both aspects of paternalist masculinity cannot exist in the same man in this new social world.

11. The attitudes and behaviors of Popeye, like those of Horace, can be linked to those of other Faulkner characters. Popeye clearly has similarities to Jason Compson, who prefers giving money to his "whore" Lorraine to having sexual relations with her, and even to Joe Christmas, who at first has intense conflict about having sexual relations with the black girl in the barn. He behaves violently toward this girl and eventually kills Joanna Burden because of her attitudes toward him and sexuality.

12. This definition of masculinity slips into criticism of Faulkner as well. Polk comments: "Doubtless part of [Horace] admires the Negro's neat, simple, passionate solution to his marital troubles [that is, cutting off his wife's head], and perhaps in his *fantasies* he wishes he were aggressive enough, *masculine* enough, passionate enough, to solve his own problems so completely" (1985, 21; my emphasis). To identify this kind of behavior with masculinity is an ideological statement influenced by a historically specific version of masculinity. Theweleit offers the best response: "The sexuality of the patriarch is less 'male' than it is deadly" (1987, 221–22).

13. The characterization of Narcissa in *Sanctuary* differs somewhat from her characterization in *Sartoris* and *Flags in the Dust*. (For those who do not know the history, when *Flags* was first rejected by the publisher, it was revised as *Sartoris* and published in 1929. That book left out much of the material dealing with Horace.) There, Narcissa is seen to have reactions of both attraction and repulsion to Byron Snopes's rather vulgar love letters, and she is thus not seen to be as pure as she is seen to be in *Sanctuary*. Even there, though, Narcissa represses her sexual feelings and thoughts so that no one in her social world ever witnesses them. In *Sanctuary*, the two sides of Narcissa that Faulkner explores in *Flags in the Dust* and in the story "There Was a Queen" are split into different characters, Narcissa and Ruby/Temple. For a discussion of Narcissa along these lines see Lahey (1996), and for a discussion of *Sanctuary* indirectly sympathetic to my insights here see Clarke (1994).

14. All the cases discussed in this section reveal just how much the novel's perspective derives from paternalism as well as how much the novel exposes the social ramifications of masculine fantasies. The subjectivities or personalities revealed by Narcissa, Popeye, Ruby, and Temple all derive from the ideology of paternalism. These are positions through which this ideology works to identify individuals. (In Temple's case, the

holders of the ideology had to work harder than in the other cases.) That Temple *would* be treated by poor, out-of-work men the way she is in *Sanctuary* is no more "true" than if she had subdued them via kung-fu and brought them to the authorities, or if she fell in love with one boy there who returned her home and was rewarded by the father with money to attend college. All of these stories *could* occur, depending on the perspective of the writer: if Temple's explorations into sexuality were narrated by Kate Chopin, say, we would probably read a very different story. Likewise, to depict reactions to a rape the way they are depicted here, as if this experience would unleash raging lust, seems particularly, and even absurdly, the perspective of a paternalist.

Even if we can find people in our world who do behave in the way these characters do, we cannot deny the perspective from which this book depicts its characters. Like the real people they might represent, these characters reveal the operations of an ideology that has successfully defined—or interpellated—human beings as very specific types of human subjects (with distinct subjectivities)—to some extent, exactly what *Sanctuary* is about.

In this context, my view parallels Minrose Gwin's claim that looking for examples of "authentic female subjectivity" in Faulkner is a fruitless activity (1988–89, 64). Rarely if ever does one find women in Faulkner who are not essentially projections of male fear and/or desire.

15. Robert Moore (1986) argues that Temple's passivity after her rape reveals her complicity with evil. But, Temple has already been taught that activity, on her part, is dangerous; how else can she behave? To blame her is to assign blame to the wrong party.

CHAPTER 5. *As I Lay Dying* and *Light in August:* The Social Realities of Liberalism

1. That Faulkner was aware of these other developments in the South is at least partially indicated by the comment of Lucas Burch in *Light in August:* "'I be dog if it aint enough to make a man turn downright bowlsheyvick'" (Faulkner 1985b, 438). The fact that the years 1929 and 1931 saw major protests in the South against white supremacy by a union of communists and blacks also must be seen as a backdrop to the narrative of *Light in August.* That this real, historical union is not to be found in Faulkner points again to his identification with the dominant ideologies of his time.

2. Ahearn explains Marx: "The concept of division of labor, initially visible in the family and attaining myriad productive and estranged guises in modern society, has its historically most fundamental role in the opposition between country and city" (1989, 5). For Marx's discussion of these ideas see *The German Ideology* and *The Manifesto of the Communist Party* in Marx (1972).

3. Of course, these two beliefs have historically always been associated with one another, the Protestant Reformation coinciding with the rise of the bourgeoisie. The connection of this historical development to ideological developments has been known since R. H. Tawney's *Religion and the Rise of Capitalism* and Max Weber's *The Protestant Ethic and the Spirit of Capitalism.* See Tawney (1962) and Weber (1958).

4. In contrast to Kinney, who believes that Anse is "prompted by his lifelong commitment to the forces of growth" (1978, 97), I see Anse's words and actions to be particularly repugnant to Faulkner.

5. Anse makes these comments in a number of places: "'I promised her'" (17); "'I give her my promise. . . . Her mind was set on it'" (114).

6. Commentaries on *As I Lay Dying* vary in their discussions of the novel between determining that its "journey from beginning to end is a travesty" (Vickery 1959, 52) to seeing that "one of Faulkner's principal themes in *As I Lay Dying*—perhaps the principal theme—is the nature of the heroic deed" (Brooks 1963, 142–43). Michael Millgate speaks for a common chorus when he says, "this simple story of poor farmers . . . is deliberately presented as being played out against a background of cosmic scale" (1966, 110), while Bleikasten perhaps expresses the only consensus: "[the novel] may be read in more than one way" (1973, 8). Most critics until recently limited their discussions to the problems of the characters' consciousness and to a discussion about which character serves as the focal point. For a different reading, one influenced by Marxist theories, see Matthews (1992).

My reading of the novel has been greatly influenced by the work of a colleague of mine in graduate school, Andrea Kwasny.

7. Kartiganer views these objects as transitionary as they afford a passage of grief to recovery. He sees their material desires as "the means by which the Bundrens simultaneously fulfill the originating narrative and revise its significance, transforming the procession of the dead into a progress of the living" (1989, 38).

8. Here, too, we must remember Grimm's comment when he sees Hightower trying to protect Christmas: "'Jesus Christ! . . . Has every preacher and old maid in Jefferson taken their pants down to the yellowbellied son of a bitch?'" (464). Obviously, he thinks that the natural order of things has been thrown into a state of perverted chaos.

9. Many critics, including Sundquist (1983), Kartiganer (1988), Bleikasten (1987), and Davis (1983), see race as the central concern of *Light in August,* and many understand Joe's plight as concerned either with choosing between being "white" or "black" or with rejecting both choices. Although I agree with the contention of Davis and Kartiganer that race is a social construct, I do not think Faulkner explores this insight in this book (as he will in *Absalom, Absalom!*).

10. In general my argument agrees with one of Gena McKinley's central points: "It is this racist ideology—that there is a 'blood' difference between blacks and whites—that Christmas also accepts and that finally destroys him" (1997, 155). I disagree, though, with the point that she and Jenkins (1981) make that Joe behaves "as if" he were black. He does so, at times, I would argue, only in that he certainly understands "black" as being inferior to "white"—as the racist ideology would have it and as he has internalized it in his thinking. (In other words, for us to say that anyone behaves as if he or she were white or black has no meaning at all.) On the other hand, Joe does not always allow society's definitions to control his behavior. Confusion about his identity seems to me the central question of the novel, and Joe explores and experiments in order to discover, he hopes, his true identity.

11. My discussion is set particularly against the discussions of Davis (1983) and Sundquist (1983), as valuable and important as those discussions are. Sundquist is primarily influenced by psychocultural theories about race. This terminology comes from Allen (1994 and 1997). Allen explains that one of the leading proponents of the psychocultural school is Winthrop Jordan, and Sundquist bases his own discussions about race on Jordan's 1969 work, *White Over Black.* Like Jordan, he implies an irrevocable distance between white and black: "Faulkner was haunted by an unanswerable question:

why were niggers and whites made? . . . And why this awful difference between white and black?" (Sundquist 1983, 95).

Davis takes less of an even stance on this issue, claiming that Faulkner explores how race is socially constructed and how the notion of "the Negro" had become an abstraction in the South. She does claim, however, that Joe Christmas does not accept the terms of his society, and she creates a Faulkner who criticizes all the negative ways in which the South thought about race. For me, those concerns in *Light in August* are balanced with the need for social cohesion and order, and I think that Faulkner's own ideas about race were not as clear and defined as Davis makes them seem. Faulkner's literary explorations, I believe, developed over time, and in *Absalom, Absalom!* he would offer a much different stance on the Southern ideology of race. But, race is one means through which people seek to define the world, and I believe Faulkner operated from within essentialist notions about race in *Light in August*.

In reference to these points, I would remind readers of my comments in note 2 in this chapter: Faulkner did not give any credibility in his fiction to the real historical union of communists and blacks protesting white supremacy and all of its attitudes. These groups, active during the time Faulkner wrote this book, were arguing vehemently that race and racial attitudes were indeed social constructs—very much like the lawyer, Max, in Richard Wright's *Native Son*. Faulkner did not give much credence to these beliefs and felt that Wright's explorations of these ideas in *Native Son* lessened the quality of his writing. (See Meriwether and Millgate 1980.)

Most critics of Faulkner understandably wish to show respect to America's greatest novelist and treat the question of racism in Faulkner with sensitivity. I think this approach is right even though I see *Light in August* as working within essentialist categories. My point, though, is that when he was confronted with the prospect of social upheaval—as the outbreaks of democracy and demands from the lower classes seemed to him to be—Faulkner became even more deeply concerned with social stability, order, and hierarchy and sought varying means to accomplish these goals in a world where paternalism had no social power. For other excellent discussions about race in Faulkner, see Towner (1995) and Weinstein (1995 and 1996).

12. Gwynn and Blotner (1959, 209–10). Again, in response to the temptation to label Faulkner a racist, I think we need to see these explorations within the context of the novel and its social world. Faulkner dearly feels the need for some kind of order in society—don't we all?—and these particular responses are possibilities when all in society is fluid and seemingly chaotic. To those who would claim that I am attempting to stand on both sides of the line, all I can say is that I am. Faulkner, to my mind, was both shaped by his world and strove against that world to work toward other visions. *Light in August* reveals more of how the world of paternalism shaped him than vice versa, I believe.

CHAPTER 6. *ABSALOM, ABSALOM!* AND NATURAL ARISTOCRACY

1. Faulkner uses these words to describe his own thinking about *Flags in the Dust*. (See Blotner 1973.)

2. I have culled the biographical information for this discussion from Blotner (1974, books 5, 6, and 7), Wittenberg (1979, esp. chap. 6), Karl (1989, esp. chaps. 14–17), and Williamson (1993).

Both Wittenberg and Karl offer interestingly relevant discussions about this period of Faulkner's life. Wittenberg tells of Faulkner's repeated trips to Memphis before his marriage, speculating that Faulkner faced marriage to the traditional Southern belle with some fears about his sexuality. These actions also can be seen to connect Faulkner to the ideology of paternalism, as discussed in chapters 3 and 4. Karl mentions Faulkner's need to be a patriarch and his desire to prove himself in the eyes of Estelle's family, an upper-class one that had once rejected him. His discussion is somewhat similar to Zender (1989).

3. This authorial ideology is also implied in the narrative complexity of *Absalom, Absalom!* This novel's narrative complexities can be seen to reiterate Faulkner's desire to be considered a great artist. Faulkner again uses individual narrators telling tales from their own particular, social vantage points. He incorporates intense monologues, flashbacks, narratives inside narratives, and frequent time shifts, unfolding the story like a detective novel, slowly unraveling information. In these ways, the novel posits an audience similar to the target audience of both *The Sound and the Fury* and *As I Lay Dying*. As David Paul Ragan states, agreeing with many other critics: "At the highest level, Faulkner designed *Absalom, Absalom!* for the most dedicated and discriminating reader, perhaps more so than any other of his books" (1987, 161). Faulkner himself commented on the book's completion: "'I think it's the best novel yet written by an American'" (qtd. in Blotner 1974, 927).

Absalom, Absalom! also differs from these other novels, however; unlike them, characters here speak their stories to others. Almost all the narrative is composed of conversations between two people. This type of oral narration—the union of speaking and listening—separates the book from earlier efforts and attaches it to an older social system based on oral narration.

4. Genovese's account of the South has established the basic terms of a debate in historical scholarship between Marxist historians and others. Marxist historians who follow Genovese include Mandle (1978), Wiener (1978, 1979), and Billings (1979). Others who believe the planters did have a decided class consciousness include Wayne (1983), Oakes (1982), and Allen (1994, 1997).

5. The tenuous hegemony of paternalism was demonstrated by the states' secession. Many states where slavery existed and plantocracy was the norm nonetheless voted not to secede. Many people in these states did not want to fight for the plantocrats' interests, even though they also never decided to fight directly against them either. The South's defeat in the Civil War was connected, then, to the paternalists' tenuous hold on hegemony.

6. Those who testify to the existence of paternalism in the South include Wyatt-Brown (1982), Hundley (1979), and, of course, the granddaddy of all paternalists, Fitzhugh (1960).

7. Here, again, as we saw in *Sanctuary*, Faulkner reveals how ideologies ostensibly concerning class contain definitions of racial and gender identity as well.

8. For a discussion of the origins of Southern settlers see Miller (1981).

9. Despite the fact that Sutpen's allegiance to white supremacy is obvious in his treatment of Eulalia and Charles Bon, his interactions with those characters, as with most of his interactions with people of African heritage, reveal his ultimate allegiance to liberalism. First, Sutpen feels as if his conscience is clear after "buying off" his first wife and their son. He does not recognize Bon's need to be identified with his father; Sutpen

feels no paternalistic responsibility. Also, in his interactions with his slaves, Sutpen wants somehow to demonstrate his superiority to them through fighting. He does not simply assume his inherent right to rule. Would Faulkner ever have depicted General Compson as one who would physically fight with his slaves?

Of course, what we are confronted with in Sutpen is also Faulkner's depiction of a lower-class white man making his way to the top, and some of this—Sutpen's surviving an assault by a couple of hundred Haitians and thereby gaining their respect and fear, as absurd as that might seem—stems from Faulkner's own attitudes toward both lower-class whites and "natives" from the Caribbean. Nonetheless, Sutpen's actions generally are consistent with an ideological heritage that does not assume *inherent* superiority. Even though Sutpen has no qualms about asserting his superior will, he usually performs some feat that justifies his superiority to himself.

I turn to a discussion of the racial issues of the novel in the following chapter.

10. This aspect of Sutpen's life may indeed have biographical overtones, revealing that *Absalom* too is close to Faulkner.

11. In the nineteenth-century American imagination, Haiti was the prime example of what could happen if the forces lurking in the lower orders of society were unleashed too quickly. Faulkner's sending Sutpen to Haiti further connects him to questions about the possible chaos of democracy and the extension of freedom to those who do not know how to use it well. (See Slotkin 1985 and Godden 1994.)

I discuss racial issues in the next chapter as well as the fact that Sutpen's acceptance into Jefferson also has much to do with the South's fear of revolution.

12. I refer here to the America created in Crèvecoeur (1964).

13. Sutpen thus treats Jones in a way similar to the way he acts toward the black Haitians: his strength justifies his superior position, not his inherent worth. That Sutpen sits and drinks with Jones in his store (after the war) also demonstrates a degree of closeness usually not admitted by paternalists. Judith and Rosa reveal just how differently Sutpen treats Jones through their refusal to allow Jones to even enter the house while Sutpen is away.

14. Whether these types of men actually did exist is not of concern to me here. On one hand, one could argue that men like Wash Jones, who believed they were indeed not as good as others, must have existed in order for the South's paternalism to last for very long. On the other, one could say that only men in the upper class believed that those in the lower class felt this way. What is important is that Faulkner obviously believed that men in the lower class felt as Jones does.

15. I differ here with Weinstein (1992), who, in describing Sutpen and Wash, comments that there are two classes here but only one ideology. My reading sees two ideologies, one with which Jones and Compson identify and another with which Sutpen identifies.

16. I need to note again that Porter (1981) discusses ideas relevant to my argument, and I need to make a distinction. Porter claims that Sutpen's story highlights *American* dilemmas in its uncovering of a broken human bond between white and black. Although I agree that the problem of race relations is probably the single most important problem facing America, I try to explain that Faulkner's South and Faulkner's America are more complicated than Porter makes them out to be. Race is a central problem in America not because of capitalism per se, as Porter would have it; it is also the legacy of a ruling-class policy that pits poor whites and blacks against each other along racial lines so they do

not see their connection along class lines. There certainly could be capitalist societies in which whites and blacks got along. We must be careful not to equate ruling-class ideology with all of America, especially since the geographical nation known as America has seen many, many instances of cooperation and even love between people of African and European descent.

17. This genetic explanation for Sutpen's inadequacy explains, for me, Faulkner's constant repetition of the word *innocence* when referring to Sutpen's character. This repetition serves as the only explanation Faulkner offers for Sutpen's behavior. Clearly, however, the word does not really explain anything. It serves, then, as an emblem, a code word for where the problem exists—in Sutpen's biological makeup.

CHAPTER 7. *ABSALOM, ABSALOM!* AND THE SOUTHERN IDEOLOGY OF RACE

1. My discussion in this chapter follows a relatively untapped avenue of investigation in Faulkner studies that has been influenced by much of the wonderful work being done in race theory. Those who are interested should consult Guillaumin (1995), Goldberg (1990), Harding (1993), Roediger (1991), hooks (1992), and Frankenberg (1993). Morrison (1992) is a book that everyone should read. Within Faulkner studies, Weinstein (1996) has again taken the lead with *What Else But Love?*

2. For example, *Faulkner and Race,* edited by Fowler and Abadie (1987), contains no citations to any of the socioeconomic historians. There is a reference to Winthrop Jordan in Snead's essay (1987, 168), and I would argue that the volume in general reveals the influence of Jordan's approach.

3. I believe this seeming split in Faulkner's own attitude is real and is revealed in the different ways he approaches the question of race in *Light in August* and *Absalom, Absalom!* The emphasis in *Light in August* is to assert the biological, genetic, and natural belief in race identity, and the emphasis in *Absalom, Absalom!* is to investigate its social construction—although both novels have vestiges of the other approach in them.

4. It should be noted that whether in *The Sound and the Fury, Absalom, Absalom!,* or *Go Down, Moses,* the Compsons, excluding Jason Compson IV, function as the voice of the upper, ruling, knowledgeable, and respectable class for Faulkner.

5. Of course, here we also find an explanation of Henry's murder of Bon. Despite his emotional attachment to Bon, Henry sees that his entire existence depends on the separation of white from black and that Bon's marriage to Judith would subvert the very structure of that world.

6. Bon can be seen as well to be noble rather than self-serving, because all he wants from Sutpen is recognition. He says he will leave Mississippi, not marry Judith, and take nothing tangible from Sutpen if Sutpen will only recognize the blood connection. That he wants to be recognized as a son and have his humanity validated by his father seems a justifiable goal.

CHAPTER 8. THE SNOPES TRILOGY AS SOCIAL VISION

1. The story of Bayard's development of an independent moral code stands in sharp contrast to Quentin Compson's plight and his inability to do the same. It also signifies Faulkner's growing independence from the ideological words of his family.

Faulkner's publishers pressured him into changing the title of *If I Forget Thee, Jerusa-*

lem to *The Wild Palms,* the title with which it was published in 1939. The original title has been restored since 1990.

2. In thinking about *A Fable* we can also see how it relates to the ideas of natural aristocracy I have already discussed. The corporal, the Christ-figure in the book, inspires his peers to act through his own character and commitment, not through coercion; he serves as an example to all. Faulkner juxtaposes him against the Colonel, who represents institutional authority gained through heritage.

As is implied in this discussion, Zender's *The Crossing of the Ways* (1989) has been suggestive to me, and it bears some relation to my project in this chapter. Zender argues that the second half of Faulkner's life was characterized by his desire to compensate for loss through teaching (as opposed to the first half of his life where he compensated for loss through imagination). Obviously, I agree with the assertion that Faulkner had a need to teach that became more manifest in the later works; however, one of the primary points of my argument is that Faulkner's entire career was characterized by his need to compensate for loss through writing and that through this writing Faulkner defined and exhibited a social identity for which he had always been striving. All of Faulkner's fiction can be seen to be struggling with sociohistorical voices, attempting to fit itself into these in some manner.

In his epilogue "The Poetics of Space," Zender discusses Faulkner's bifurcated settings in the novels of his late career. The conflict produces "a search for a high place—the 'pinnacle' of the Nobel Prize speech, the mountain of *A Fable*—from which to engage once again in comprehensive, authoritative, and time-defying acts of visionary seeing. On the other hand, it produces the prison setting, into which Faulkner repeatedly inserts mute relics of an earlier age, who either must learn to speak across a generational or ideological gap or who must resign themselves to bearing silent witness to the obliteration of the meaning they embody" (1989, 143–44). What I hope to show in this chapter is that this latter condition is caused, for Faulkner, by the former—that these two seemingly separate settings are part of the same problem—the demise of natural aristocrats and benevolent paternalists from the South. Those figures of authority can recognize the value of the mute relics and give them voice. Faulkner specifically adopts this role, claims it for himself, while showing the societal effects of this demise. The conflict, as I see it, is between Faulkner's vision of the way the world should be and the way he thought the world was.

3. Both sources quoted here, Grimwood (1987) and Snead (1986), offer arguments related to my own. Grimwood gives an excellent explanation of the narrative and linguistic structures of *The Hamlet,* showing how they connect to Faulkner's political fears about the rise of the rednecks. He situates his argument in the context of the narrative structures of southwestern humor. Snead argues that the trilogy epitomizes the social divisions inherent in Frenchman's Bend and that the threat to this hamlet is the self-destruction of its figures of authority, not the evil of Snopes. In the sense that the economic systems of Frenchman's Bend place Varner and de Spain in precarious positions, vulnerable to those who can master these systems better than they, I would agree with Snead. My argument also claims that Faulkner nonetheless asserts another possible authority that would not self-destruct or be vulnerable to these forces.

4. Interesting in this regard are Faulkner's comments about the difference between Sutpen and Flem Snopes: "Only Sutpen had a grand design. Snopes's design was pretty base—he just wanted to get rich" (Gwynn and Blotner 1959, 97).

5. As Woodward explains it, barn-burning was a form of protest by tenant farmers against their exploitation (1951, 415). Indeed, it was their only possible form of protest in an intensely labor-repressive system.

6. Two points need to be made about the ideas expressed in this paragraph. First, the story of Ab's involvement with the Sartorises has also led to his being soured. He had been involved with Rosa Millard, Bayard Sartoris's grandmother, selling horses during the Civil War. Eventually Rosa gets killed, and Bayard Sartoris, along with his black companion Ringo, hunts Ab down and exacts some retribution. Faulkner's attitude toward these actions remains debatable. On one hand, he obviously does not idealize Sartoris and his kind; on the other, it is not clear that he condemns Sartoris's actions either. In a sense, Ab broke a code of honor by getting a woman involved with his dealings and not protecting her. Faulkner would seemingly support this punishment. Also, paternalism for Faulkner had lost some social power and those who adopt some of its values in his novels have lost their ability to act—Quentin Compson and Gavin Stevens are the obvious examples. That Sartoris can act in defense of honor may not be completely wrong in Faulkner's eyes.

In other places, Faulkner seems to offer support for Colonel John Sartoris, Bayard's father, for his pursuits after the Civil War, which involve a vision of the entire South, not just himself as Sutpen's plans do. See *The Unvanquished* (Faulkner 1966, 256).

Second, regarding paternalists' treatment of those who work for them, Kerr discusses William Percy's comments about the economic system of his family: "William Percy . . . speaks as a member of one of the best families of the old tradition; with unquestioned benevolence and integrity, he worked his plantation on a fifty-fifty sharecropping basis with his Negro workers. . . . Even while defending this system, Percy elaborates on the abuses of it under inferior upstarts 'on the make.' His attitude toward Negroes is that of benevolent paternalism" (1969, 146). This quote, though obviously somewhat self-serving, shows that there were different attitudes projected by landowners. It should not be at all surprising that Faulkner himself comes to believe in benevolent paternalism as described here; after all, he identified with the Percys.

7. Various critics, including Stroble (1980), Wilson (1980), Matthews (1982), and Marcus (1960), have discussed Flem's similarities to Varner.

8. Critics who discuss Ratliff in these terms include Millgate (1966), Brooks (1963), Vickery (1959), Kerr (1969), Kinney (1978), Snead (1986), Taylor (1983), and Matthews (1982).

9. Faulkner emphasizes Ratliff's opinion about Varner by having him repeat it twice during the course of the novel. Ratliff makes almost identical comments at the opening of "The Long Summer" section (174). Faulkner wants to stress that Flem alone did not beat Ratliff.

10. Faulkner will later hint at the reason why Ratliff has proven unworthy—he is from the wrong class; his language only reaches so far and stops (see Faulkner 1957, 260–61).

11. It should be remembered that the people who support de Spain are the people of Faulkner's "third race," whom Faulkner does not value very highly in his scheme of Yoknapatawpha.

In the quotation of Gavin Stevens's comments, he is not literally describing the actions of de Spain and Varner; he addresses these words to the actions of Wall Street Panic Snopes. The trilogy makes clear, however, that Wall Snopes is not this kind of person.

He gets supported in his business by Ratliff, marries a woman who hates Flem, and remains happily in his class helping the community flourish. Faulkner would later comment very positively about him. My claim stems from an obvious truth about Gavin's conversation as stated by Chick Mallison in *The Town:* "when you heard it you realised it was always true, only a little cranksided" (182).

12. In *Culture and Society* (1983), Raymond Williams discusses the changes from notions of culture as interconnected relationships among people to notions of a society whose members exist more as separate entities pursuing individual goals. These developments coincide with the developments of capitalist societies and are part of the ideological structures within capitalism.

13. Brooks (1963) discusses a tradition of a code of honor in both the folk culture of lower classes and the aristocratic culture of upper classes and claims that these shared principles unify the two classes. To a certain extent, he is right; however, he does not point to the fact that this unity is a hierarchical one in which the upper class keeps power. Mink has a definite value for Faulkner precisely because he does recognize his "rightful" place in the system as inferior. Faulkner's vision always remained hierarchical.

14. Gregory (1976) discusses the positive potentials of the values of communism represented by both Mink and Linda. These claims seem to me to be a bit stretched, for Faulkner's vision remains primarily romantic. As I explain, the ultimate cause for both Mink's and Linda's revenge lies in their recognition of kinship ties. This recognition connects them to social structures of the past rather than those of the future, which a communist society would represent. Brooks (1963) discusses *The Mansion* as Attic tragedy and speaks indirectly to this point.

CHAPTER 9. *THE REIVERS:* IMAGINARY
RESOLUTIONS AND UTOPIAN YEARNINGS

1. Slotkin (1985) discusses these ideas under the rubric of "The New Paternalism"—an attitude that developed during and after Reconstruction (see esp. 306–9.)

2. Both Bleikasten (1990) and Mortimer (1983) discuss Faulkner in this way.

3. This whole process is discussed in Williams (1983). It was this process that Marx was trying to counterbalance with his critiques of life within capitalism.

Works Cited

Ahearn, Edward J. 1989. *Marx and Modern Fiction.* New Haven and London: Yale University Press.

Allen, Theodore W. 1994. *The Invention of the White Race,* vol. 1: *Racial Oppression and Social Control.* London and New York: Verso.

———. 1997. *The Invention of the White Race,* vol. 2: *The Origin of Racial Oppression in Anglo-America.* London and New York: Verso.

Althusser, Louis. 1971. "Ideology and Ideological State Apparatuses." In his *Lenin and Philosophy and Other Essays.* Translated by Ben Brewster. New York and London: Monthly Review Press.

Aristotle. 1984. *The Politics.* Chicago: University of Chicago Press.

Ayers, Edward L. 1992. *The Promise of the New South: Life after Reconstruction.* Oxford and New York: Oxford University Press.

Bakhtin, M. M. 1981. "Discourse in the Novel." In his *The Dialogic Imagination.* Translated by Caryl Emerson and Michael Holquist. Austin: University of Texas Press.

Bennett, Lerone, Jr. 1967. *Black Power, USA: The Human Side of Reconstruction, 1867–1877.* Chicago: Johnson Publishing Co.

Berman, Marshall. 1988 [1982]. *All That Is Solid Melts into Air: The Experience of Modernity.* New York: Penguin.

Billings, Dwight B., Jr. 1979. *Planters and the Making of a "New South": Class, Politics, and Development in North Carolina, 1865–1900.* Chapel Hill: University of North Carolina Press.

Bleikasten, Andre. 1973. *Faulkner's* As I Lay Dying. Translated by Roger Little. Bloomington and London: Indiana University Press.

———. 1976. *The Most Splendid Failure: Faulkner's* The Sound and the Fury. Bloomington and London: Indiana University Press.

———. 1983. "For/Against an Ideological Reading of Faulkner's Novels." In *Faulkner and Idealism: Perspectives from Paris,* edited by Michel Gresset and Patrick Samway, S.J. Jackson and London: University Press of Mississippi.

———. 1985. "Terror and Nausea: Bodies in *Sanctuary.*" *Faulkner Journal* 1.1: 17–29.

———. 1990. *The Ink of Melancholy: Faulkner's Novels from* The Sound and the Fury *to* Light in August. Bloomington and Indianapolis: Indiana University Press.

Blotner, Joseph. 1973. "William Faulkner's Essay on the Composition of *Sartoris.*" *Yale University Library Gazette* 47: 121–24.

——. 1974. *Faulkner: A Biography.* 2 vols. New York: Random House.

——, ed. 1977. *Selected Letters of William Faulkner.* New York: Random House.

Brandfon, Robert L. 1967. *Cotton Kingdom of the New South: A History of the Yazoo Mississippi Delta from Reconstruction to the Twentieth Century.* Cambridge, Mass., and London: Harvard University Press.

Brooks, Cleanth. 1963. *William Faulkner: The Yoknapatawpha Country.* New Haven and London: Yale University Press.

——. 1978. "Thomas Sutpen: A Representative Southern Planter?" In his *William Faulkner: Toward Yoknapatawpha and Beyond.* New Haven and London: Yale University Press.

Carlyle, Thomas. 1891. *On Heroes, Hero-worship, and the Heroic in History.* New York: Crowell.

Cash, W. J. 1969 [1941]. *The Mind of the South.* New York: Vintage.

Clark, Thomas D., and Albert D. Kirwan. 1967. *The South since Appomattox: A Century of Regional Change.* Oxford and New York: Oxford University Press.

Clarke, Deborah. 1994. *Robbing the Mother: Women in Faulkner.* Jackson: University Press of Mississippi.

Clinton, Catherine. 1982. *The Plantation Mistress: Woman's World in the Old South.* New York: Pantheon.

Cobb, James C. 1992. *The Most Southern Place on Earth: The Mississippi Delta and the Roots of Regional Identity.* Oxford and New York: Oxford University Press.

Collins, Carvel, ed. 1962. *William Faulkner: Early Prose and Poetry.* Boston and Toronto: Little, Brown.

Cooper, James Fenimore. 1986 [1826]. *The Last of the Mohicans.* New York and London: Penguin.

Cowley, Malcolm. 1966. *The Faulkner-Cowley File: Letters and Memories, 1944–1962.* New York: Viking.

Crèvecoeur, St. John de. 1964 [1782]. *Letters from an American Farmer.* Garden City, N.Y.: Doubleday.

Davis, Thadious M. 1983. *Faulkner's "Negro": Art and the Southern Context.* Baton Rouge and London: Louisiana State University Press.

Degler, Carl N. 1959. "Slavery and the Origin of American Race Prejudice." *Comparative Studies in Society and History* 2.1: 49–66.

——. 1971. *Neither Black nor White: Slavery and Race Relations in Brazil and the United States.* New York: Macmillan.

Dollard, John. 1957 [1937]. *Caste and Class in a Southern Town.* Garden City, N.Y.: Doubleday.

DuBois, W. E. B. 1969 [1935]. *Black Reconstruction in America, 1860–1880.* New York: Atheneum.

Eagleton, Terry. 1978 [1975]. *Criticism and Ideology: A Study in Marxist Literary Theory.* London and New York: Verso.

———. 1991. *Ideology: An Introduction*. London and New York: Verso.

Ehrenreich, Barbara. 1987. Foreword. In *Male Fantasies*, vol. 1: *Women, Bodies, Floods, History*, by Klaus Theweleit. Minneapolis: University of Minnesota Press.

Faulkner, William. 1948. *Intruder in the Dust*. New York: Random House.

———. 1954. *A Fable*. New York: Random House.

———. 1957. *The Town*. New York: Vintage.

———. 1959. *The Mansion*. New York: Vintage.

———. 1962. *The Reivers: A Reminiscence*. New York: Random House.

———. 1966 [1938]. *The Unvanquished*. New York: Vintage-Random House.

———. 1973. *Flags in the Dust*. Edited by Douglas Day. New York: Vintage.

———. 1981. *Sanctuary*. The Original Text edited by Noel Polk. New York: Random House.

———. 1983a. *Father Abraham*. Edited with an introduction by James B. Meriwether. New York: Random House.

———. 1983b [1929]. *Sartoris*. New York: New American Library.

———. 1984 [1929]. *The Sound and the Fury*. The Corrected Text edited by Noel Polk. New York: Vintage International.

———. 1985a [1930]. *As I Lay Dying*. The Corrected Text edited by Noel Polk. New York: Vintage International.

———. 1985b [1932]. *Light in August*. The Corrected Text edited by Noel Polk. New York: Vintage International.

———. 1985c [1931]. *Sanctuary*. The Corrected Text edited by Noel Polk. New York: Vintage.

———. 1986 [1936]. *Absalom, Absalom!* The Corrected Text edited by Noel Polk. New York: Vintage International.

———. 1990a [1942]. *Go Down, Moses*. New York: Vintage International.

———. 1990b [1940]. *The Hamlet*. The Corrected Text edited by Noel Polk. New York: Vintage International.

———. 1990c [1939]. *If I Forget Thee, Jerusalem* [*The Wild Palms*]. In *William Faulkner, Novels, 1936–1940*, edited by Noel Polk. New York: Library of America.

Fitzhugh, George. 1960 [1854]. *Cannibals All! or, Slaves Without Masters*. Edited by C. Vann Woodward. Cambridge, Mass., and London: Harvard University Press.

Foner, Eric. 1988. *Reconstruction: America's Unfinished Revolution, 1863–1877*. New York: Harper and Row.

Fowler, Doreen, and Ann J. Abadie, eds. 1987. *Faulkner and Race: Faulkner and Yoknapatawpha, 1986*. Jackson: University Press of Mississippi.

Frankenberg, Ruth. 1993. *White Women, Race Matters: The Social Construction of Whiteness*. Minneapolis: University of Minnesota Press.

Gaston, Paul. 1970. *The New South Creed: A Study in Southern Mythmaking*. Baton Rouge and London: Louisiana State University Press.

Genovese, Eugene. 1961. *The Political Economy of Slavery: Studies in the Economy and Society of the Slave South*. New York: Vintage.

———. 1969. *The World the Slaveholders Made: Two Essays in Interpretation*. New York: Pantheon.

———. 1972. *Roll, Jordan, Roll: The World the Slaves Made*. New York: Pantheon.

Godden, Richard. 1989. "Iconic Narrative: Or, How Faulkner Fought the Second Civil War." In *Faulkner's Discourse: An International Symposium*, edited by Lothar Hönnighausen. Tubingen: Max Niemayer Verlag.

———. 1993. "*Absalom, Absalom!* and Rosa Coldfield: Or, What Is in the Dark House." *Faulkner Journal* 8.2: 31–66.

———. 1994. "*Absalom, Absalom!*, Haiti, and Labor History: Reading Unreadable Revolutions." *ELH* 61: 685–720.

Goodwyn, Lawrence. 1976. *Democratic Promise: The Populist Movement in America*. Oxford and New York: Oxford University Press.

Goldberg, David Theo, ed. 1990. *The Anatomy of Racism*. Minneapolis: University of Minnesota Press.

Goldfield, Michael. 1991. "The Color of Politics in the United States: White Supremacy as the Main Explanation for the Peculiarities of American Politics from Colonial Times to the Present." In *The Bounds of Race: Perspectives on Hegemony and Resistance*, edited by Dominick LaCapra. Ithaca and London: Cornell University Press.

Gramsci, Antonio. 1988. "Hegemony, Relations of Force, Historical Bloc." In *An Antonio Gramsci Reader*, edited by David Forgacs. New York: Schocken.

Grantham, Dewey W. 1983. *Southern Progressivism: The Reconciliation of Progress and Tradition*. Knoxville: University of Tennessee Press.

Gregory, Eileen. 1976. "The Temerity to Revolt: Mink Snopes and the Dispossessed in *The Mansion*." *Mississippi Quarterly* 29: 401–22.

Grimwood, Michael. 1987. *Heart in Conflict: Faulkner's Struggles with Vocation*. Athens and London: University of Georgia Press.

Guillaumin, Collette. 1995. *Racism, Sexism, Power, and Ideology*. London: Routledge.

Gutman, Herbert G. 1976. *The Black Family in Slavery and Freedom, 1750–1925*. New York: Vintage.

Gwin, Minrose. 1988–89. "Feminism and Faulkner: Second Thoughts, or What's a Radical Feminist Doing with a Canonical Male Writer Anyway?" *Faulkner Journal* 4.1–2: 55–66.

Gwynn, Frederick L., and Joseph Blotner. 1959. *Faulkner in the University*. Charlottesville: University of Virginia Press.

Handlin, Mary F., and Oscar Handlin. 1950. "Origins of the Southern Labor System." *William and Mary Quarterly*, 3rd series, 7: 212–35.

Hannon, Charles. 1991–92. "Signification, Simulation, and Containment in *If I Forget Thee, Jerusalem*." *Faulkner Journal* 4.1–2: 133–50.

———. 1997. "Race Fantasies: The Filming of *Intruder in the Dust*." In *Faulkner in Cultural Context: Faulkner and Yoknapatawpha, 1995*, edited by Donald M. Kartiganer and Ann J. Abadie. Jackson: University Press of Mississippi.

Harding, Sandra. 1993. *The "Racial" Economy of Science: Toward a Democratic Future*. Bloomington: University of Indiana Press.

hooks, bell. 1992. *Black Looks: Race and Representation.* Boston: South End Press.

Hundley, Daniel. 1979 [1860]. *Social Relations in Our Southern States.* Edited by William J. Cooper. Baton Rouge: Louisiana State University Press.

Irwin, John T. 1992. "Horace Benbow and the Myth of Narcissa." *American Literature* 64.3: 543–66.

Jameson, Fredric. 1981. *The Political Unconscious: Narrative as Socially Symbolic Act.* Ithaca and London: Cornell University Press.

Jehlen, Myra. 1976. *Class and Character in Faulkner's South.* Secaucus, N.J.: Citadel Press.

———. 1986. "Introduction: Beyond Transcendence." In *Ideology and Classic American Literature,* edited by Sacvan Bercovitch and Myra Jehlen. Cambridge and New York: Cambridge University Press.

Jenkins, Lee. 1981. *Faulkner and Black-White Relations: A Psychoanalytic Approach.* New York: Columbia University Press.

Jones, Anne Goodwyn. 1981. "Dixie's Diadem." In her *Tomorrow Is Another Day: The Woman Writer in the South, 1859–1936.* Baton Rouge and London: Louisiana State University Press.

Jordan, Winthrop D. 1969. *White Over Black: American Attitudes Toward the Negro, 1550–1812.* Baltimore: Penguin.

Karl, Frederick R. 1989. *William Faulkner: American Writer: A Biography.* New York: Weidenfeld and Nicolson.

Kartiganer, Donald M. 1988. "The Meaning of Form in *Light in August.*" In *William Faulkner's* Light in August, edited by Harold Bloom. New York: Chelsea House.

———. 1989. "Faulkner's Art of Repetition." In *Faulkner and the Craft of Repetition: Faulkner and Yoknapatawpha, 1987,* edited by Doreen Fowler and Ann J. Abadie. Jackson: University Press of Mississippi.

Kartiganer, Donald M., and Ann J. Abadie, eds. 1995. *Faulkner and Ideology: Faulkner and Yoknapatawpha, 1992.* Jackson: University Press of Mississippi.

Kavanaugh, James. 1985. "Shakespeare in Ideology." In *Alternative Shakespeares,* edited by John Drakikis. London and New York: Methuen.

Kerr, Elizabeth M. 1969. *Yoknapatawpha: Faulkner's "Little Postage Stamp of Native Soil."* New York: Fordham University Press.

Kinney, Arthur F. 1978. *Faulkner's Narrative Poetics: Style as Vision.* Amherst: University of Massachusetts Press.

Kirwan, Albert D. 1951. *Revolt of the Rednecks: Mississippi Politics, 1876–1925.* Lexington: University of Kentucky Press.

Knights, Pamela E. 1989. "The Cost of Single-mindedness: Consciousness in *Sanctuary.*" *Faulkner Journal* 5.1: 3–10.

Kwasny, Andrea. N.d. "Subject/Abject Relations: Poor Whites in *As I Lay Dying.*" Paper presented at the 1994 NEMLA conference in Philadelphia, Pa.

Lahey, Michael E. 1996. "Narcissa's Love Letters: Illicit Space and the Writing of Female Identity in 'There Was a Queen.'" In *Faulkner and Gender: Faulkner and Yoknapatawpha, 1994,* edited by Donald M. Kartiganer and Ann J. Abadie. Jackson: University Press of Mississippi.

Lester, Cheryl. 1987. "To Market, to Market: The Portable Faulkner." *Criticism: A Quarterly for Literature and the Arts* 29.3: 371–89.

———. 1988. "From Place to Place in *The Sound and the Fury:* The Syntax of Interrogation." *Modern Fiction Studies* 34.2: 141–55.

———. 1995. "Racial Awareness and Arrested Development: *The Sound and the Fury* and the Great Migration (1915–1928)." In *The Cambridge Companion to William Faulkner,* edited by Philip M. Weinstein. Cambridge and New York: Cambridge University Press.

———. 1997. "*If I Forget Thee, Jerusalem* and the Great Migration: History in Black and White." In *Faulkner in Cultural Context: Faulkner and Yoknapatawpha, 1995,* edited by Donald M. Kartiganer and Ann J. Abadie. Jackson: University Press of Mississippi.

Lind, Ilse Dusoir. 1986. "The Mutual Relevance of Faulkner Studies and Women Studies: An Interdisciplinary Inquiry." In *Faulkner and Women: Faulkner and Yoknapatawpha, 1985,* edited by Doreen Fowler and Ann J. Abadie. Jackson: University Press of Mississippi.

Litwack, Leon F. 1979. *Been in the Storm So Long: The Aftermath of Slavery.* New York: Knopf.

Loewen, James W., and Charles Sallis, et al. 1974. *Mississippi: Conflict and Change.* New York: Pantheon.

Mandle, Jay R. 1978. *The Roots of Black Poverty: The Southern Plantation Economy after the Civil War.* Durham: Duke University Press.

Marcus, Steven. 1960. "Snopes Revisited." In *William Faulkner: Three Decades of Criticism,* edited by Frederick J. Hoffman and Olga Vickery. East Lansing: Michigan State University Press.

Marx, Karl. 1972. *The Marx-Engels Reader.* 2nd edition, edited by Robert C. Tucker. New York: Norton.

Matthews, John T. 1982. *The Play of Faulkner's Language.* Ithaca and London: Cornell University Press.

———. 1984. "The Elliptical Nature of *Sanctuary.*" *Novel* 17: 246–66.

———. 1992. "*As I Lay Dying* in the Machine Age." *boundary 2* (Spring): 69–94.

Meriwether, James B., ed. 1972. "William Faulkner: An Introduction to *The Sound and the Fury.*" *Southern Review* 8: 705–10.

———. 1973. "An Introduction to *The Sound and the Fury.*" *Mississippi Quarterly* 26: 410–15.

Meriwether, James B., and Michael Millgate. 1980 [1968]. *The Lion in the Garden: Interviews with William Faulkner, 1926–1962.* Lincoln: University of Nebraska Press.

McKinley, Gena. 1997. "*Light in August:* A Novel of Passing?" In *Faulkner in Cultural Context: Faulkner and Yoknapatawpha, 1995,* edited by Donald M. Kartiganer and Ann J. Abadie. Jackson: University Press of Mississippi.

Miller, Perry. 1981. *Errand in the Wilderness.* Cambridge, Mass., and London: Belknap Press of Harvard University Press.

Millgate, Michael. 1966. *The Achievement of William Faulkner*. New York: Random House.

Minter, David. 1980. *William Faulkner: His Life and Work*. Baltimore and London: Johns Hopkins University Press.

Moore, Robert T. 1986. "Desire and Despair: Temple Drake's Self-Victimization." In *Faulkner and Women: Faulkner and Yoknapatawpha, 1985*, edited by Doreen Fowler and Ann J. Abadie. Jackson: University Press of Mississippi.

Morgan, Edmund. 1975. *American Slavery, American Freedom: The Ordeal of Colonial Virginia*. New York: Norton.

Morrison, Toni. 1992. *Playing in the Dark: Whiteness and the Literary Imagination*. Cambridge, Mass., and London: Harvard University Press.

Mortimer, Gail L. 1983. *Faulkner's Rhetoric of Loss: A Study of Perception and Meaning*. Austin: University of Texas Press.

Oakes, James. 1982. *The Ruling Race: A History of American Slaveholders*. New York: Knopf.

Oates, Stephen B. 1987. *William Faulkner, the Man and the Artist: A Biography*. New York: Harper and Row.

Oshinsky, David M. 1996. *Worse than Slavery: Parchman Farm and the Ordeal of Jim Crow Justice*. New York: Free Press.

Osterweis, Rollin G. 1973. *The Myth of the Lost Cause, 1865–1900*. Hamden, Conn.: Archon.

Percy, Walker. 1962. *The Moveigoer*. New York: Knopf.

Percy, William Alexander. 1941. *Lanterns on the Levee: Recollections of a Planter's Son*. New York: Knopf.

Petesch, Donald. 1979. "Temple Drake: Faulkner's Mirror for the Social Order." *Studies in American Fiction* 7.1: 37–48.

Polk, Noel. 1983. "Idealism in *The Mansion*." In *Faulkner and Idealism: Perspectives from Paris*, edited by Michel Gresset and Patrick Samway, S.J. Jackson and London: University Press of Mississippi.

———. 1984. "'The Dungeon was Mother Herself': William Faulkner, 1927–1931." In *New Directions in Faulkner Studies: Faulkner and Yoknapatawpha, 1983*, edited by Doreen Fowler and Ann J. Abadie. Jackson and London: University Press of Mississippi.

———. 1985. "The Space Between *Sanctuary*." In *Intertexuality in Faulkner*, edited by Michel Gresset and Noel Polk. Jackson and London: University Press of Mississippi.

Porter, Carolyn. 1981. "Faulkner's America." In her *Seeing and Being: The Plight of the Participant Observer in Emerson, James, Adams, and Faulkner*. Middletown, Conn.: Wesleyan University Press.

Ragan, David Paul. 1987. *William Faulkner's Absalom, Absalom!: A Critical Study*. Ann Arbor and London: UMI Research Press.

Ransom, Roger L., and Richard Sutch. 1977. *One Kind of Freedom: The Economic Con-*

sequences of Emancipation. Cambridge, London, and New York: Cambridge University Press.

Rhodes, Pamela, and Richard Godden. 1985. "*The Wild Palms:* Degraded Culture, Devalued Texts." In *Intertexuality in Faulkner,* edited by Michel Gresset and Noel Polk. Jackson and London: University Press of Mississippi.

Roberts, Diane. 1988–89. "Ravished Belles: Stories of Rape and Resistance in *Flags in the Dust* and *Sanctuary.*" *Faulkner Journal* 4.1–2: 21–36.

———. 1994. *Faulkner and Southern Womanhood.* Athens and London: University of Georgia Press.

Roediger, David. 1991. *The Wages of Whiteness: Race in the Making of the American Working Class.* New York: Verso.

Saldivar, Ramon. 1990. *Chicano Narrative: The Dialectics of Difference.* Madison: University of Wisconsin Press.

Scott, Anne Firor. 1970. *The Southern Lady: From Pedestal to Politics, 1830–1930.* Chicago and London: University of Chicago Press.

Sensibar, Judith L. 1984. *The Origins of Faulkner's Art.* Austin: University of Texas Press.

Slotkin, Richard. 1985. *The Fatal Environment: The Myth of the Frontier in the Age of Industrialization, 1800–1890.* Middletown, Conn.: Wesleyan University Press.

Snead, James A. 1986. *Figures of Division: William Faulkner's Major Novels.* New York: Methuen.

———. 1987. "*Light in August* and the Rhetorics of Racial Division." In *Faulkner and Race: Faulkner and Yoknapatawpha, 1986,* edited by Doreen Fowler and Ann J. Abadie. Jackson and London: University Press of Mississippi.

Stroble, Woodrow. 1980. "Flem Snopes: A Crazed Mirror." In *Faulkner: The Unappeased Imagination: A Collection of Critical Essays,* edited by Glenn O. Carey. Troy, N.Y.: Whitson.

Sundquist, Eric J. 1983. *Faulkner: The House Divided.* Baltimore and London: Johns Hopkins University Press.

Tawney, R. H. 1962 [1926]. *Religion and the Rise of Capitalism.* Gloucester, Mass.: Peter Smith.

Taylor, Walter. 1983. *Faulkner's Search for a South.* Urbana: University of Illinois Press.

Taylor, William R. 1979. *Cavalier and Yankee: The Old South and American National Character.* Cambridge, Mass., and London: Harvard University Press.

Theweleit, Klaus. 1987. *Male Fantasies,* vol. 1: *Women, Bodies, Floods, History.* Minneapolis: University of Minnesota Press.

———. 1989. *Male Fantasies,* vol. 2: *Male Bodies: Psychoanalyzing the White Terror.* Minneapolis: University of Minnesota Press.

Tindall, George. 1967. *The Emergence of the New South, 1913–1945.* Baton Rouge and London: Louisiana State University Press.

Towner, Theresa M. 1995. "'How Can a Black Man Ask?': Race and Self-Representation in Faulkner's Later Fiction." *Faulkner Journal* 10.2: 3–22.

Trachtenberg, Alan. 1982. *The Incorporation of America: Culture and Society in the Gilded Age.* New York: Hill and Wang.

Vickery, Olga. 1959. *The Novels of William Faulkner: A Critical Interpretation.* Baton Rouge: Louisiana State University Press.

Warren, Robert Penn. 1941. "The Snopes World." *Kenyon Review* 3: 253–57.

Wayne, Michael. 1983. *The Reshaping of Plantation Society: The Natchez District, 1860–1880.* Baton Rouge and London: Louisiana State University Press.

Weber, Max. 1958 [1930]. *The Protestant Ethic and the Spirit of Capitalism.* Translated by Talcott Parsons. New York: Charles Scribner and Sons.

Weinstein, Philip M. 1992. *Faulkner's Subject: A Cosmos No One Owns.* Cambridge, Mass., and London: Cambridge University Press.

———. 1995. "Diving into the Wreck: Faulknerian Practice and the Imagination of Slavery." *Faulkner Journal* 10.2: 23–54.

———. 1996. *What Else But Love?: The Ordeal of Race in Faulkner and Morrison.* New York: Columbia University Press.

Wiebe, Robert H. 1967. *The Search for Order, 1877–1920.* New York: Hill and Wang.

Wiener, Jonathan M. 1978. *Social Origins of the New South: Alabama, 1860–1885.* Baton Rouge and London: Louisiana State University Press.

———. 1979. "Class Structure and Economic Development in the American South, 1865–1955." *American Historical Review* 84: 970–1006.

Williams, Eric. 1961. *Capitalism and Slavery.* New York: Russell and Russell.

Williams, Raymond. 1977. *Marxism and Literature.* Oxford: Oxford University Press.

———. 1983 [1958]. *Culture and Society 1780–1950.* New York: Columbia University Press.

Williamson, Joel. 1993. *William Faulkner and Southern History.* Oxford and New York: Oxford University Press.

Wilson, Raymond J., III. 1980. "Imitative Flem Snopes and Faulkner's Causal Sequence in *The Town.*" *Twentieth Century Literature* 26: 432–44.

Wittenberg, Judith B. 1979. *Faulkner: The Transfiguration of Biography.* Lincoln: University of Nebraska Press.

Woodward, C. Vann. 1951. *Origins of the New South, 1877–1913.* Baton Rouge: Louisiana State University Press.

Wright, Richard. 1945. *Black Boy: A Record of Childhood and Youth.* New York: Harper and Row.

———. 1969 [1940]. *Native Son.* New York: Harper and Row.

Wyatt-Brown, Bertram. 1982. *Southern Honor: Ethics and Behavior in the Old South.* Oxford and New York: Oxford University Press.

Zender, Karl F. 1989. *The Crossing of the Ways: William Faulkner, the South, and the Modern World.* New Brunswick and London: Rutgers University Press.

Index

(bourgeois ideology, *continued*)
liberal, bourgeois values. *See also* capitalism; liberalism
bourgeois subjectivity, 92, 93
bourgeoisie, 62, 114, 115, 158. *See also* capitalism; liberalism
Brooks, Cleanth, 112, 159, 161, 195 (n. 13)
Brown, John, 136
Bunch, Byron, 96, 99, 101
Bundren, Addie, 44, 95, 96, 102; and capitalism, 92–93
Bundren, Anse, xii, 66, 89–90, 110, 136; as caricature of paternalist, 92–94, 102, 103; and Faulkner's authorial ideology, 44; relation to Thomas Sutpen, 116, 117. *See also* Compson, Jason (IV), as caricature of paternalist
Bundren, Darl, 93, 102
Bundrens, the, 44, 89–96, 102, 103; and capitalism, 94–95; and middle class values, 89–92, 93
Burch, Lucas, 96, 103
Burden, Joanna, 99, 100, 101, 127

capitalism: and Benjy Compson, 52, 53; changes for women in, 56–57; Faulkner's criticism of, 58, 88, 89, 94, 104, 117; and Faulkner's utopian yearning, 172, 173; and Mr. Compson, 59; and Old South social formations, 112, 114, 119; and Quentin Compson, 58; and *The Sound and the Fury*, 66. *See also* bourgeoisie; liberalism; middle class values
Carlyle, Thomas, 169, 174
Cash, W. J., 63
Cavalier ideology, 119, 182 (n. 4)
Cavalier paternalism, 64, 182 (n. 2); and Quentin Compson, 53–60. *See also* paternalism
Cavaliers, 121
Christmas, Joe, 96, 99, 104, 127; and essentialist thinking, 97–98, 101; and race, 97–98, 188 (n. 10); relation to liberalism of, 101–103; and Thomas Sutpen, 102, 134–35
Clinton, Catherine, 55
Coldfield, Goodhue, 119; and Christianity, 120–21; and liberalism, 120; and Thomas Sutpen, 134, 135, 136
Coldfield, Rosa, 122, 134, 135
Compson, Benjy, 51–53; and aesthetic ideology, 51–52; contrasted to Jason Compson (IV), 61, 65

Compson, Caddy, 45, 65, 66, 95; and Benjy Compson, 52; and Jason Compson, 62, 64; and Quentin Compson, 55, 57
Compson, General (Jason II), 158, 171; and Charles Etienne Saint Valery Bon, 132–33; and Faulkner's authorial ideology, 44, 121–22, 123, 125; and *Go Down, Moses*, 141; and natural artistocracy, 124–25; and paternalism, 121–22; and Southern ideology of race, 133; and Thomas Sutpen, 119, 120, 121–22, 134, 135, 138
Compson, Jason (IV), xii, 60–65, 89, 141, 183 (n. 11); attitudes about race of, 64; as caricature of paternalist, 61–62; contrasted to Quentin Compson, 64; and liberalism, 62; and Progressivism, 62–64; and the savage ideal, 63–64; and Thomas Sutpen, 116, 117
Compson, Mr. (Jason III), 52, 58, 62, 64, 65, 122
Compson, Mrs., 62, 65
Compson, Quentin, xii, 53–60, 182 (n. 2); attitude about race of, 54; attitude about women of, 57–58; and the Bundrens, 89, 94; and democracy, 58–59; and Horace Benbow, 69, 71, 77, 84; relation to Faulkner's authorial ideology, 41, 45, 52
Constitutional Convention of 1890, 19, 22
convict-lease system, 19, 179 (n. 6)
Cooper, James Fenimore, 104

Davis, Thadious, 66, 103, 184 (n. 12), 188–89 (n. 11)
Degler, Carl, 128
Delta, the, 6, 9, 10, 11. *See also* Black Counties
"Delta Autumn," 98, 141
democracy, 58, 65, 149, 151, 172, 174, 175
Democratic Party, 13–14, 15
de Spain, Major, 44, 150
de Spain, Manfred, 150, 156, 157, 160; as representative of Redeemers, 151
Dilsey. *See* Gibson, Dilsey
Doc Hines, 97, 99
dominant ideology, xi, 4, 22, 45, 95, 114; definition of, 4–5
Drake, Judge, 75, 84
Drake, Temple, 57, 69, 79, 81; and mobility, 82–83, 87; and patriarchy, 82–83, 84; and sexuality, 75–76
Dreiser, Theodore, 89
Du Bois, W. E. B.: and economic democracy, 178 (n. 3)

Eagleton, Terry, 3, 30; critique of Althusser of, 31–32
Ehrenreich, Barbara, 70
Eliot, T. S., 40
emergent ideology, xi, 4, 21, 22, 45, 114; definition of, 5

Fable, A, 44, 45, 147, 193 (n. 2)
Falkner, John, 35
Falkner, John Wesley Thompson, 32, 33; attachment to paternalism, 34–35; biography of, 34–35; influence on Faulkner, 36
Falkner, Murray, 35
Falkner, William Clark, 34, 112; attachment to liberalism, 33–34; biography of, 32–34
Farmers' Alliance, 19, 36
fascism: and paternalism, 70
Father Abraham, 148–49
Fathers, Sam, 140, 141
Faulkner, Estelle Oldham, 36, 37, 42, 44, 109
Faulkner, William: assessments of liberalism, 41, 43–44, 65, 88, 94–96, 115–16, 117, 125–26; assessments of paternalism, 116–17, 125–26, 194 (n. 6); authorial ideology of, 43–46, 111–12, 124–26, 138, 139, 147, 156, 167, 161, 170, 172, 173, 174, 190 (n. 3); and construction of racial identity, 127–28; development of public role of, 145–48; early influences on, 39–40; family background of, 32–37; ideological development of, 41–45, 53, 66–67, 85–86, 88, 95–96, 103–105, 124, 125–26, 140, 167, 172–73, 173–74; ideological position of, 31–32, 41–42, 169, 170; and Klaus Theweleit, 70–71, 185 (n. 5); in the 1930s, 109–111; and natural aristocracy, 43–46, 111–12, 125–26, 136, 147, 166, 167, 172, 173, 174; as natural aristocrat, 166, 167; paternalism's effects on, 37–40, 51, 60, 66, 110, 115–16, 171; social vision of, 166, 167, 169, 171, 173, 175; and Southern ideology of race, 127, 133, 136–37, 139, 192 (n. 3); subject formation of, 3, 36–42, 109–111. See also *Absalom, Absalom!; As I Lay Dying; Fable, A; Father Abraham; Flags in the Dust; Go Down, Moses; Hamlet, The; Light in August; Mansion, The; Reivers, The; Sanctuary; Snopes Trilogy; Sound and the Fury, The; Town, The*
Flags in the Dust, 111, 148, 170; derivative nature of, 50, 51; publishers' rejection of, 40, 41

Frenchman's Bend, 148, 149, 151, 153, 160, 161

Gatsby, Jay: and Joe Christmas, 102
Genovese, Eugene, 112, 113
George, J. Z., 16
Gibson, Dilsey, 44, 52, 64, 65–66, 184 (n. 12)
Gibson, Luster, 61, 65, 66
Go Down, Moses, 49, 111, 128, 145, 150; place in Faulkner's canon, 140, 141
Goodwin, Lee, 71
Goodwin, Ruby, 76, 78, 81
Grimm, Percy, 96, 141, 185 (n. 5), 188 (n. 8); and race hatred, 132; as undeserving authority figure, 103, 104. *See also* Bundren, Anse, as caricature of paternalist; Compson, Jason (IV), as caricature of paternalist
Grimwood, Michael, 164, 193 (n. 3)
Grove, Lena, 44, 96, 102; and social mobility, 103

Haiti, 131, 133; significance for plantocrats, 135
Hamilton, Alexander, 174
Hamlet, The, 36, 145, 147, 149–56, 161, 163. *See also* Snopes Trilogy
Handlin, Mary and Oscar, 128
Head, Herbert: and Quentin Compson, 55, 56
hegemony, 4, 5, 7, 114, 172; definition of, 4
Hightower, Gail, 71, 99, 100, 101, 104
Hollywood, 43
honor: relation to paternalism, 38–39; effects on Faulkner, 39
Houston, Jack: and Mink Snopes, 162, 163
humanism, 166. *See also* Stevens, Gavin, and humanism

ideology, 3, 4, 41, 69, 73, 85; affective account of, 3, 29–32; Althusser's theory of, 30–32; definition of, 30; rationalist account of, 3–5. *See also* aesthetic ideology; authorial ideology; dominant ideology; emergent ideology; hegemony; ideology of gender; interpellation; residual ideology; Southern ideology of race
ideology of gender, 73, 185 (n. 6)
ideology of race. *See* Southern ideology of race
If I Forget Thee, Jerusalem, 146
interpellation, xi, 30, 37, 40, 67, 95, 173
Intruder in the Dust, 169
Invention of the White Race, The, 128
Irwin, John, 69